W9-AQL-669

A NEAR EAST STUDIES HANDBOOK, 570-1974

A Near East Studies Handbook, 570-1974

BY JERE L. BACHARACH

3421

UNIVERSITY OF WASHINGTON PRESS
Seattle and London

Copyright © 1974 by the University of Washington Press
Printed in the United States of America

All rights reserved. No part of this publication may be reproduced or transmitted in any form or by any means, electronic or mechanical, including photocopy, recording, or any information storage or retrieval system, without permission in writing from the publisher.

Library of Congress Cataloging in Publication Data

Bacharach, Jere L 1938-
A Near East studies handbook, 570-1974.

1. Islamic Empire--History--Handbooks, manuals, etc. 2. Near East--History--1517- --Handbooks, manuals, etc. I. Title.
DS61.B3 956'.002'02 74-14547
ISBN 0-295-95329-2
ISBN 0-295-95361-6 (pbk.)

To

Andrew S. Ehrenkreutz

Teacher, Scholar, Friend

PREFACE

This handbook concentrates on the geographical area of Iran, Egypt, Turkey, the Fertile Crescent and the Arabian Peninsula; that is, Southwest Asia and Egypt. Occasionally material touching on Libya, the Sudan, the Ottomans in Europe and Muslims in Afghanistan is mentioned. However, in order to avoid confusion with Southeast Asia, the geographically vague but popular term of "Near East" has been used in the title. The time dimension begins with 570 A.D. and ends with June 1, 1974.

As there is no single accepted transliteration system from the Arabic script to the Latin alphabet, the first chapter identifies some of the common Latin variations for particular Arabic script letters and vowel sounds, as well as the transliteration system used by the *Middle East Studies Association*. Sixty-nine abbreviations of major periodicals and reference works are listed in Chapter II, while the following chapter identifies the abbreviation for sixty-five Twentieth Century political, economic and social groups. In this chapter each abbreviation is followed by its full title and some pertinent data.

The next three chapters are concerned with the names, dates and genealogies of dynasties and rulers. The first section, Chapter IV, includes the names of over one-hundred dynasties with their initial and terminal dates given in the Muslim and Christian calendars. Chapter V, a Table of Rulers, has thirty eight lists, including the names of Turkish Presidents, Israeli Prime Ministers, British officials in Egypt and Palestine and French officials in Syria, as well as the rulers of over thirty Muslim dynasties. The last chapter for this section includes twenty-five genealogy tables for the major Medieval Islamic dynasties and families. All three chapters are indexed in the General Index.

Chapter VII is an historical atlas of thirty-one maps with almost two-thirds of them covering proposed and actual divisions of Southwest Asia in this century. The special Map Index includes variant spellings of many of the names. The next chapter is the standard table for converting Muslim and Christian dates from one calendar to the other, while Chapter IX is a Glossary of approximately two hundred fifty words. The last chapter is a chronology of over five hundred data fully indexed.

This handbook does not include a bibliography. In introductory paragraphs to most of the chapters, major references are listed. For Medieval studies, the best annotated bibliography is Jean Sauvaget's *Introduction to the History of the Muslim East: A Bibliographical Guide*, edited and revised by Claude Cahen (Berkeley: University of California Press, 1965). In order to locate appropriate periodical articles, the continuing volumes of *Index Islamicus*, edited by James Pearson, are essential. A new reference work is *Middle East and Islam: A Bibliographical Introduction*, edited by Derek Hopwood and Diana Grimwood-Jones (Zurich: Inter Documentation Co., 1972).

There is nothing equivalent to Sauvaget for modern studies. One bibliography of almost five thousand items is *Arab Culture and Society in Change: A Partially Annotated Bibliography* (Beirut: Saint Joseph's University, 1973). Annotated bibliographies of particular regions or topics have been produced by the Middle East Institute, Washington, D.C. and the American Institute of Islamic Studies, Denver. A few modern works include annotated bibliographies such as Sidney N. Fisher's *The Middle East: A History* (New York: Alfred A. Knopf, 1969) and Abid A. Al-Marayati's *The Middle East: Its Governments and Politics* (Belmont, Cal.: Duxbury Press, 1972). For a survey of current periodical material, there is a "Bibliography of Periodical Literature" in each quarterly issue of the *Middle East Journal.*

Besides my debt to scholarly works which I acknowledge in each chapter, a number of individuals have aided me and I wish to thank them, recognizing that others could have been added to this list: Calvin Allen, Andrew S. Ehrenkreutz, Nicholas Heer, Judith S. Heide, Michael M. Pixley, Stephanie Sayers and Farhat J. Ziadeh.

The maps and genealogy tables were drawn by Alice Alden, while this photographed text was typed by Barb Shurin and I am indebted to both of them for the fine quality of their work. Obviously, any errors remain my responsibility.

A number of the maps were adapted from previously produced works:

From *An Atlas of Middle Eastern Affairs*, by Robert C. Kingsbury and Norman J.G. Pounds (New York: Frederick A. Praeger, Inc., Copyright 1963). Excerpted and adapted by permission.

From *History of the Arabs*, by Philip Hitti (New York: Copyright 1965 by St. Martin's Press, Inc. and Macmillan Co., Ltd., London). Excerpted and adapted by permission.

From *The Historical Atlas of the Muslim Peoples*, by R. Roolvink (Amsterdam: Djambatan, Inc., 1957). Excerpted and adapted by permission.

From *South West Asia*, by William C. Brice (London: Copyright 1967 by The University of London Press, Ltd.). Excerpted and adapted by permission.

CONTENTS

A NEAR EAST STUDIES HANDBOOK, 570-1974

TRANSLITERATION SYSTEMS

Because there is no single, universally accepted system of transliteration from the Arabic script to the Roman alphabet, one often finds variant spellings of words that can confuse the unwary. As an example, for the holy book of the Muslims (or Moslems), one will see "Koran" or "Qur'ān."

The following remarks indicate some of the problems one may face when coming across Arabic, Persian and Ottoman words written in a Western script. The section concludes with the transliteration system used by the Middle East Studies Association, as well as a number of other important variants.

For words from Arabic the major variants are q or k, j or dj, u or o, i or y or e. In the preceding example there was Koran and Qur'ān which illustrate two variants. *The Encyclopedia of Islam*, in the manner of the old European system, uses "k" and "dj" for "q" and "j," respectively. Therefore, the modern Muslim reformist, Jamal al-Dīn al-Afghanī, is found in the *Encyclopedia of Islam* under "dj." There is also the problem of the article "al." It is either always written with the "l," or when it precedes certain letters; that is, t, th, d, dh, r, z, s, sh, ṣ, ḍ, ṭ, ẓ and n, the "l" changes to that letter; e.g., al-dīn or ad-dīn.

The transliteration system used for Persian has been heavily influenced by the forms used for Arabic. As a whole, this has not caused serious problems, except in the transliteration of vowels and a few consonants. One may find Isfahan or Esfahan, Mulk or Molk, Firdawsi or Ferdosi, and Qazwin or Qazvin; that is, i or e, u or o, w or v, and various forms for diphthongs.

Ottoman Turkish is the most troublesome, and even the Library of Congress has not adopted an official transliteration system. The fullest discussion can be found in an article by Eleazar Birnbaum, "The Transliteration of Ottoman Turkish for Library and General Purposes," *Journal of the American Oriental Society*, 87 (1967), 122-156, where he suggests his own system. The modern Turks, having adopted a Roman script in 1928, have their own system of transliterating Ottoman. Therefore, if one were to take the Ottoman word for a member of the old Turkish dynasty, عثمانلى, it could be transliterated as ^{c}Uthmānlī, ^{c}Osmānlī or Osmanl*ı* using an Arabic based system, MESA rules and modern Turkish forms, respectively.

Finally, a graphic but special example of transliteration: the Persian word for a "teacher" or "educated person" is خواجه, and it can be found as "hoca" in modern Turkish, but will be found in the *Encyclopedia of Islam* under k̲h̲^{w}ādja!

MESA SYSTEMS PLUS VARIATIONS

Arabic		Persian	Ottoman Turkish	Modern Turkish	Variations: Other Systems
ا	ʾ	ʾ	ʾ	—	
ب	b	b	b	b or p	
پ	—	p	p	p	
ت	t	t	t	t	
ث	th	s̲	s̲	s	th, t̲
ج	j	j	c	c	dj, d̲j̲, g, dsch, y, c
چ	—	ch	ç	ç	ch, tsch, cʹ, tj
ح	ḥ	ḥ	ḥ	h	
خ	kh	kh	ẖ	h	kh, k
د	d	d	d	d	
ذ	d̲h̲	z̲	z̲	z	dh, d̲
ر	r	r	r	r	
ز	z	z	z	z	
ژ	—	zh	j	j	z, z̲h̲
س	s	s	s	s	
ش	s̲h̲	s̲h̲	ş	ş	sh, ch, sj, s
ص	ṣ	ṣ	ṣ	s	
ض	ḍ	ż	ż	z	d
ط	ṭ	ṭ	ṭ	t	
ظ	ẓ	ẓ	ẓ	z	
ع	ʿ	ʿ	ʿ	—	ʿ
غ	g̲h̲	g̲h̲	g or ğ	g or ğ	gh, ġ

Arabic		Persian	Ottoman Turkish	Modern Turkish	Variations: Other Systems
ف	f	f	f	f	
ق	q	q	ḳ	k	
ك	k	k or g	k,ñ,y,ǧ	k,n,y,ǧ	g
گ	—	g	g	g	
ل	l	l	l	l	
م	m	m	m	m	
ن	n	n	n	n	
ه	h	h	h*	h*	
و	w	v or u	v	v	ou
ى	y	y	y	y	
ة	-a**				
ال	al-,'l-***				

V O W E L S

Arabic and Persian			Ottoman Turkish	Modern Turkish
Long	ا or ى	â	â words of Arabic	â
	و	û	û and Persian	û
	ي	î	î origin only	î
Doubled	ـيّـ	iyy(final form î)	iy (final form î)	iy (final form î)
	وّ	uww(final form û),etc.	uvv	uvv
Diphthongs	وَ	au or aw	ev	ev
	يَ	ai or ay	ey	ey
Short	َ	a	a or e	a or e
	ُ	u	u or ü	u or ü
			o or ö	o or ö
	ِ	i	ı or i	ı or i

* When not final.
** -at when in construct state.
*** The "l" in the article may change to t, th, d, dh, r, z, s, sh, ṣ, ḍ, ṭ, ẓ or n if the word it is attached to begins with that letter; e.g., al-dīn or ad-dīn.

ABBREVIATIONS: MAJOR PERIODICALS AND REFERENCES

More extensive lists of periodical abbreviations can be found in James D. Pearson, *Index Islamicus, 1906-1955* (Cambridge: Heffer, 1953), *Middle East Journal* and *Muslim World*. The best introduction to reference sources including abbreviations is Jean Sauvaget, *Introduction to the History of the Muslim East: A Bibliographical Guide,* 2nd edition recast by Claude Cahen (Berkeley: University of California Press, 1965).

AHR *American Historical Review*

AHS *African Historical Studies*

AI *Ars Islamica*

And. *al-Andalus*

AO *Acta orientalia*

ArO *Archiv orientální*

ArOtt *Archivum Ottomanicum*

BEO *Bulletin d'études orientales*

BGA *Bibliotheca geographorum Arabicarum*

BIE *Bulletin de l'Institut d'Égypte*

BIFAO *Bulletin de l'Institut Français d'Archéologie Orientale*

BSOAS *Bulletin of the School of Oriental & African Studies* (London University)

BZ *Byzantinische Zeitschrift*

CH *Current History*

CIA *Corpus Inscriptionum Arabicarum*

CSSH *Comparative Studies in Society and History*

DI *Der Islam*

EHR *English Historical Review/Economic Historical Review*

EI[1] *The Encyclopaedia of Islam.* 4 vols., supp. Leiden, 1913-1942

EI[2] *The Encyclopaedia of Islam.* 2nd ed. Leiden, 1954-

GAL Brockelmann, C. *Geschichte der arabischen Litteratur.* 2nd ed., 2 vols. Leiden, 1943-1949.

GALS Brockelmann, C. *Geschichte der arabischen Litteratur Supplement.* 3 vols. Leiden, 1937-1942.

GAS Sezgin, F. *Geschichte des arabischen Schrifttums.* Leiden, 1967-

GMS *Gibb Memorial Series*

HO Spuler, B.(ed.). *Handbuch der Orientalistik.* Leiden, 1952

IC *Islamic Culture*

IEJ *Israel Exploration Journal*

IJAHS *International Journal of African Historical Studies*

IJMES *International Journal of Middle East Studies*

IQ *Islamic Quarterly*

IS *Islamic Studies*

JA *Journal asiatique*

JAH *Journal of African History*

JAL *Journal of Arab Literature*

JAOS *Journal of the American Oriental Society*

JCH *Journal of Contemporary History*

JESHO *Journal of the Economic and Social History of the Orient*

JJS *Journal of Jewish Studies*

JMAS *Journal of Modern African Studies*

JMH *Journal of Modern History*

JNES *Journal of Near Eastern Studies*

JRAS *Journal of the Royal Asiatic Society of Great Britain and Ireland*

JSS *Journal of Semitic Studies*

JWH *Journal of World History*

MEED *Middle East Economic Digest*

MEF *Middle East Forum*

MEJ *Middle East Journal*

MESA Bulletin *Middle East Studies Association Bulletin*

MIDEO *Mélanges de l'Institut Dominicain d'Études Orientales du Caire*

MIFAO *Mémoires de l'Institut Français d'Archéologie Orientale*

MW *Muslim World*

OM *Oriente moderno*

Ois *Oriens*

PO *Patrologia Orientalis*

RAAD *Revue de l'Académie Arabe de Damas*

REI *Revue des études islamiques*

REJ *Revue des études juives*

RH *Revue historique*

RHC *Recueil des historiens des croisades*

RIMA *Revue de l'Institut des Manuscripts Arabes*

RMM	*Revue de monde musulman*
ROC	*Revue de l'Orient chrétien*
RSO	*Rivista degli studi orientali*
SEI	*Shorter Encyclopaedia of Islam*
SI	*Studia Islamica*
Spec.	*Speculum*
WI	*Die Welt des Islams*
WO	*Die Welt des Orients*
ZDMG	*Zeitschrift der Deutschen Morgenländischen Gesellschaft*

ABBREVIATIONS: TWENTIETH CENTURY
SOCIAL, POLITICAL AND ECONOMIC UNITS

There is no single extensive collection of abbreviations dealing with the political, social and economic groups formed in the Twentieth Century. Each new resistance movement, military junta, political party, oil company, interstate organization, etc. brings with it a new abbreviation. The easiest way to locate the full name of an undefined abbreviation, which by context is connected with Twentieth Century Southwest Asia and Egypt, is to turn to the index of any of the standard works on the modern era such as: Abid A. Al-Marayati, ed., *The Middle East: Its Governments and Politics* (Belmont, Cal.: Duxbury Press, 1972); Michael Adams, ed., *The Middle East: A Handbook* (London: Anthony Blond, Ltd., 1971); and Tareq Y. Ismael, *Governments and Politics of the Contemporary Middle East* (Homewood, Ill.: The Dorsey Press, 1970).

AIOC — Anglo-Iranian Oil Co.: 1935-51; British controlled oil company; superseded APOC.

AL — Arab League: 1945-; Members as of 1974 were Algeria, Bahrain, Egypt, Iraq, Jordan, Kuwait, Lebanon, Libya, Morocco, Qatar, Saudi Arabia, South Yemen, Sudan, Syria, Tunisia, United Arab Emirates, Yemen, Oman and Mauritania. Also League of Arab States.

ALF — Arab Liberation Front: 1969-; A Palestinian *fidā'īyīn* group sponsored by Iraq.

ANM — Arab Nationalist Movement: 1950's-; An Arab, particularly Palestinian, group dominated by George Habash; precursor to PFLP.

APOC — Anglo-Persian Oil Co.: 1930-35; Earliest Western oil company in the area.

ARAMCO — Arabian-American Oil Co.: 1946-; Owned by Standard Oil of California, Standard Oil of New Jersey, Mobil and Texaco.

ARE — Arab Republic of Egypt: 1971-; Official name of Egypt.

ASU — Arab Socialist Union: 1957-; The only legal Egyptian political party.

BP — British Petroleum: 1951-; Superseded AIOC.

CENTO — Central Treaty Organization: 1958-; Members as of 1974 were Britain, Iran, Pakistan and Turkey; previously called Baghdad Pact, 1955-58, and included Iraq.

CUP — Committee of Union and Progress: 1908-18; Known as "Young Turks"; this group of Turkish military leaders ran Ottoman government and reinstated 1876 Constitution.

DP	Democratic Party: 1946-60; A Turkish political party during first Republic dominated by Adnan Menderes and in power 1950-60.
EGPC	Egyptian General Petroleum Co.: 1960-; Egyptian national oil company.
FLOSY	Front for Liberation of Occupied South Yemen: 1966-67; Radical group opposed to British occupation of Aden and South Yemen.
IBRD	International Bank for Reconstruction and Development: 1944-; Created to provide and facilitate international investment.
INOC	Iraq National Oil Co.: 1958-; Iraqi national oil company.
IPC	Iraq Petroleum Co.: 1929-58; A.P.O.C. (B.P.), Shell, Compagnie Française, Standard Oil of New Jersey, Mobil and Gulbenkian interests in oil consortium; superseded TPC.
JNF	Jewish National Fund: 1901-; *Keren Kayemeth*, concerned with fund raising and acquisition of land in Palestine and then Israel for Jewish people.
JP	Justice Party: 1961-; A major Turkish political party in the Second Turkish Republic led by Süleyman Demirel.
KNPC	Kuwait National Petroleum Co.: 1960-; National oil company financed by State of Kuwait.
KOC	Kuwait Oil Co.: 1933-; Western oil consortium of A.P.O.C. (B.P.) and Gulf Oil Corporation.
MEPL	Middle East Pipeline, Ltd.: 1947; A company controlled by AIOC and American oil companies that sought to build a pipeline from Iran to the Mediterranean, but failed.
NATO	North Atlantic Treaty Organization: 1949-.
NF	National Front: 1) 1964-; A major radical political party in South Yemen; 2) 1951-53; A nationalist Iranian political group dominated by Mosaddeq.
NIOC	National Iranian Oil Company: 1951-; Iranian national oil company.
NLF	National Liberation Front: 1954-64; A radical anti-British political party in Aden.
NUC	National Unity Committee: 1961-62; The military group that ran Turkey for the period between the two republics.
OAPEC	Organization of Arab Petroleum Exporting Countries: 1968-; Membership as of 1974 was Abu Dhabi, Algeria, Bahrain, Egypt, Iraq, Kuwait, Libya, Qatar, Saudi Arabia and Syria.
OAU	Organization of African Unity: 1963-; Organization of African states, excluding European controlled areas, to further African unity and solidarity.
OPEC	Organization of Petroleum Exporting Countries: 1960-; Membership as of 1974 was Abu Dhabi, Algeria, Ecuador, Indonesia, Iran, Iraq, Kuwait, Libya, Nigeria, Qatar, Saudi Arabia and Venezuela.
PDFLP	Popular Democratic Front for Liberation of Palestine: 1969-; Rad-

ical Palestinian *fidā'īyīn* group founded by Nayif Hawatmeh; broke off from PFLP.

PDRY — People's Democratic Republic of Yemen: 1970-; The official name for the government of South Yemen.

PFLP — Popular Front for Liberation of Palestine: 1968-; Marxist Palestinian *fida'iyin* group founded by George Habash.

PFLP - Gen. Comm. — Popular Front for Liberation of Palestine - General Command: 1968-; Radical Palestinian *fida'iyin* group founded by Aḥmad Jibril; broke off from PFLP.

PFLOAG — Popular Front for Liberation of Occupied Arab Gulf: 1970-; A radical group opposed to the existing governments of Oman, UAE and other Gulf States sponsored by the PDRY.

PLA — Palestine Liberation Army: 1964-; The official army of the PLO.

PLF — Palestine Liberation Front: 1965(?)-68; A Palestinian *fidā'īyīn* group founded by Aḥmad Jibril; later merged with part of ANM and other groups to form PFLP.

PLO — Palestine Liberation Organization: 1964-; Umbrella organization of various Palestinian groups.

POLP — Popular Organization for Liberation of Palestine: Maoist Palestinian *fidā'īyīn* group.

PPS — Parti Populaire Syrien: 1932-; Syrian national party founded by Anṭun Saᶜada; also known as SSNP.

PRSY — Peoples Republic of South Yemen: See PDRY.

PSP — Progressive Socialist Party: 1949-; Major Lebanese Druze political party associated with Kamāl Jumblaṭ.

RCC — Revolutionary Command Council: 1952-56; Egyptian military group led by Gamāl Abd al-Nāṣir, which planned the 1952 coup and then ran the government under leadership of Muḥammad Naguib.

RPP — Republican People's Party: 1923-; Major Turkish political party founded by Mustafa Kemal Atatürk.

SAR — Syrian Arab Republic: 1961-; Official name of Syria.

SAVAK — Sāzeman-e Attilᶜāt va Amniyat-e Keshvar: Organization for the information and security of the country; Iranian security forces combining roles of FBI and CIA.

SSNP — Syrian Social Nationalist Party: See PPS.

Tapline — Trans-Arabian Pipeline Co.: 1947-; Subsidiary of Aramco that built a 1,068.2 mile pipeline from Saudi Arabia to Sidon.

TPC — Turkish Petroleum Co.: 1912-29; Western dominated oil company that became basis for IPC.

UAA — Union of Arab Amirates: Also known as UAE (United Arab Emirates).

UAE — Union of Arab Emirates: 1971-; Members as of 1974 include Abu Dhabi, Dubai, Sharjah, Ajman, Umm al-Qaywayn and al-Fujayrah. (also United Arab Emirates).

UAR	United Arab Republic: 1958-61; Union of Egypt and Syria with former keeping name until 1971 when it became the ARE.
UJA	United Jewish Appeal: A major pro-Israeli Jewish fund-raising group in the United States.
UNCC	United Nations Conciliation Commission: 1948-49; Commission composed of France, Turkey and United States aimed at achieving a peace settlement between Israel and the Arab States.
UNDOF	United Nations Disengagement Observer Force: 1974-; An international military force established in June 1974 to patrol the buffer region separating Israeli and Syrian forces on the Golan Heights.
UNEF	United Nations Emergency Force: 1957-67; 1974-; An international military force established after 1956 Suez War between Egypt and Israel and reactivated after the 1974 War.
UNESCO	United Nations Educational, Scientific and Cultural Organization.
UNGA	United Nations General Assembly.
UNMAC	United Nations Mixed Armistice Commission: 1949-; International groups to supervise and investigate truce violations between Egypt and Israel-UNEIMAC, Jordan and Israel-UNJIMAC, Syria and Israel-UNSIMAC, and Lebanon and Israel, UNLIMAC.
UNOGIL	United Nations Observer Group in Lebanon: 1958; International group to investigate possible Syrian interference during Lebanese Civil War.
UNRPR	United Nations Relief for Palestinian Refugees: 1948-49; To provide immediate relief for Palestinian refugees; superseded by UNRWA.
UNRWA	United Nations Relief and Works Agency: 1949-; International group to temporarily house, feed and train Palestinian refugees.
UNSCOP	United Nations Special Committee on Palestine: 1947; U.N. Committee whose majority recommended partition of Palestine.
UNTSO	United Nations Truce Supervision Organization: 1948-49; Established to supervise the Arab-Israeli armistice.
WZO	World Zionist Organization: 1897-; Major Zionist body.
YAR	Yemen Arab Republic: 1962-; Official name of Northern Yemen.

TABLE OF DYNASTIES

The most important reference work for a list of Muslim dynasties, the names of their rulers and, in many cases, a genealogy table is E. de Zambaur's *Manuel de Généalogie et de Chronologie pour l'histoire de l'Islam* (Hanover, 1927, Reprinted 1955). The accompanying list follows the order established by Zambaur, but all dates have been checked against other sources. In many cases there is no agreement among scholars as to the beginning and, less frequently, the end of many dynasties:

Dynasties	Muslim Dates	Christian Dates
I. Sunnī Caliphs:		
A. Rāshidūn	11 - 40	632 - 661
B. Umayyads	41 - 132	661 - 750
C. ᶜAbbāsids	132 - 656	750 - 1258
D. ᶜAbbāsids of Cairo	659 - 923	1261 - 1517
II. Egypt and Southern Syria:		
A. Ṭūlūnids	254 - 292	868 - 905
B. Ikhshīdids	323 - 358	935 - 969
C. Fāṭimids	297 - 567	909 - 1171
D. Ayyūbids	564 - 9th Cent.	1169 - 15th C.
1. Egypt	564 - 650	1169 - 1252
2. Damascus	582 - 658	1186 - 1260
3. Aleppo	579 - 658	1183 - 1260
4. Mayyāfāriqīn, Sinjār	581 - 658	1185 - 1260
5. Baᶜlbakk	568 - 658	1172 - 1260
6. Hama	574 - 732	1178 - 1332
7. Ḥimṣ	574 - 661	1178 - 1262
8. Yemen	569 - 626	1174 - 1229
9. Ḥiṣn Kayfā and Āmid	629 - 9th Cent.	1232 - 15th C.
E. Mamlūks	648 - 922	1250 - 1517
1. Baḥrī	648 - 792	1250 - 1390
2. Circassian (Burji)	784 - 922	1382 - 1517
F. Muḥammad ᶜAlī Family	1220 - 1372	1805 - 1953
III. Arabian Peninsula:		
A. Ziyādids	204 - 409	819 - 1018
B. Yaᶜfurids	247 - 345	861 - 956
C. Qarāmiṭa	281 - 5th Cent.	894 - 11th C.
D. Zuray'ids	476 - 569	1083 - 1173
E. Najāhids	412 - 553	1021 - 1158
F. Mahdids	554 - 569	1159 - 1173
G. Ṣulayḥids	439 - 532	1047 - 1138
H. Ḥamdānids of Ṣanᶜā'	492 - 569	1098 - 1173
I. Ayyūbids	See Egypt	--- ---

Dynasties	Muslim Dates	Christian Dates
J. Rasūlids	626 - 858	1229 - 1454
K. Ṭāhirids of Yemen	850 - 923	1446 - 1517
L. Ṙassid Zaydī Imāms	246 - 680	860 - 1281
M. Qāsimid Zaydī Imāms of Ṣan^{c}ā'	1000 - 1382	1592 - 1962
N. Waḣhābīs	1159 -	1746 -
O. Rashīdids	1248 - 1342	1832 - 1923
P. Sa^{c}ūdī Family	1154 -	1741 -
IV. Iraq and Northern Syria:		
A. Ḥamdānids	293 - 394	905 - 1004
1. Mosul	293 - 391	905 - 1000
2. Aleppo	333 - 394	945 - 1004
B. Mirdāsids	414 - 472	1023 - 1079
C. ^{c}Uqaylids	380 - 489	990 - 1096
D. Marwānids	372 - 478	983 - 1085
E. Mazyadids	350 - 545	961 - 1150
F. Inālids	490 - 579	1096 - 1183
V. Asia Minor:		
A. Seljuks of Rūm	470 - 707	1077 - 1307
B. Menqüchekids	464 - ca.650	1071 - 1252
C. Dānishmandids	464 - 573	1071 - 1177
D. Isfendiyarids	690 - 866	1291 - 1461
E. Ṣārū Khānids	700 - 813	1300 - 1410
F. Åydīnids	708 - 829	1308 - 1425
G. Germiyāndis	699 - 832	1300 - 1429
H. Ḥamīdids	700 - 826	1239 - 1423
I. Menteshādids	700 - 829	1300 - 1426
J. Eretnaids	736 - 782	1335 - 1380
K. Ramaḍānids	780 - 819	1378 - 1416
L. Dhū-l-Qadrids	738 - 928	1337 - 1522
M. Karamānids	654 - 888	1256 - 1483
N. Ottomans	680 - 1342	1281 - 1924
VI. Caucasuses Before the Seljuks:		
A. Sājids	266 - 318	879 - 930
B. Musāfirids (or Sallarids or Kangarids)	304 - 483	916 - 1090
C. Rawwādids	4th Cent - 463	10th Cent - 1071
D. Sharwān Shāhs		
1. First Dynasty	183 - 381	799 - 991
2. Second Dynasty	418 - 455	1027 - 1063
3. Fourth Dynasty	1180 - 1236	1766 - 1821
E. Shaddādids	340 - 571	951 - 1174
F. Dābūyids	40 - 142	660 - 760
G. Bāwandids	45 - 750	665 - 1349
1. Kā'ūsīya Line	45 - 466	665 - 1074
2. Ispahbadīya Line	466 - 606	1074 - 1210
3. Kinkhwārīya Line	635 - 750	1238 - 1349
H. Bādūspānids	40 - 1006	665 - 1599
I. Zaydī ^{c}Alīds of Ṭabaristān	250 - 316	864 - 928

Dynasties	Muslim Dates	Christian Dates
VII. Iran Before the Seljuks:		
A. Ṭāhirids	205 - 259	821 - 873
B. Dulafids	210 - 284	825 - 898
C. Ṣaffārids	253 - ca.900	867 - ca.1495
D. Sāmānids	204 - 395	819 - 1005
E. Banijurids	233 - 337	848 - 948
F. Qarakhānids (Īlek Khāns)	382 - 607	992 - 1211
G. Khwarazm Shāhs		
1. Afrīghids	? - 385	? - 995
2. Ma'mūnids	385 - 408	995 - 1017
3. Governors	408 - 425	1017 - 1034
4. Anūshtigin Line	470 - 624	1077 - 1231
H. Ziyārids	315 - 483	927 - 1090
I. Ḥasanwayhids	348 - 405	959 - 1014
J. Būyids (Buwayhids)	320 - 447	932 - 1055
1. Baghdad	334 - 447	945 - 1055
2. Fars	322 - 454	934 - 1062
3. Kirmān	324 - 440	936 - 1048
4. Jabal	320 - 366	932 - 977
5. Hamadān	366 - 419	977 - 1028
6. Rayy	366 - 420	977 - 1029
7. ᶜUmān	363 - 388	974 - 998
K. Ilyāsids	320 - 357	932 - 968
L. Kākūyids (Kākwayhids)	398 - 443	1008 - 1051
VIII. Seljuks and Atabegs:		
A. Seljuks	429 - 700	1037 - 1300
1. Great Seljuks	429 - 552	1037 - 1157
2. Seljuks of Iraq	511 - 590	1117 - 1194
3. Seljuks of Syria	471 - 511	1078 - 1117
4. Seljuks of Kirmān	433 - 583	1041 - 1187
5. Seljuks of Rūm	See Asia Minor	
B. Būrids	497 - 549	1104 - 1154
C. Zangids		
1. Mosul	521 - 619	1127 - 1222
2. Syria	541 - 577	1146 - 1181
3. Sinjār	566 - 617	1170 - 1220
4. Jazira	576 - 648	1180 - 1250
D. Begteginids	539 - 630	1145 - 1233
E. Artugids	491 - 811	1098 - 1408
1. Ḥisn Kayfā Line	491 - 629	1098 - 1232
2. Mārdīn Line	497 - 811	1104 - 1408
F. Suqman Shāhs	493 - 604	1100 - 1207
G. Eldeguzids (or Ildenizids)	531 - 622	1136 - 1225
H. Salghurids	543 - 668	1148 - 1270
I. Faḍlawayhids	448 - 718	1056 - 1318
J. Hazarāspids	550 - 827	1155 - 1424
K. Qutlugh Khāns	619 - 706	1222 - 1306
IX. Mongols:		
A. Great Mongols	603 - 1043	1206 - 1634
B. Il-Khānids	654 - 754	1256 - 1353
C. Golden Horde	621 - 760	1224 - 1359

Dynasties	Muslim Dates	Christian Dates
D. White Horde	623 - 831	1226 - 1428
E. Chaghatayids	624 - 771	1227 - 1370
F. Khans of Kazan	841 - 959	1438 - 1552
G. Khans of Kasimof	854 - 1089	1450 - 1678
H. Khans of the Crimea	823 - 1197	1420 - 1783
X. Iran After the Mongols:		
A. Jalāyirids	736 - 835	1336 - 1432
B. Muzaffarids	713 - 795	1314 - 1393
C. Īnjūids	703 - 758	1303 - 1357
D. Sarbadārids	758 - 781	1357 - 1379
E. Karts	643 - 791	1245 - 1389
F. Qara Qoyunlu	782 - 873	1380 - 1468
G. Aq Qoyunlu	780 - 914	1378 - 1508
H. Ṣafavids	907 - 1145	1501 - 1732
I. Afshārids	1148 - 1210	1736 - 1795
J. Zands	1163 - 1209	1750 - 1794
K. Qājārs	1193 - 1342	1779 - 1924
L. Pahlavi	1342 -	1924 -
XI. Transoxiana and Afghanistan - India:		
A. Tīmūrids	771 - 912	1370 - 1506
B. Shaybānids	905 - 1007	1500 - 1598
C. Jānids	1009 - 1199	1559 - 1785
D. Mangits	1170 - 1339	1757 - 1920
E. Khāns of Khiva	921 - 1290	1515 - 1872
F. Ghaznavids	366 - 582	977 - 1186
G. Ghūrids	390 - 612	1000 - 1215

TABLE OF RULERS

A critical tool for any analysis of political developments is the list of caliphs, sultans, governors, presidents, prime ministers, etc. who ruled over Southwest Asia and Egypt. Students of pre-Twentieth Century Islamic history are very fortunate in having the excellent work by C.E. Bosworth, *The Islamic Dynasties* (Chicago: Aldine Publishing Co., 1967), University of Edinburgh Islamic Surveys No. 5. In 82 tables, Professor Bosworth lists every major and many minor dynasties from Spain through India. Each section lists the rulers, their regnal dates (in Muslim and Christian years), and then presents a brief historical sketch followed by a few pertinent references. The only weakness of this well-written and fully-indexed work is its lack of any genealogical tables.

If one wishes more extensive tables of rulers for medieval Islamic history, including numerous lists of wazirs and governors, full Muslim dates for the beginning of a rule and, when possible, Muslim dates of death, the best source is Edward von Zambaur, *Manuel de Généalogie et de Chronologie pour l'histoire de l'Islam* (Hanover, 1927; reprinted Berlin, 1955). There is also an Arabic translation of Zambaur by Zaki M. Ḥasan Bey, Ḥasan Aḥmad Maḥmūd *et al.*, *Mu^{c}jām al-ansāb wa l-usarāt al-ḥākima fī l-ta'rīkh al-Islāmī*, (Cairo: Arab League, 1370/1951). However, unlike Bosworth, neither Zambaur nor the translation of his work includes Christian dates, historical summaries or a bibliography.

One other important source for information on medieval dynasties, wazirs, etc. is *EI*[1] and *EI*[2]. On the other hand, Stanley Lane-Poole's pioneer work, *The Mohammadan Dynasties* (London, 1893; reprinted New York: Frederick Ungar Publishing Co., 1965) is outdated and inaccurate in places, although it includes dynasties not in Bosworth:

TABLES OF RULERS

I. The Caliphs

1. Orthodox or Rightly Guided Caliphs

11/632	Abū-Bakr	23/644	^{c}Uthmān b. ^{c}Affān
13/634	^{c}Umar b. al-Khaṭṭāb	35-40/656-61	^{c}Alī b. Abī-Ṭālib

2. Umayyad Caliphs

41/661	Mu^{c}āwiya I	99/717	^{c}Umar II
60/680	Yazīd I	101/720	Yazīd II
64/683	Mu^{c}āwiya II	105/724	Hishām
64/684	Marwān I	125/743	al-Walīd II
65/685	^{c}Abd al-Malik	126/744	Yazīd III
86/705	al-Walīd I	126/744	Ibrāhīm
96/715	Sulaymān	127-32/744-50	Marwān II

3. ᶜAbbāsid Caliphs

(a) In Iraq and Baghdad

132/749	al-Saffāḥ	322/934	al-Rāḍī
136/754	al-Manṣūr	329/940	al-Muttaqī
158/775	al-Mahdī	333/944	al-Mustakfī
169/785	al-Hādī	334/946	al-Mutīᶜ
170/786	Hārūn al-Rashīd	363/974	al-Ṭā'iᶜ
193/809	al-Amīn	381/991	al-Qādir
198/813	al-Ma'mūn	422/1031	al-Qā'im
218/833	al-Muᶜtaṣim	467/1075	al-Muqtadī
227/842	al-Wāthiq	487/1094	al-Mustaẓhir
232/847	al-Mutawakkil	512/1118	al-Mustarshid
247/861	al-Muntaṣir	529/1135	al-Rāshid
248/862	al-Mustaᶜīn	530/1136	al-Muqtafī
252/866	al-Muᶜtazz	555/1160	al-Mustanjid
255/869	al-Muhtadī	566/1170	al-Mustaḍī'
256/870	al-Muᶜtamid	575/1180	al-Nāṣir
279/892	al-Muᶜtaḍid	622/1225	al-Ẓāhir
289/902	al-Muktafī	623/1226	al-Mustanṣir
295/908	al-Muqtadir	640-56/1242-58	al-Mustaᶜṣim
320/932	al-Qāhir		

(b) In Cairo

659/1261	al-Mustanṣir	791/1389	al-Mutawakkil I, 3rd Reign
660/1261	al-Ḥākim I	808/1406	al-Mustaᶜīn
701/1302	al-Mustakfī I	816/1414	al-Muᶜtaḍid II
740/1340	al-Wāthiq I	845/1441	al-Mustakfī II
741/1341	al-Ḥākim II	855/1451	al-Qā'im
753/1352	al-Muᶜtaḍid I	859/1455	al-Mustanjid
763/1362	al-Mutawakkil I, 1st Reign	884/1479	al-Mutawakkil II
779/1377	al-Muᶜtaṣim , 1st Reign	903/1497	al-Mustamsik, 1st Reign
779/1377	al-Mutawakkil I, 2nd Reign	914/1508	al-Mutawakkil III, 1st Reign
785/1383	al-Wāthiq II	922/1516	al-Mustamsik, 2nd Reign
788/1385	al-Muᶜtaṣim, 2nd Reign	923/1517	al-Mutawakkil III, 2nd Reign

II. Egypt, Syria and Iraq

4. The Ṭūlūnids

254/868	Aḥmad b. Ṭūlūn	283/896	Hārūn
270/884	Khumārawayh	292/905	Shaybān
282/896	Jaysh		

5. The Ikhshīdids

323/935	Muḥammad b. Ṭughj al-Ikhshīd		
334/946	Ūnūjūr	355/966	Kāfūr
349/961	ᶜAlī	357-8/968-9	Aḥmad

6. The Fāṭimids

297/909	ᶜUbaydullāh al-Mahdī	487/1094	al-Mustaᶜlī
322/934	al-Qā'im	495/1101	al-Āmir
334/946	al-Manṣūr	524/1130	Interregnum
341/953	al-Muᶜizz	525/1131	al-Ḥāfiẓ
365/975	al-ᶜAzīz	544/1149	al-Ẓāfir
386/996	al-Ḥākim	549/1154	al-Fā'iz
411/1021	al-Ẓāhir	555-67/1160-71	al-ᶜĀḍid
427/1036	al-Mustanṣir		

7. The Ḥamdānids

(a) Mosul Branch

317/929	Nāṣir al-Dawla al-Ḥasan	379-401/	Ibrāhīm) Joint Rulers
358/969	ᶜUddat al-Dawla Abū Taghlib	989-1010	al-Ḥusayn)

(b) Aleppo Branch

333/945	Sayf al-Dawla ᶜAlī I	392/1002	ᶜAlī II
356/967	Saᶜd al-Dawla Sharīf I	394/1004	Sharīf II
381/991	Saᶜīd al-Dawla Saᶜīd		

8. The Zangids

(a) Mosul and Aleppo Lines

521/1127	ᶜImād al-Dīn Zangī b. Aq Sonqur		
541/1146	Sayf al-Dīn Ghāzī I	589/1193	Nūr al-Dīn Arslan Shāh I
544/1149	Quṭb al-Dīn Mawdūd	607/1211	ᶜIzz al-Dīn Masᶜūd II
564/1169	Sayf al-Dīn Ghāzī II	615/1218	Nūr al-Dīn Arslan Shāh II
572/1176	ᶜIzz al-Dīn Masᶜūd I	616-19/1219-22	Nāṣir al-Dīn Maḥmūd

(b) Damascus Line, Then Aleppo

541/1146	Nūr al-Dīn Maḥmūd b. Zangī
569-77/1174-81	Nūr al-Dīn Ismāᶜīl

9. The Ayyūbids

(a) In Egypt

564/1169	al-Malik al-Nāṣir Ṣalāḥ-al-Dīn (Saladin)		
589/1193	al-Malik al-ᶜAzīz	635/1238	al-Malik al-ᶜĀdil II
595/1198	al-Malik al-Manṣūr	637/1240	al-Malik al-Ṣāliḥ Najm al-Dīn Ayyūb
596/1200	al-Malik al-ᶜĀdil I	647/1249	al-Malik al-Muᶜaẓẓam Tūrān-Shāh
615/1218	al-Malik al-Kāmil	648-50/1250-2	al-Malik al-Ashraf II

(b) In Damascus

582/1186	al-Malik al-Afḍal	635/1238	al-Malik al-ᶜĀdil II

(b) In Damascus

592/1196	al-Malik al-ᶜĀdil I
615/1218	al-Malik al-Muᶜaẓẓam
624/1227	al-Malik al-Nāṣir Ṣalāḥ al-Dīn Dā'ūd
626/1229	al-Malik al-Ashraf
634/1237	al-Malik al-Ṣāliḥ Ismāᶜīl, 1st Reign
635/1238	al-Malik al-Kāmil
636/1239	al-Malik al-Ṣāliḥ Najm al-Dīn Ayyūb, 1st Reign
637/1239	al-Malik al-Ṣāliḥ Ismāᶜīl, 2nd Reign
643/1245	al-Malik al-Ṣāliḥ Najm al-Dīn Ayyūb, 2nd Reign
647-1249	al-Malik al-Muᶜaẓẓam Tūrān Shāh
648-58/1250-60	al-Malik al-Nāṣir II Ṣalāḥ al-Dīn

(c) In Aleppo

579/1183	al-Malik al-ᶜĀdil I
582/1186	al-Malik al-Ẓāhir Ghiyāth al-Dīn
613/1216	al-Malik al-ᶜAzīz Ghiyāth al-Dīn
634-58/1237-60	al-Malik al-Nāṣir II Ṣalāḥ al-Dīn

(d) The Yemen

569/1174	al-Malik al-Muᶜaẓẓam Shams al-Dīn Tūrān-Shāh
577/1181	al-Malik al-ᶜAzīz Ẓahīr al-Dīn Tughtigīn
593/1197	Muᶜizz al-Dīn Ismāᶜīl
598/1202	al-Malik al-Nāṣir Ayyūb
611/1214	al-Malik al-Muẓaffar Sulaymān
612-26/1215-29	al-Malik al-Masᶜūd Ṣalāḥ al-Dīn

NOTE: On other branches, see Bosworth and Zambaur.

10. The Mamlūks

(a) Baḥrī Line

648/1250	Shajar al-Durr
648/1250	Aybak
655/1257	ᶜAlī
657/1259	Quṭuz
658/1260	Baybars I
676/1277	Baraka Khān
678/1280	Salāmish
678/1280	Qalā'ūn
689/1290	Khalīl
693/1294	al-Nāṣir Muḥammad, 1st Reign
694/1295	Kitbughā
696/1297	Lājīn
698/1299	al-Nāṣir Muḥammad, 2nd Reign
708/1309	Baybars II
709/1309	al-Nāṣir Muḥammad, 3rd Reign
741/1340	Abū-Bakr
742/1341	Kūjūk
743/1342	Aḥmad
743/1342	Ismāᶜīl
746/1345	Shaᶜbān I
747/1346	Ḥājjī I
748/1347	al-Nāṣir al-Ḥasan, 1st Reign
752/1351	Ṣāliḥ
755/1354	al-Nāṣir al-Ḥasan, 2nd Reign
762/1361	al-Manṣūr Muḥammad
764/1363	Shaᶜbān II
778/1376	al-Manṣūr ᶜAlī
783/1382	al-Ṣāliḥ Ḥājjī II 1st Reign
(784/1382	Barqūq)
791/1389	Ḥājjī II, 2nd Reign

(b) Circassian Line

784/1382	Barqūq, 1st Reign	857/1453	^{c}Uthmān
(791/1389	Ḥājjī II)	857/1453	Ināl
792/1390	Barqūq, 2nd Reign		
801/1399	Faraj, 1st Reign	865/1461	al-Mu'ayyad Aḥmad
808/1405	al-Manṣūr ^{c}Abd al-^{c}Azīz	865/1461	Khūshqadam
808/1405	Faraj, 2nd Reign	872/1467	Bilbay
815/1412	al-^{c}Ādil al-Musta^{c}īn	872/1468	Timurbughā
815/1412	al-Mu'ayyad Shaykh	872/1468	al-Ashraf Qāyitbāy
824/1421	al-Muẓaffar Aḥmad	901/1496	al-Nāṣir Muḥammad
824/1421	Ṭaṭār	903/1498	Qānṣūh
824/1421	al-Ṣāliḥ Muḥammad	905/1500	Jānbalāṭ
825/1422	Barsbay	906/1501	al-^{c}Ādil Tūmān Bay
841/1437	Yūsuf	906/1501	Qānṣūh al-Ghawrī
842/1438	al-Ẓāhir Jaqmaq	922/1517	al-Ashraf Tūmān Bay

11. Muḥammad ^{c}Alī's Line

Egypt

1220/1805	Muḥammad ^{c}Alī Pasha	1309/1892	^{c}Abbās II Hilmī
1264/1848	Ibrāhīm Pasha	1333/1914	Ḥusayn Kāmil (Sultan)
1264/1848	^{c}Abbās I Pasha	1335/1917	Aḥmad Fu'ād I (King from 1340/1922)
1270/1854	Sa^{c}īd Pasha	1355/1936	Fārūq
1280/1863	Ismā^{c}īl (Khedive from 1284/1867)	1371-2/1952-3	Fu'ād II
1296/1878	Tawfīq		

12. British Consul Generals, High Commissioners For Egypt 1879-1936

Consul Generals

1879	Sir Edward Malet	1907	Sir Eldon Gorst
1883	Evelyn Baring (Lord Cromer)	1911	Sir Herbert Kitchener

High Commissioners

1914	Sir Henry MacMahon	1925	Lord George Lloyd
1916	Sir Reginald Wingate	1929	Sir Percy Loraine
1919	Sir Edmund Allenby	1933-36	Sir Miles Lampson (Lord Killearn)

13. British High Commissioners For Palestine

1920	Sir Herbert Samuel	1937	Sir Harold MacMichael
1925	Field Marshal Lord Plumer	1944	Field Marshal Lord Gort
1928	Sir John Chancellor	1945-48	Sir Alan Cunningham
1931	Sir Arthur Wauchope		

14. French High Commissioners and Delegate Generals For Syria – Lebanon

High Commissioners

1919	General Henri Gouraud	1926	Henri Ponsot

High Commissioners

1923	General Maxime Weygand	1940	General Henri-Fernand Dentz
1925	General Maurice Sarrail	1941	General Georges Catroux
1925	Henri de Jouvenal	1943	Yves Chataigneau
1933	Damien de Martel	1943	Jean Helleu
1938	Gabriel Puaux	1944-46	General Paul Emile Beynet

15. Presidents of Lebanon

1926	Charles Dabbas	Sharl Dabbās
1934	Habib Sa'd	Ḥabīb al-Saᶜd
1936	Emile Edde	Imīl Iddi
1941	Alfred Naccache	Alfrad Naqqāsh
1943	Eyub Tabet	ᶜAyyūb Thābit
1943	Petro Trad	Batru Trād
1943	Bishara Khuri	Bishārah al-Khūrī
1952	Camille Chamoun	Kamīl Shimᶜūn
1958	General Fouad Chehab	Fu'ād Shihāb
1964	Charles Helou	Sharl Ḥilū
1970	Suleiman Franjieh	Sulaymān Franjīyah

16. Hāshimites of Hejaz, Jordan and Iraq

Hejaz

1908-16	al-Ḥusayn (Amīr)		
1916-24	al-Ḥusayn (King)	1924-25	ᶜAlī

Transjordan — Jordan

1921-46	ᶜAbdallāh (Amīr)	1951-52	Ṭalāl
1946-51	ᶜAbdallāh (King)	1952-	al-Ḥusayn

Iraq

1921-33	Fayṣal I	1939-58	Fayṣal II
1933-39	Ghāzī		

17. Prime Ministers of Israel

February 14, 1949	David Ben-Gurion
December 7, 1953	Moshe Sharett
November 3, 1955	David Ben-Gurion
June 16, 1963	Levi Eshkol (Died February 26, 1969)
March 17, 1969	Golda Meir
June 3, 1974	Yitzhak Rabin

III. Arabian Peninsula

18. The Ṣulayḥids

Yemen

429/1037	ᶜAlī b. Muḥammad	484/1091	al-Manṣūr Sabā'
459/1067	al-Mukarram Aḥmad	492-532/1099-1138	al-Sayyida Arwā
477/1084	al-Mukarram ᶜAlī		

19. The Rasūlids

Yemen

626/1229	al-Malik al-Manṣūr cUmar I	803/1400	al-Malik al-Nāṣir Aḥmad
647/1250	al-Malik al-Muẓaffar Yūsuf I	827/1424	al-Malik al-Manṣūr cAbdullāh
694/1295	al-Malik al-Ashraf cUmar II	830/1427	al-Malik al-Ashraf Ismācīl II
696/1296	al-Malik al-Mu'ayyad Dā'ūd	831/1428	al-Malik al-Ẓāhir Yaḥyā
721/1322	al-Malik al-Mujāhid cAlī	842/1439	al-Malik al-Ashraf Ismācīl III
764/1363	al-Malik al-Afḍal al-cAbbās	845/1442	al-Malik al-Muẓaffar Yūsuf II
778/1377	al-Malik al-Ashraf Ismācīl I		

846/1442	al-Malik al-Mufaḍḍal Muḥammad)	RIVALS
846/1442	al-Malik al-Nāṣir cAbdullāh)	
854/1450	al-Malik al-Mascūd)	
855/1451	al-Malik al-Mu'ayyad)	

20. Zaydī Imāms - Modern Period (Qāsimid Line)

1000/1592	al-Qāsim al-Manṣūr	1160/1747	al-cAbbās al-Mahdī
1029/1620	Muḥammad al-Mu'ayyad I	1190/1776	cAlī al-Manṣūr
1054/1644	Ismācīl al-Mutawakkil	1221/1806	Aḥmad al-Mahdī
1087/1676	Muḥammad al-Mu'ayyad II	? ?	cAlī al-Manṣūr, 2nd Reign
1092/1681	Muḥammad al-Hādī	1257/1841	al-Qāsim al-Mahdī
1097/1686	Muḥammad al-Mahdī	1261/1845	Muḥammad Yaḥyā
1128/1716	al-Qāsim al-Mutawakkil	1289/1872	Ottoman Occupation
1139/1726	al-Ḥusayn al-Manṣūr, 1st Reign	1308/1890	Ḥamīd al-Dīn Yaḥyā
1139/1726	Muḥammad al-Hādī al-Majīd	1322/1904	Yaḥyā Maḥmūd al-Mutawakkil
1140/1728	al-Ḥusayn al-Manṣūr, 2nd Reign	1367/1948	Sayf al-Islām Aḥmad
		1382/1962	Muḥammad Badr

21. Sacūdī Family

1159/1746	Muḥammad b. Sacūd	1287/1871	Sacūd b. Fayṣal
1179/1765	cAbd al-cAzīz I	1291/1874	cAbdullāh III, 2nd Reign
1218/1803	Sacūd b. cAbd al-cAzīz	1305/1887	Conquest by Rashīdids
1229/1814	cAbdullāh I b. Sacūd	1307/1889	cAbd al-Raḥmān b. Fayṣal, Vassal Governor
1233-8/1818-22	Ottoman Occupation	1308/1891	Muḥammad b. Fayṣal al-Mutawwic, Vassal Governor
1238/1823	Turkī	1319/1902	cAbd al-cAzīz II
1249/1834	Fayṣal I, 1st Reign	1373/1953	Sacūd
1253/1837	Khālid b. Sacūd	1384/1964	Fayṣal II
1257/1841	cAbdullāh II b. Thunayyān		
1259/1843	Fayṣal I, 2nd Reign		
1282/1865	cAbdullāh III b. Fayṣal, 1st Reign		

IV. Iran and Afghanistan

22. The Ṭāhirids

205/821	Ṭāhir I b. al-Ḥusayn	230/845	Ṭāhir II
207/822	Ṭalḥa	248-59/862-73	Muḥammad
213/828	^{c}Abdullāh		

23. The Sāmānids

204/819	Aḥmad I b. Asad b. Sāmān	343/954	al-Amīr al-Mu'ayyad ^{c}Abd al-Malik I
250/864	Naṣr I b. Aḥmad	350/961	al-Amīr al-Sadīd Manṣūr I
279/892	Ismā^{c}īl I b. Aḥmad	365/976	al-Amīr al-Riḍā Nūḥ II
295/907	Aḥmad II b. Ismā^{c}īl	387/997	Manṣūr II
301/914	al-Amīr al-Sa^{c}īd Naṣr II	389/999	^{c}Abd al-Malik II
331/943	al-Amīr al-Ḥamīd Nūḥ I	390-5/1000-5	Ismā^{c}īl II al-Muntaṣir

24. The Ṣaffārids

253/867	Ya^{c}qūb b. Layth al-Ṣaffār	296/908	Layth b. ^{c}Alī
265/879	^{c}Amr b. Layth	298/910	Muḥammad b. ^{c}Alī
288/901	Ṭāhir b. Muḥammad b. ^{c}Amr		

NOTE: A full list can be found in Bosworth, p. 103.

25. The Būyids (Buwayhids)

(a) Line in Fārs and Khūzistān

322/932	^{c}Imād al-Dawla ^{c}Alī	403/1012	Sulṭān al-Dawla
338/949	^{c}Aḍud al-Dawla Fanā-Khusraw	412/1021	Musharrif al-Dawla Ḥasan
372/983	Sharāf al-Dawla Shīrzīl	415/1024	^{c}Imād al-Dīn Marzubān
380/990	Ṣamṣām al-Dawla Marzubān	440/1048	al-Malik al-Raḥīm Khusraw-Fīrūz
388/998	Bahā' al-Dawla Fīrūz	447-54/1055-62	Fūlād-Sutūn (Fārs only)

(b) Line in Kirmān

324/936	Mu^{c}izz al-Dawla Aḥmad	388/998	Bahā'al-Dawla Fīrūz
338/949	^{c}Aḍud al-Dawla Fanā-Khusraw	403/1012	Qawām al-Dawla
372/983	Ṣamṣām al-Dawla Marzubān	419-40/1028-48	^{c}Imād al-Dīn Marzubān

(c) Line in Jibāl

320/932	^{c}Imād al-Dawla ^{c}Alī	335-66/947-77	Rukn al-Dawla Ḥasan

1. Branch in Hamadan and Isfahān

366/977	Mu'ayyid al-Dawla Būya	387/997	Shams al-Dawla
373/983	Fakhr al-Dawla ^{c}Alī	412-c.419/1021-c.1029	Samā' al-Dawla

2. Branch in Rayy

366/977	Fakhr al-Dawla ^{c}Alī	387-420/997-1029	Majd al-Dawla Rustam

(d) Line in Iraq

334/945	Mu^c^izz al-Dawla Aḥmad	403/1012	Sulṭān al-Dawla
356/967	^c^Izz al-Dawla Bakhtiyār	412/1021	Musharrif al-Dawla Ḥasan
367/978	^c^Aḍud al-Dawla Fanā-Khusraw	416/1025	Jalāl al-Dawla Shīrzīl
372/983	Ṣamṣām al-Dawla Marzubān	435/1044	^c^Imād al-Dīn al-Marzubān
376/987	Sharāf al-Dawla Shīrzīl	440-7/1048-55	al-Malik al-Raḥīm Khusraw-Fīrūz
379/989	Bahā' al-Dawla Fīrūz		

26. Great Seljuks

429/1038	Rukn al-Dunyā wa-l-Dīn Toghril I (Tughril)
455/1063	^c^Aḍud al-Dawla Alp-Arslān
465/1072	Jalāl al-Dawla Malik-Shāh I
485/1092	Nāṣir al-Dīn Maḥmūd I
487/1094	Rukn al-Dīn Berk-yāruq (Barkiyāruq)
498/1105	Mu^c^izz al-Dīn Malik-Shāh II
498/1105	Ghiyāth al-Dīn Muḥammad I
511-52/1118-57	Mu^c^izz al-Dīn Sanjar

List of other families can be found in Bosworth, pp. 115-116.

27. Khwārazm-Shāhs - Anūshtigin Line

c.470/c.1077	Anūshtigin Gharcha'ī	567/1172	^c^Alā' al-Dīn Tekish
490/1097	Turkish Governor	567-89/1172-93	Rival Ruler
490/1097	Quṭb al-Dīn Muḥammad	596/1200	^c^Alā' al-Dīn Muḥammad
521/1127	^c^Alā' al-Dīn Atsīz	617-28/1220-31	Jalāl al-Dīn
551/1156	Īl-Arslān		

28. The Ghaznavids

366/977	Nāṣir al-Dawla Sebüktigīn	444/1053	Qawām al-Dawla Toghril, Usurper
387/997	Ismā^c^īl	444/1053	Farrukhzād
388/998	Maḥmūd	451/1059	Ibrāhīm
421/1030	Muḥammad, 1st Reign	492/1099	Mas^c^ūd III
421/1031	Mas^c^ūd I	508/1115	Shīrzād
432/1041	Muḥammad, 2nd Reign	509/1115	Arslān Shāh
432/1041	Shihāb al-Dawla Mawdūd	512/1118	Bahrām Shāh
441/1050	Mas^c^ūd II	547/1152	Khusraw Shāh
441/1050	^c^Alī	555-82/1160-86	Khusraw Malik
441/1050	^c^Abd al-Rashīd		

29. The Īl-Khānids

654/1256	Hülegü (Hūlagū)	694/1295	Maḥmūd Ghāzān
663/1265	Abaqa	703/1304	Muḥammad Khudābanda Öljeytü
680/1282	Aḥmad Tegüder (Takūdār)	716/1317	Abū Sa^c^īd
683/1284	Arghūn	736/1335	Arpa
690/1291	Gaykhatu	736/1336	Mūsā
694/1295	Baydu	(736-54/1336-53 Period of several rival Khāns)	

30. The Tīmūrids

Supreme Rulers

771/1370	Tīmūr (Temur)	854/1450	ʿAbdullāh
807/1405	Khalīl (till 812/1409)	855/1451	Abu Saʿīd
807/1405	Shāh Rukh	873/1469	Ahmad
850/1447	Ulugh Beg	899-906/1494-1500	Maḥmūd b. Abī Saʿīd
853/1449	ʿAbd al-Laṭīf		

31. The Ṣafavids

907/1501	Ismāʿīl I	1105/1694	Ḥusayn I
930/1524	Ṭahmāsp I	1135/1722	Ṭahmāsp II
984/1576	Ismāʿīl II	1145/1732	ʿAbbās III
985/1578	Muḥammad Khudābanda	1163/1749	Sulaymān II
996/1588	ʿAbbās I	1163/1750	Ismāʿīl III
1038/1629	Safī I	1166/1753	Ḥusayn II
1052/1642	ʿAbbās II	1200/1786	Muḥammad
1077/1666	Sulaymān I(Ṣafī II)		

32. The Afshārids

1148/1736	Nādir Shāh, Ṭahmāsp Qulī Khān	1161/1748	Ibrāhīm
1160/1747	ʿĀdil Shāh, ʿAlī Qulī Khān	1161-1210/1748-95	Shāh Rukh (in Khurasan)

33. The Zands

1163/1750	Muḥammad Karīm Khān	1193-9/1779-85	ʿAlī Murād (in Iṣfahān)
1193/1779	Abū l-Fatḥ) Muḥammad ʿAlī) Conjointly	1199/1785	Jaʿfar
1193-5/1779-81	Ṣādiq (in Shīrāz)	1203-9/1789-94	Luṭf ʿAlī

34. The Qājārs

1193/1779	Āghā Muḥammad	1313/1896	Muẓaffar al-Dīn
1212/1797	Fatḥ ʿAlī Shāh	1324/1907	Muḥammad ʿAlī
1250/1834	Muḥammad	1327-42/1909-24	Aḥmad
1264/1848	Nāṣir al-Dīn		

35. Pahlavi Dynasty

December 13, 1925	Reza Shāh	September 18, 1941	Mohammed Reza Shāh

V. Anatolia

36. Seljuks of Rūm

470/1077	Sulaymān b. Quṭlumush	588/1192	Ghiyāth al-Dīn Kay-Khusraw I, 1st Reign
479/1086	Interregnum		
485/1092	Qilich Arslān I	592/1196	Rukn al-Dīn Sulaymān II
500/1107	Malik-Shāh	600/1204	ʿIzz al-Dīn Qilich Arslān III
510/1116	Rukn al-Dīn Masʿūd I		
551/1156	ʿIzz al-Dīn Qilich Arslān II	601/1204	Ghiyāth al-Dīn Kay-Khusraw I, 2nd Reign

36. Seljuks of Rūm (cont)

607/1210	^{c}Izz al-Dīn Kay-Kā'ūs I	681/1282	Ghiyāth al-Dīn Mas^{c}ūd II, 1st Reign
616/1219	^{c}Alā' al-Dīn Kay-Qubādh I	683/1284	^{c}Alā' al-Dīn Kay-Qubādh III, 1st Reign
634/1237	Ghiyāth al-Dīn Kay-Khusraw II	683/1284	Mas^{c}ūd II, 2nd Reign
644/1246	^{c}Izz al-Dīn Kay-Kā'ūs II	692/1293	Kay-Qubādh III, 2nd Reign
646/1248	Kay-Kā'ūs II) Rukn al-Dīn Qilich) Jointly Arslān IV)	693/1294	Mas^{c}ūd II, 3rd Reign
647/1249	Kay-Kā'ūs II,) Qilich Arslān IV)Jointly ^{c}Alā' al-Dīn Kay-Qubādh II)	700/1301	Kay-Qubādh III, 3rd Reign
655/1257	Qilich Arslān IV	702/1303	Mas^{c}ūd II, 4th Reign
663/1265	Ghiyāth al-Dīn Kay-Khusraw III	704/1305	Kay-Qubādh III, 4th Reign
		707/1307	Ghiyāth al-Dīn Mas^{c}ūd III

37. The Ottomans

680/1281	Osman	1049/1640	Ibrāhīm
724/1324	Orhān	1058/1648	Meḥmet IV
761/1360	Murād I	1099/1687	Süleymān II
791/1389	Bāyezīd I	1102/1691	Aḥmed II
805/1403	Interregnum	1106/1695	Muṣṭafā II
816/1413	Meḥmet I Chelebi	1115/1703	Aḥmed III
824/1421	Murād II, 1st Reign	1143/1730	Maḥmūd I
848/1444	Meḥmet II Fâtiḥ, 1st Reign	1168/1754	Osmān III
850/1446	Murād II, 2nd Reign	1171/1757	Muṣṭafā III
855/1451	Meḥmet II, 2nd Reign	1187/1774	^{c}Abdülhamīd I
886/1481	Bāyezīd II	1203/1789	Selīm III
918/1512	Selīm I Yavuz	1222/1807	Muṣṭafā IV
926/1520	Süleymān I Kānūnī	1223/1808	Maḥmūd II
974/1566	Selīm II	1255/1839	^{c}Abdülmecīd I
982/1574	Murād III	1277/1861	^{c}Abdülezīz
1003/1595	Meḥmet III	1293/1876	Murād V
1012.1603	Aḥmed I	1293/1876	^{c}Abdülḥamīd II
1026/1617	Muṣṭafā I, 1st Reign	1327/1909	Meḥmet V Reshād
1027/1618	Osmān II	1336/1918	Meḥmet VI
1031/1622	Muṣṭafā I, 2nd Reign	1341-42/1922-4	^{c}Abdülmecīd II (Caliph only)
1032/1623	Murād IV		

38. Presidents of Turkey

1923	Muṣṭafā Kemal Ataturk	1961	Cemal Gürsel
1938	İsmet İnönü	1966	Cevdet Sunay
1950	Celal Bayar	1973	Fahri Korutürk

GENEALOGIES

For an understanding of many political events in Islamic history, a knowledge of the genealogical relationships among individuals is critical. The most extensive collection of genealogies was prepared by Edward de Zambaur as part of his *Manuel de Généalogie et de Chronologie pour l'histoire de l'Islam* (Hanover, 1927; reprinted in Berlin, 1955). He also prepared a supplement with twenty very extensive tables.

Stanley Lane-Poole's *The Mohammadan Dynasties* (London, 1893; reprinted New York: Frederich Ungar Publishing Co., 1965) includes numerous genealogy tables which can be used. Numerous articles in *EI*[1] and *EI*[2] include valuable tables, while A.D. Alderson's *The Structure of the Ottoman Dynasty* (Oxford: Clarendon Press, 1956) is the best Western source for genealogy tables related to the Ottoman family.

A recent reference work in Arabic is by Dr. Aḥmad al-Saᶜīd Sulaymān, entitled *Ta'rīkh al-Duwal al-Islāmiya wa Muᶜjam al-Asr al-Hakima* (Cairo: Dār al-Maᶜārif [n.d.]). His book includes 115 dynasties with a brief historical introduction, the names and dates of the rulers and, whenever possible, a genealogy table.

The following genealogy tables cover some of the major Islamic dynasties, as well as a few others which have proved useful for teaching purposes. As in the Table of Rulers, only the most common name of an individual is given rather than his full title. The geographical-chronological ordering established in the Table of Dynasties is followed.

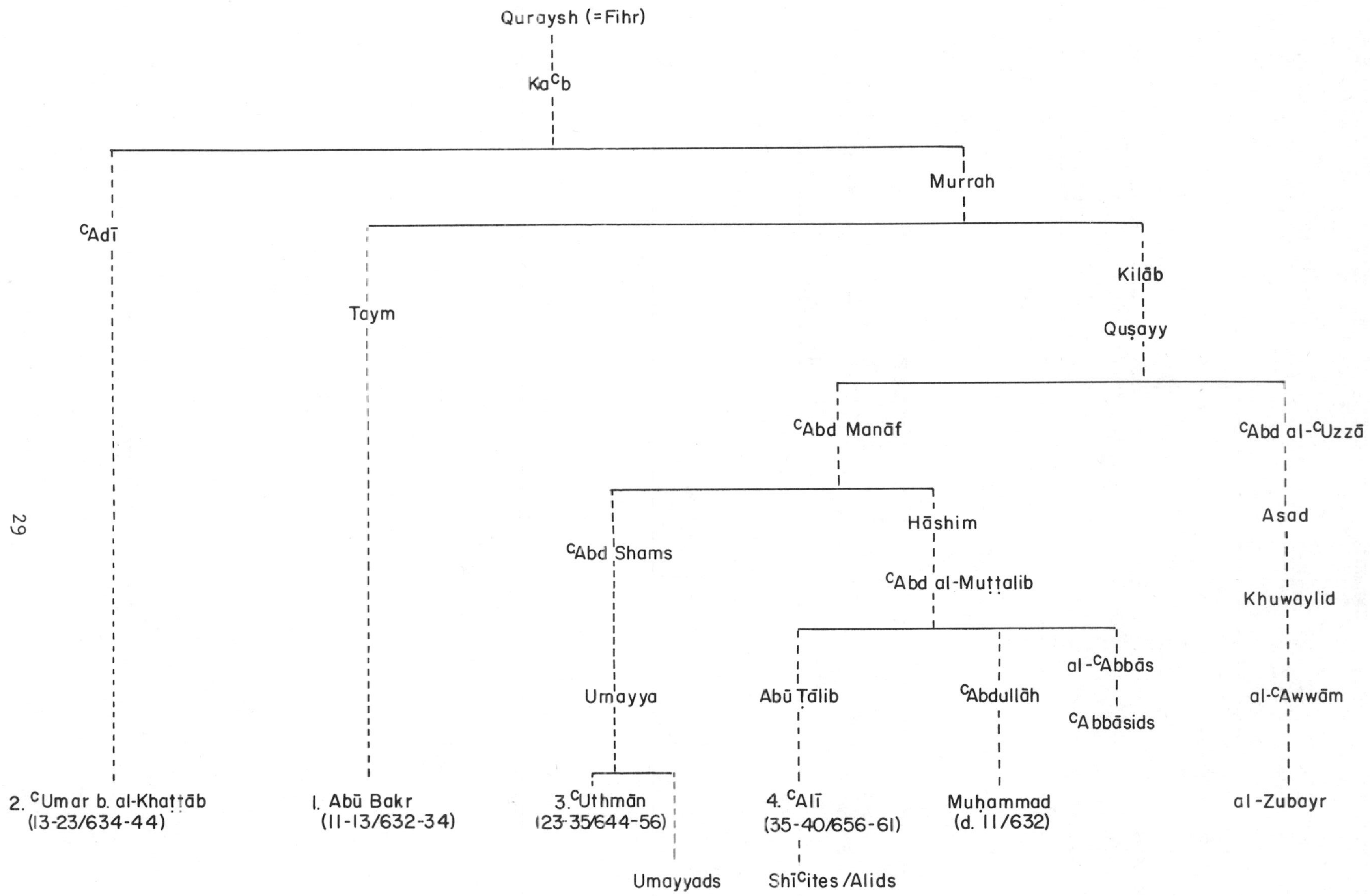

I LEADING FAMILIES OF MECCA

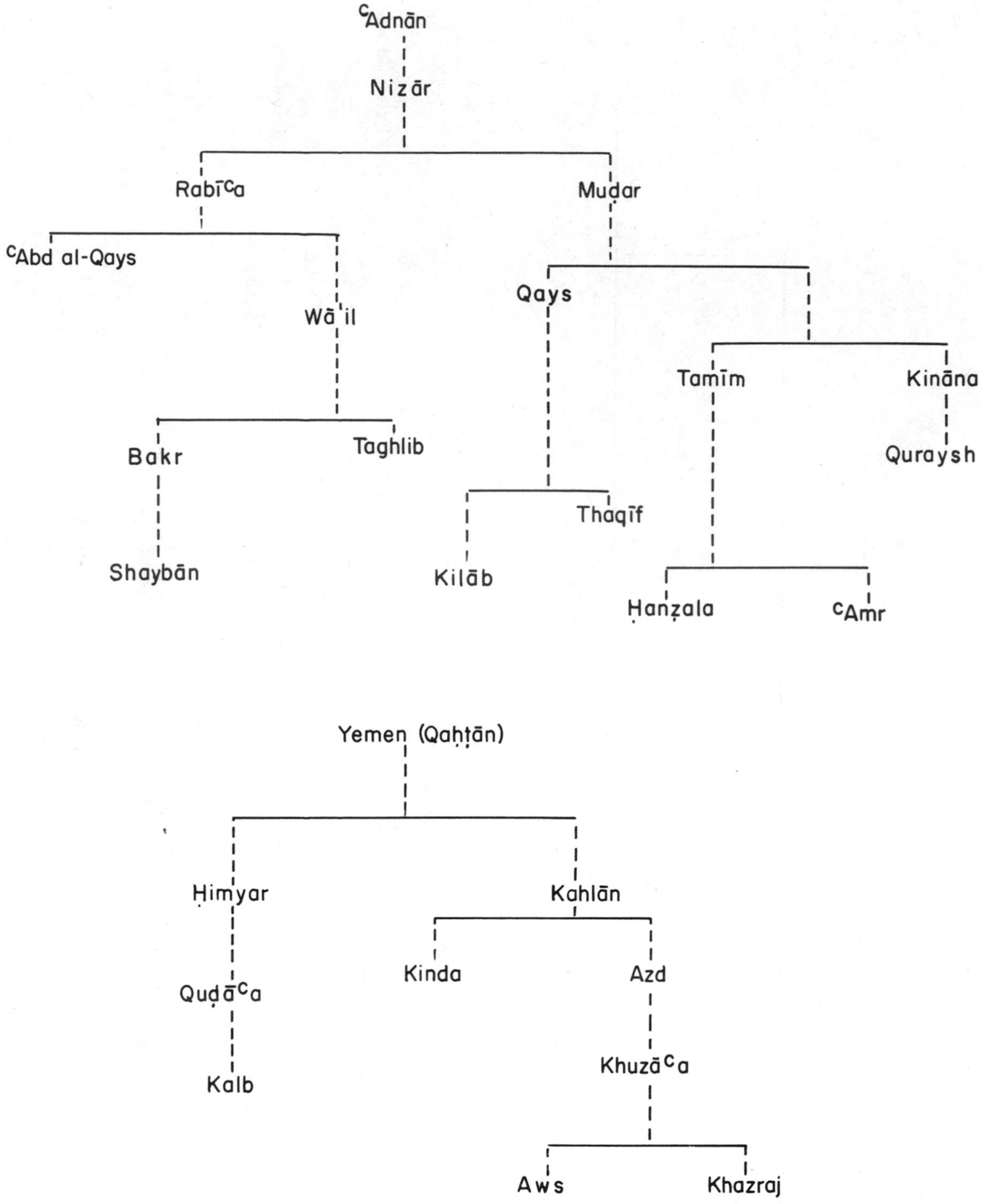

II MAJOR ARAB TRIBES: SKELETON OUTLINE

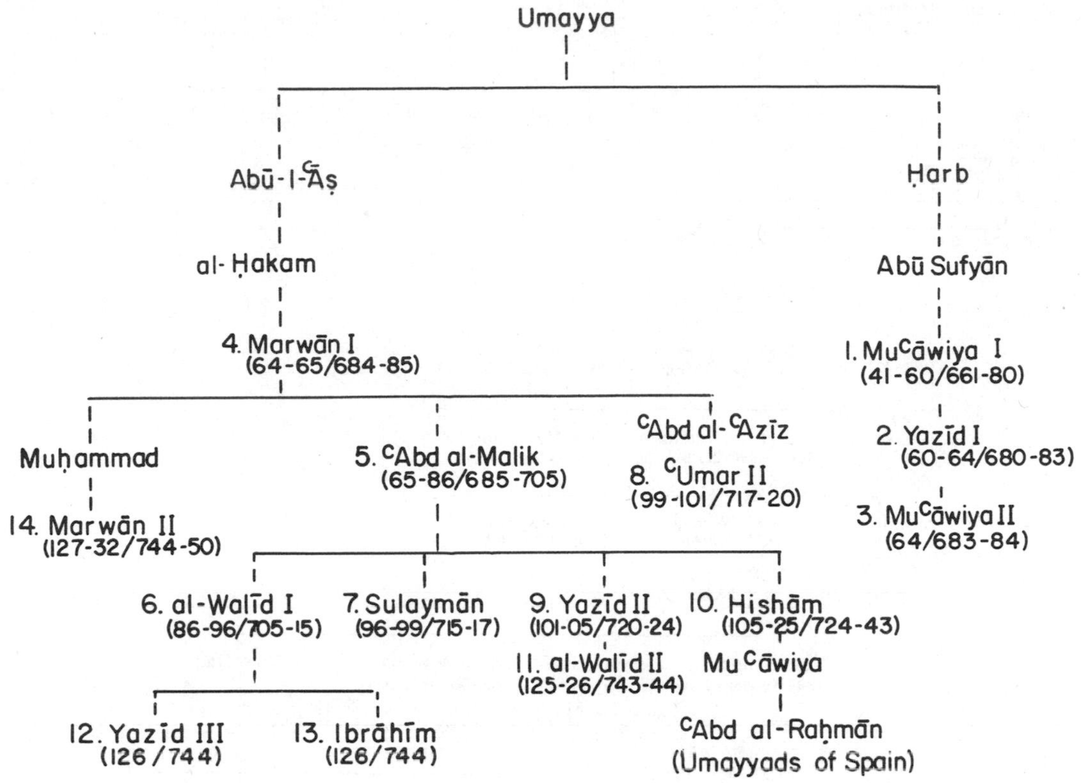
Umayya
Abū-l-ᶜĀṣ
Ḥarb
al-Ḥakam
Abū Sufyān
4. Marwān I
(64-65/684-85)
1. Muᶜāwiya I
(41-60/661-80)
Muḥammad
5. ᶜAbd al-Malik
(65-86/685-705)
ᶜAbd al-ᶜAzīz
8. ᶜUmar II
(99-101/717-20)
2. Yazīd I
(60-64/680-83)
3. Muᶜāwiya II
(64/683-84)
14. Marwān II
(127-32/744-50)
6. al-Walīd I
(86-96/705-15)
7. Sulaymān
(96-99/715-17)
9. Yazīd II
(101-05/720-24)
10. Hishām
(105-25/724-43)
11. al-Walīd II
(125-26/743-44)
Muᶜāwiya
12. Yazīd III
(126/744)
13. Ibrāhīm
(126/744)
ᶜAbd al-Raḥmān
(Umayyads of Spain)

III UMAYYADS
(41-132/661-750)

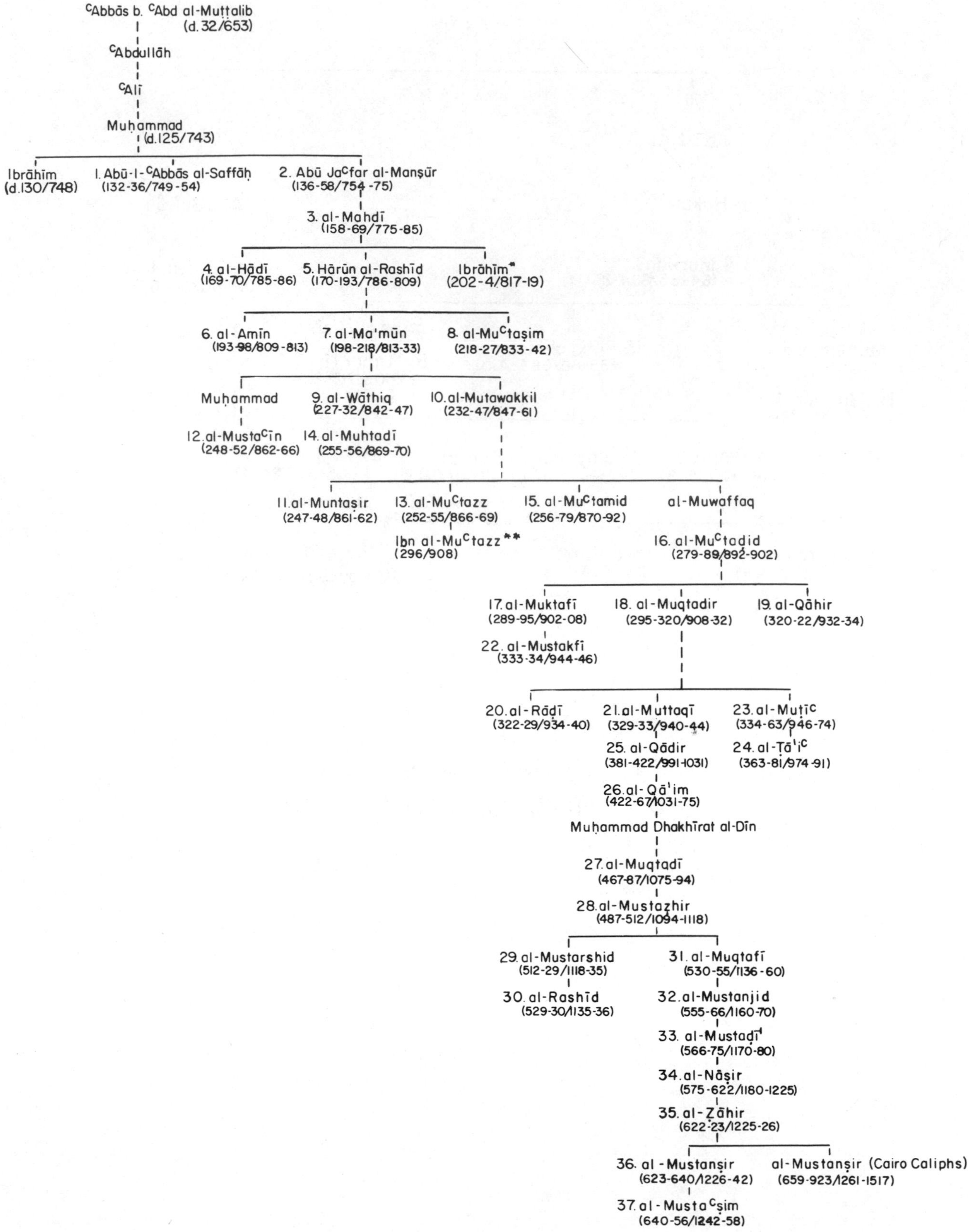
ʿAbbās b. ʿAbd al-Muṭṭalib (d.32/653)
ʿAbdullāh
ʿAlī
Muḥammad (d.125/743)
Ibrāhīm (d.130/748)
1. Abū-l-ʿAbbās al-Saffāḥ (132-36/749-54)
2. Abū Jaʿfar al-Manṣūr (136-58/754-75)
3. al-Mahdī (158-69/775-85)
4. al-Hādī (169-70/785-86)
5. Hārūn al-Rashīd (170-193/786-809)
Ibrāhīm* (202-4/817-19)
6. al-Amīn (193-98/809-813)
7. al-Ma'mūn (198-218/813-33)
8. al-Muʿtaṣim (218-27/833-42)
Muḥammad
9. al-Wāthiq (227-32/842-47)
10. al-Mutawakkil (232-47/847-61)
12. al-Mustaʿīn (248-52/862-66)
14. al-Muhtadī (255-56/869-70)
11. al-Muntaṣir (247-48/861-62)
13. al-Muʿtazz (252-55/866-69)
15. al-Muʿtamid (256-79/870-92)
al-Muwaffaq
Ibn al-Muʿtazz** (296/908)
16. al-Muʿtaḍid (279-89/892-902)
17. al-Muktafī (289-95/902-08)
18. al-Muqtadir (295-320/908-32)
19. al-Qāhir (320-22/932-34)
22. al-Mustakfī (333-34/944-46)
20. al-Rāḍī (322-29/934-40)
21. al-Muttaqī (329-33/940-44)
23. al-Muṭīʿ (334-63/946-74)
25. al-Qādir (381-422/991-1031)
24. al-Ṭā'iʿ (363-81/974-91)
26. al-Qā'im (422-67/1031-75)
Muḥammad Dhakhīrat al-Dīn
27. al-Muqtadī (467-87/1075-94)
28. al-Mustaẓhir (487-512/1094-1118)
29. al-Mustarshid (512-29/1118-35)
31. al-Muqtafī (530-55/1136-60)
30. al-Rashīd (529-30/1135-36)
32. al-Mustanjid (555-66/1160-70)
33. al-Mustaḍī' (566-75/1170-80)
34. al-Nāṣir (575-622/1180-1225)
35. al-Ẓāhir (622-23/1225-26)
36. al-Mustanṣir (623-640/1226-42)
al-Mustanṣir (Cairo Caliphs) (659-923/1261-1517)
37. al-Mustaʿṣim (640-56/1242-58)

IV ʿABBĀSIDS

(132-650/749-1258)

* In Baghdad

** Caliph for part of a day

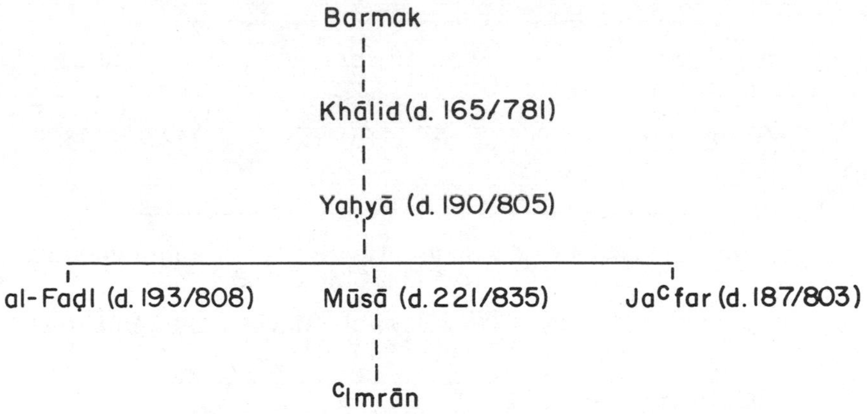

V BARMAKIDS

(^{c}Abbāsid wazīrs, military leaders, and governors)

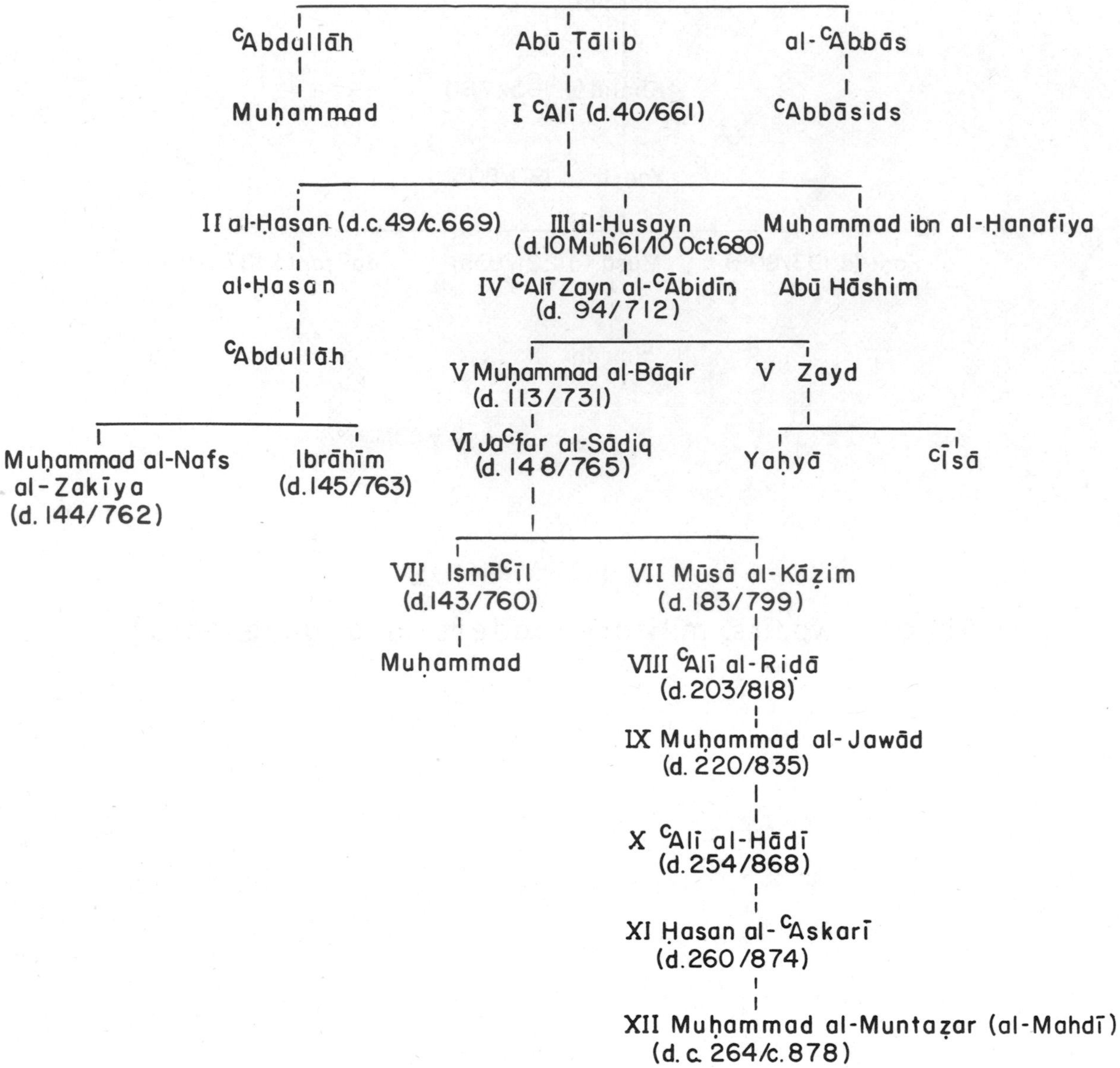

VI EARLY SHĪʿITES

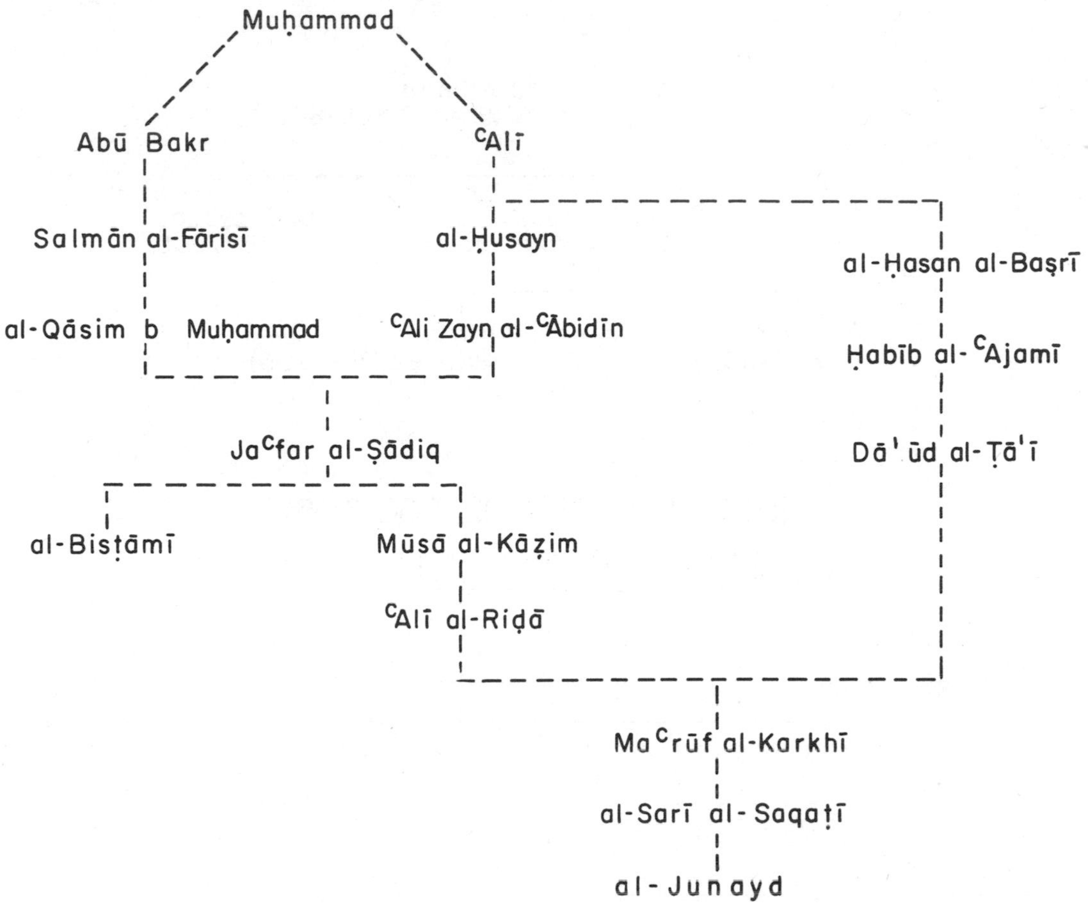

VII MAJOR SŪFĪ ISNĀDS

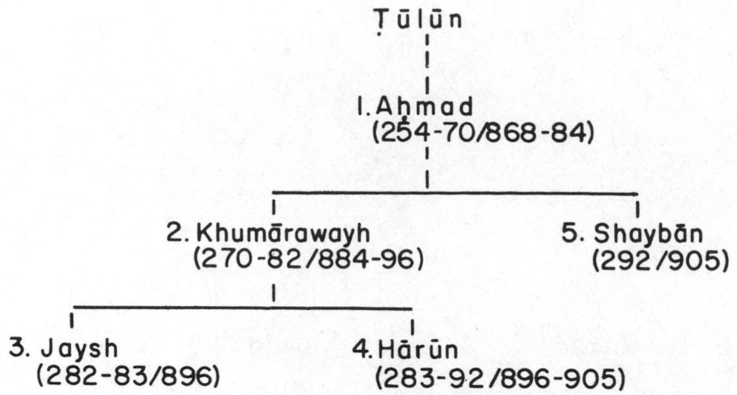

VIII ṬŪLŪNIDS (254-92/868-905)
EGYPT AND SYRIA

1. ʿUbaydullāh al-Mahdī (297-322/909-34)

2. al-Qā'im (322-34/934-46)

3. al-Manṣūr (334-41/946-53)

4. al-Muʿizz (341-65/953-75)

5. al-ʿAzīz (365-86/975-96)

6. al-Ḥākim (386-411/996-1021)

7. al-Ẓāhir (411-27/1021-36)

8. al-Mustanṣir (427-87/1036-94)

- Abū Manṣūr Nizār (d. 488/1095)
  - Abū ʿAbdullāh al-Ḥasan (d. 557/1162)
- Abū-l-Qāsim Muḥammad
  - 11. al-Ḥāfiẓ* (525-44/1131-49)
    - 12. al-Ẓāfir (544-49/1149-54)
      - 13. al-Fā'iz (549-55/1154-60)
    - Yūsuf
      - 14. al-ʿĀḍid (555-67/1160-71)
- 9. al-Mustaʿlī (487-95/1094-1101)
  - 10. al-Āmir (495-524/1101-30)

* Interregnum (524-25/1130-31)

IX FĀṬIMIDS (297-567/909-1171)
NORTH AFRICA, EGYPT AND SYRIA

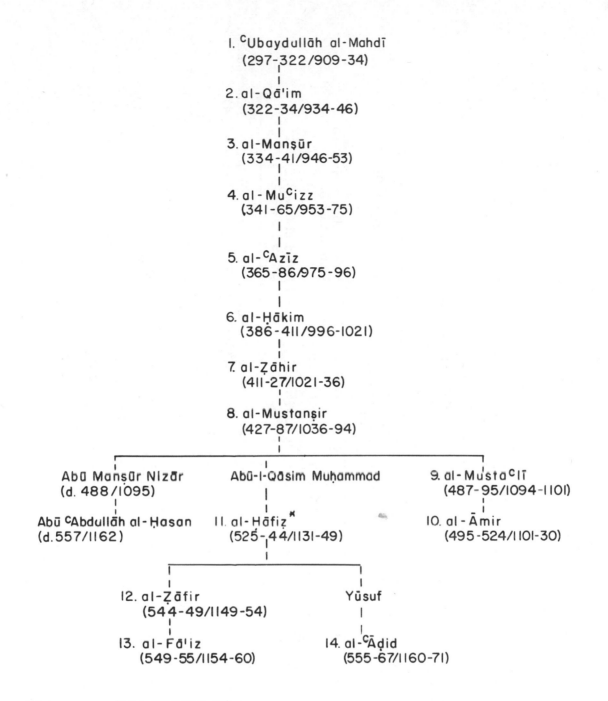

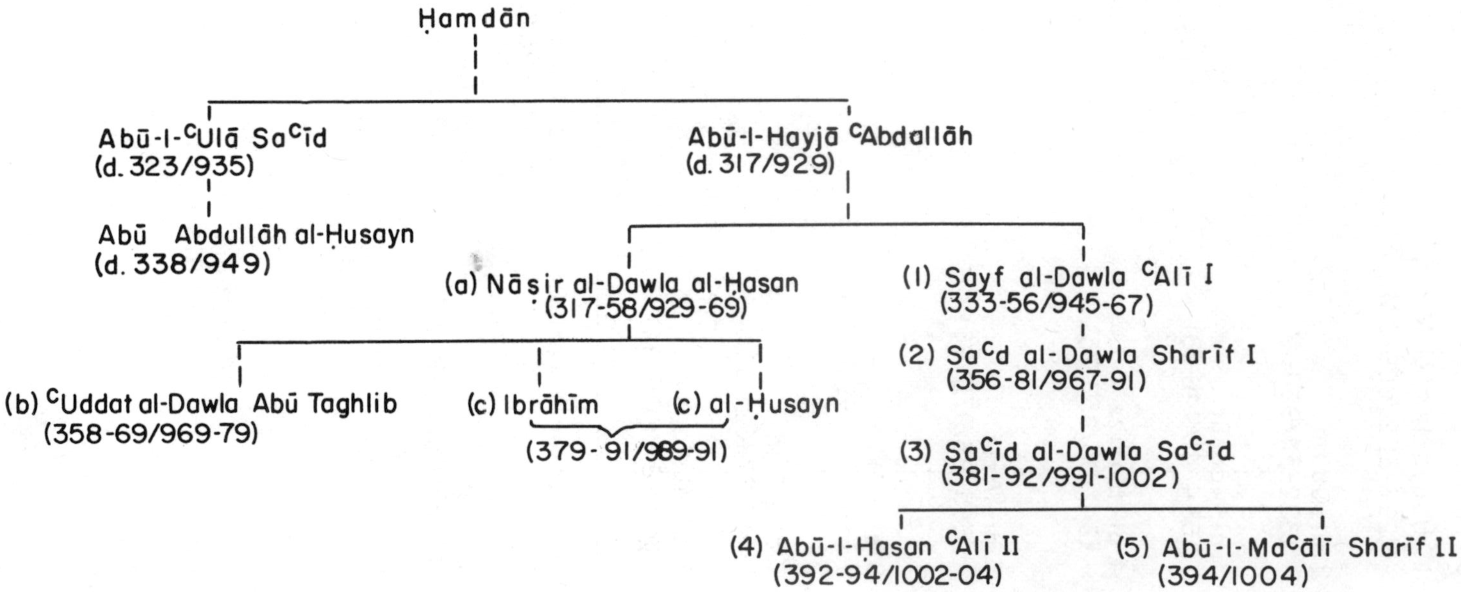

X ḤAMDĀNIDS (317-394/929-1004)

a-c MOṢUL

1-5 ALEPPO

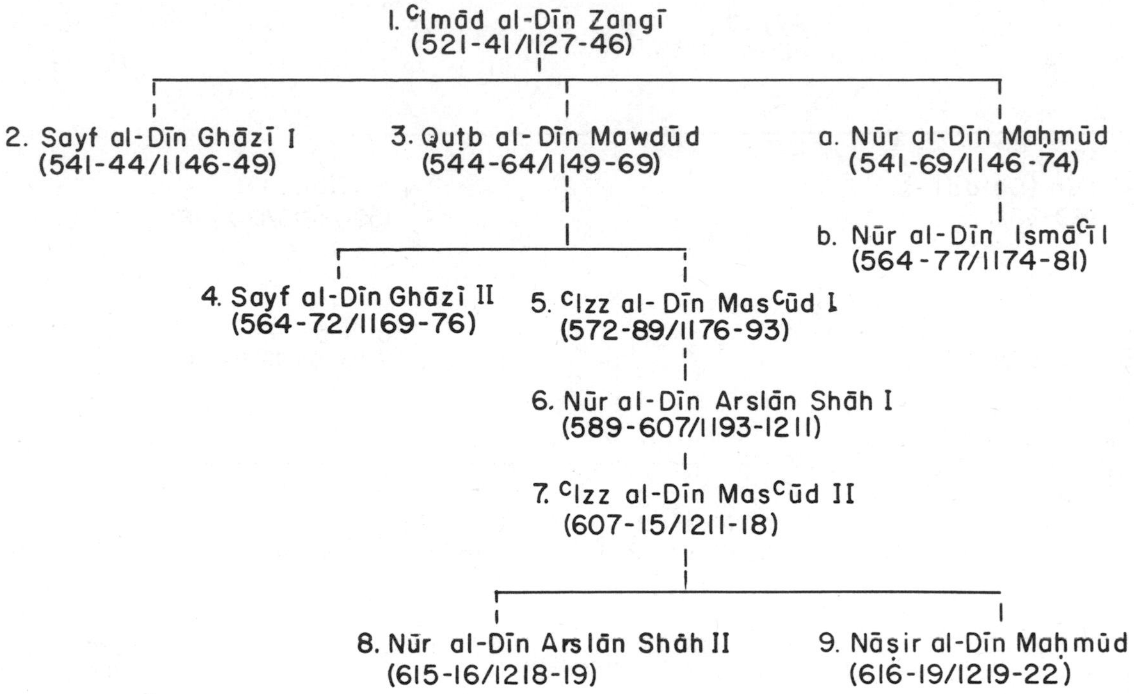

XI ZANGIDS (521-619/1127-1222)
1-9 MOSUL
a-b ALEPPO

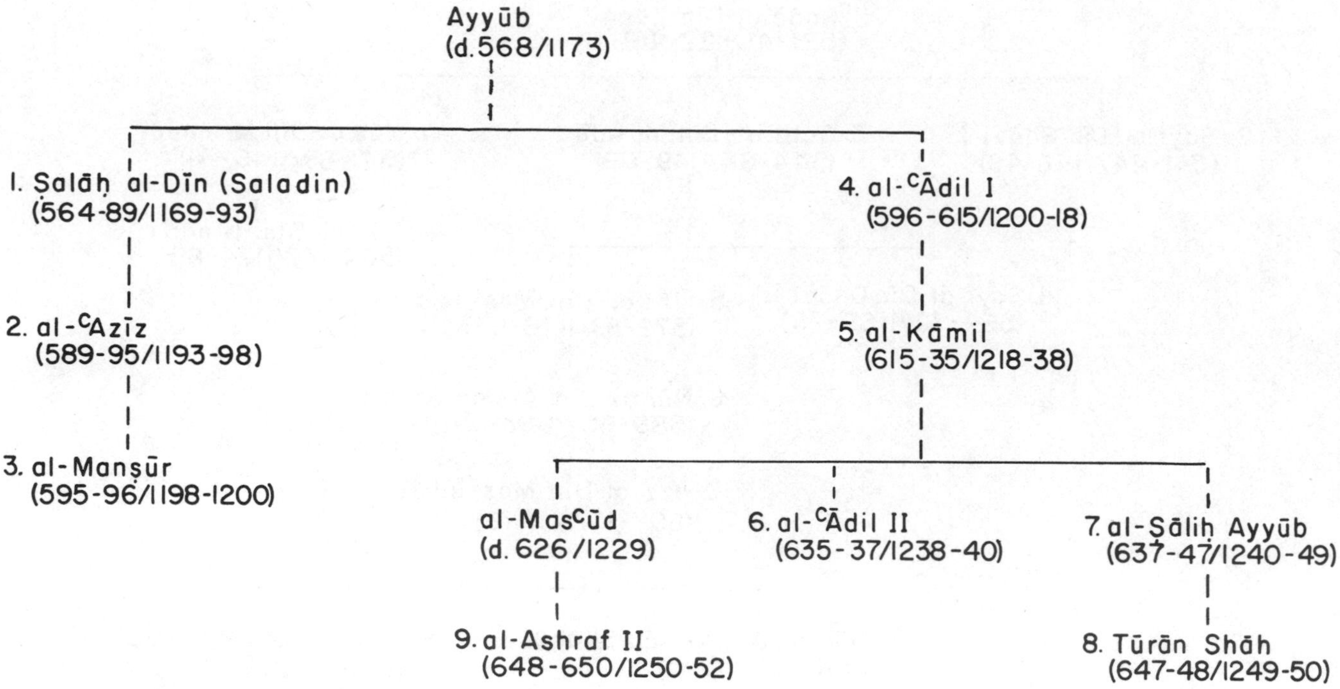

XII AYYŪBIDS OF EGYPT
(564-650/1169-1252)

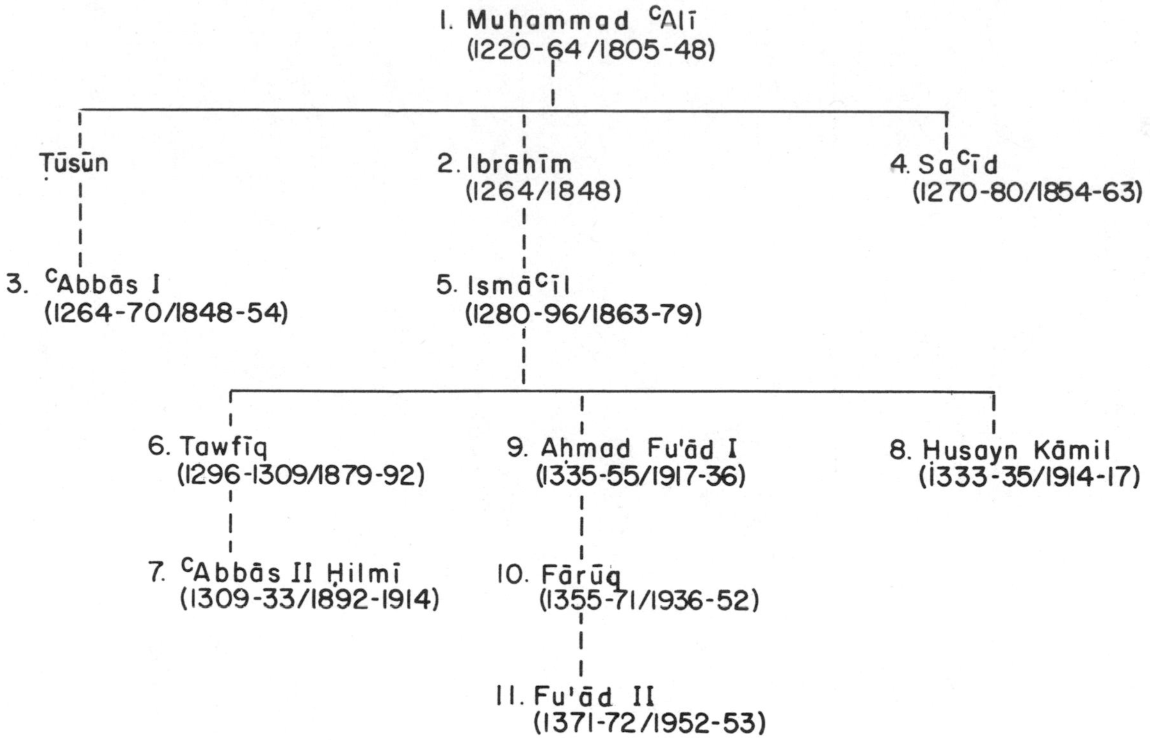

XIII MUḤAMMAD ʿALĪ'S LINE (1220-1372/1805-1953)
EGYPT

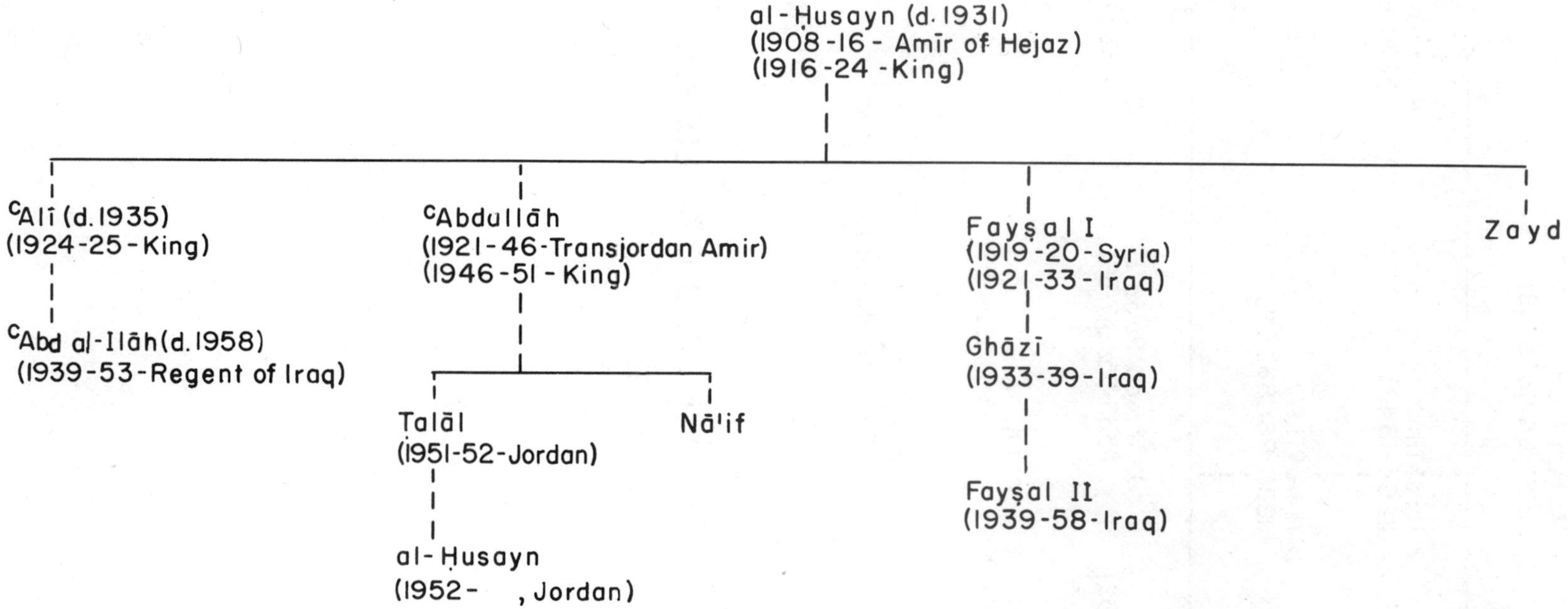

XIV ḤĀSHIMITES (1908-)

FERTILE CRESCENT

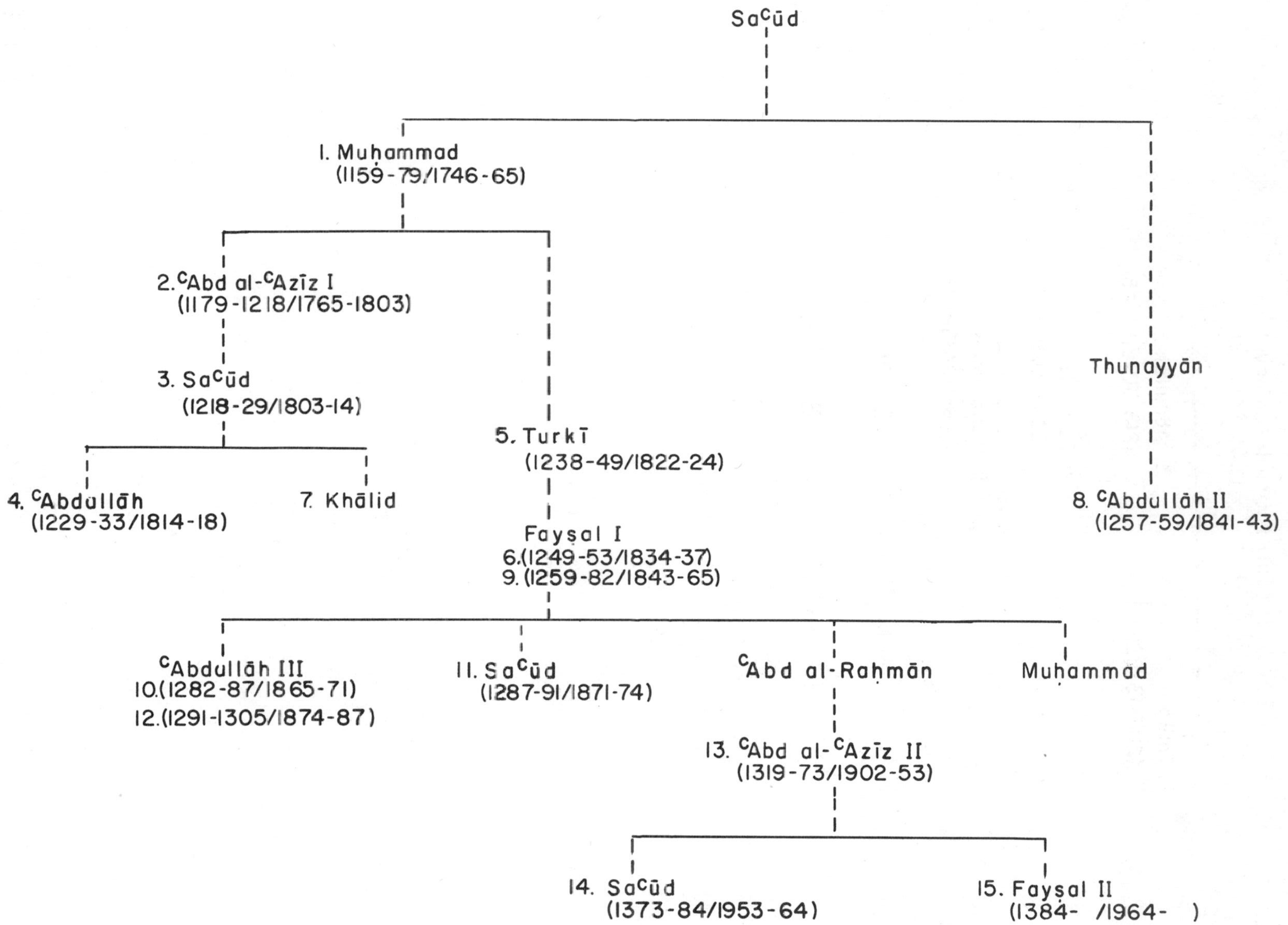

XV SAʿŪDĪ FAMILY (1159- /1746-)

ARABIA

1. Ṭāhir I (Dhū-l-Yamīnayn) (205-7/821-2)

- 2. Ṭalḥa (207-13/822-28)
- 3. ᶜAbdullāh (213-30/828-45)
  - 4. Ṭāhir II (230-48/845-62)
    - 5. Muḥammad (248-59/862-73)

XVI TĀHIRIDS (205-59/821-73)
KHURASĀN

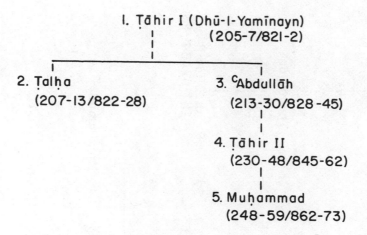

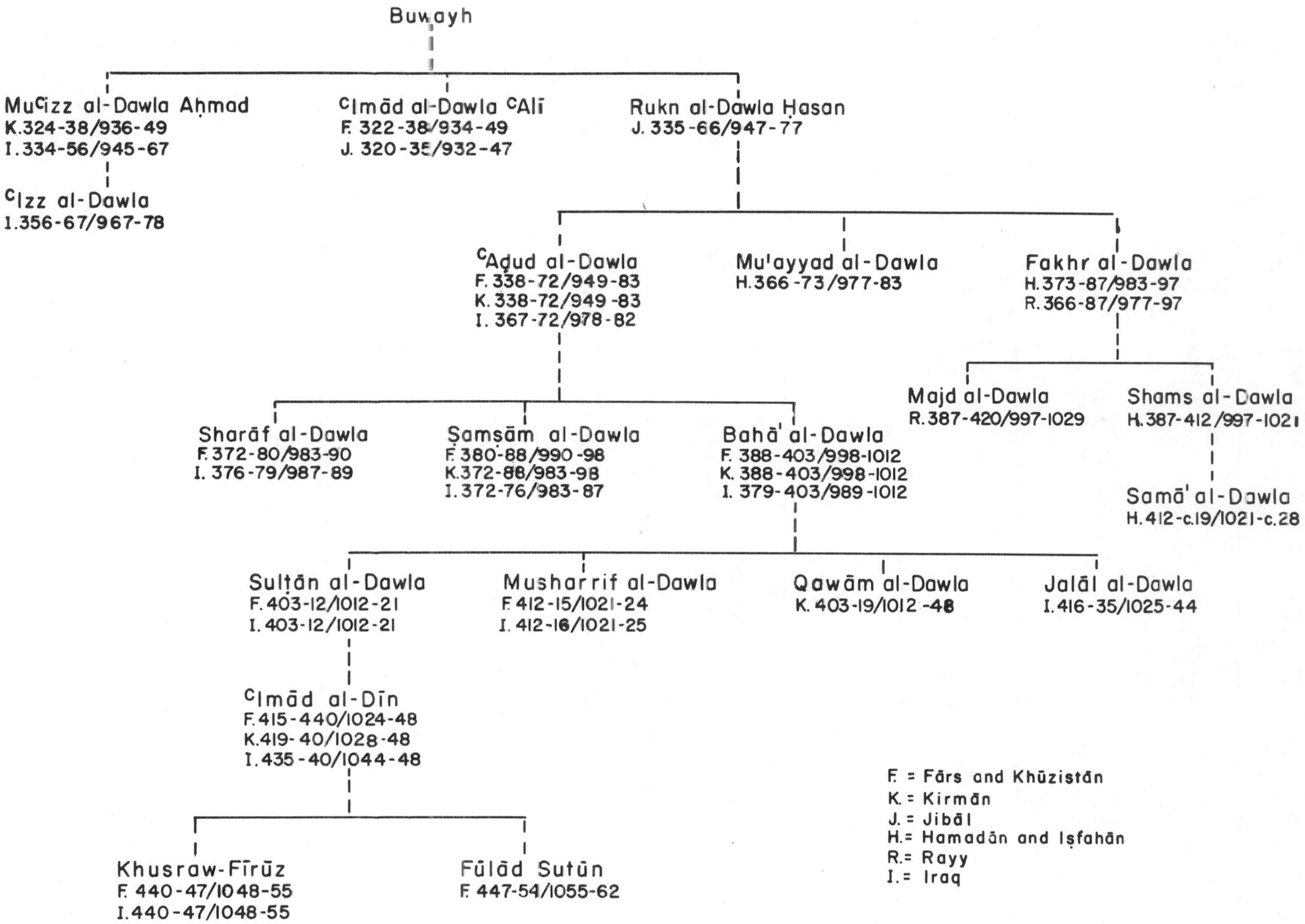
Buwayh
Muᶜizz al-Dawla Aḥmad
K.324-38/936-49
I.334-56/945-67
ᶜIzz al-Dawla
I.356-67/967-78
ᶜImād al-Dawla ᶜAlī
F. 322-38/934-49
J. 320-35/932-47
Rukn al-Dawla Ḥasan
J. 335-66/947-77
ᶜAḍud al-Dawla
F. 338-72/949-83
K. 338-72/949-83
I. 367-72/978-82
Mu'ayyad al-Dawla
H.366-73/977-83
Fakhr al-Dawla
H.373-87/983-97
R.366-87/977-97
Majd al-Dawla
R.387-420/997-1029
Shams al-Dawla
H.387-412/997-1021
Samā' al-Dawla
H.412-c.19/1021-c.28
Sharāf al-Dawla
F.372-80/983-90
I. 376-79/987-89
Ṣamṣām al-Dawla
F.380-88/990-98
K.372-88/983-98
I.372-76/983-87
Bahā' al-Dawla
F. 388-403/998-1012
K. 388-403/998-1012
I. 379-403/989-1012
Sulṭān al-Dawla
F. 403-12/1012-21
I. 403-12/1012-21
Musharrif al-Dawla
F. 412-15/1021-24
I. 412-16/1021-25
Qawām al-Dawla
K. 403-19/1012-48
Jalāl al-Dawla
I. 416-35/1025-44
ᶜImād al-Dīn
F.415-440/1024-48
K.419-40/1028-48
I.435-40/1044-48
Khusraw-Fīrūz
F. 440-47/1048-55
I.440-47/1048-55
Fūlād Sutūn
F. 447-54/1055-62
F. = Fārs and Khūzistān
K. = Kirmān
J. = Jibāl
H. = Hamadān and Iṣfahān
R. = Rayy
I. = Iraq

XVII BŪYIDS-BUWAYHIDS (320-454/932-1062)
IRAQ AND IRAN

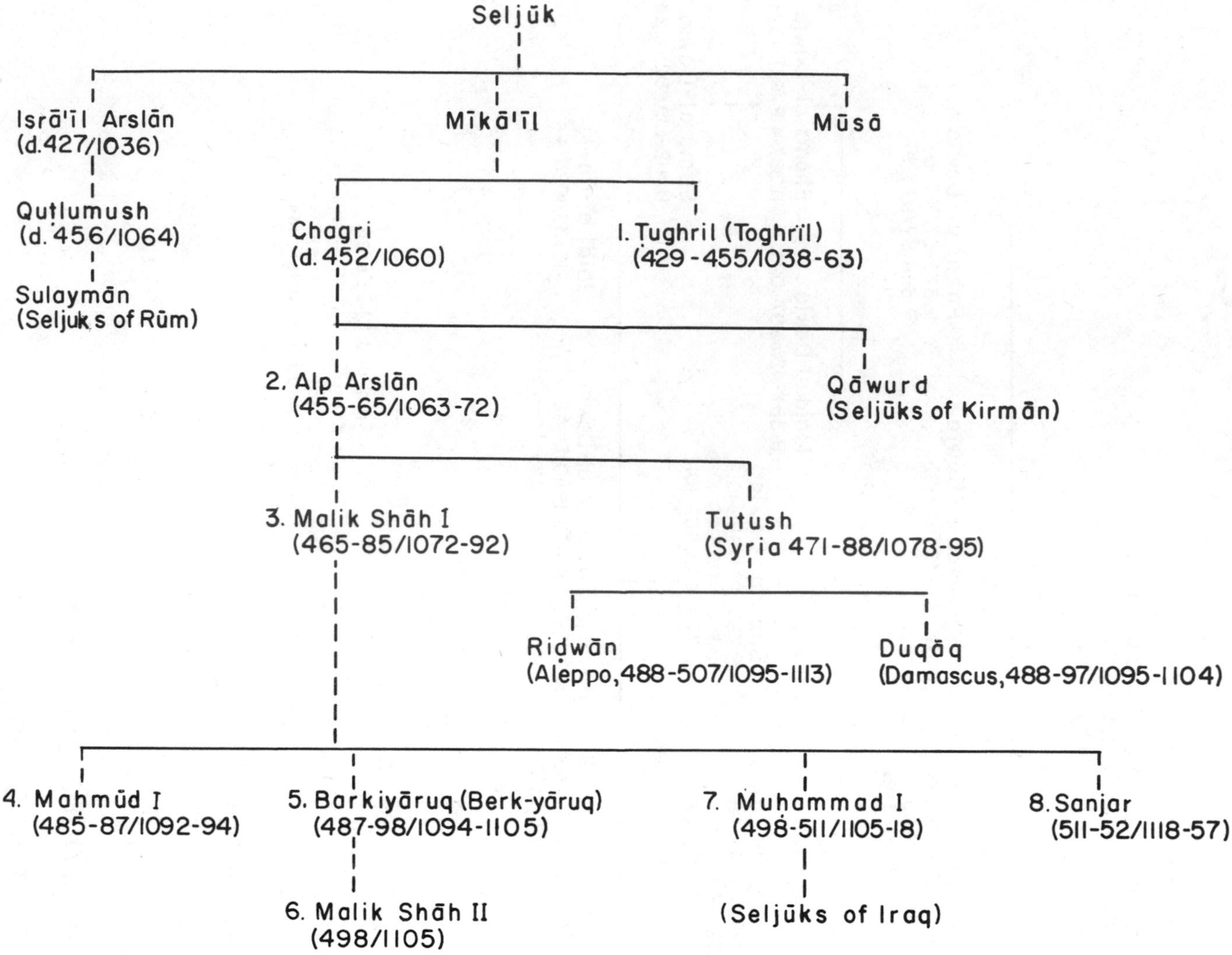

XVIII GREAT SELJUKS (429-590/1038-1194)
IRAN AND IRAQ

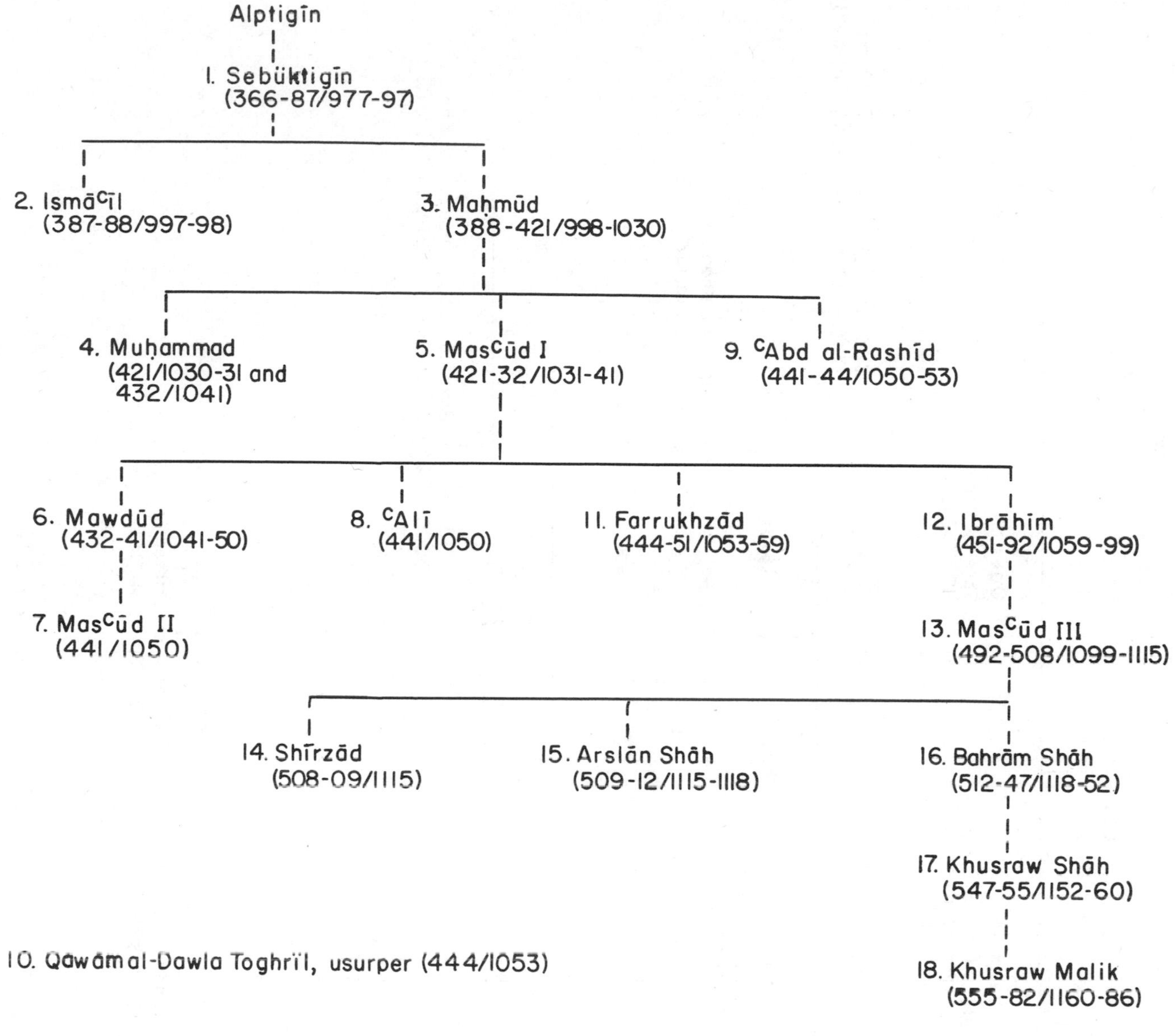

XIX GHAZNAVIDS (366-582/977-1186)

KHURASAN, AFGHANISTAN, AND NORTHERN INDIA

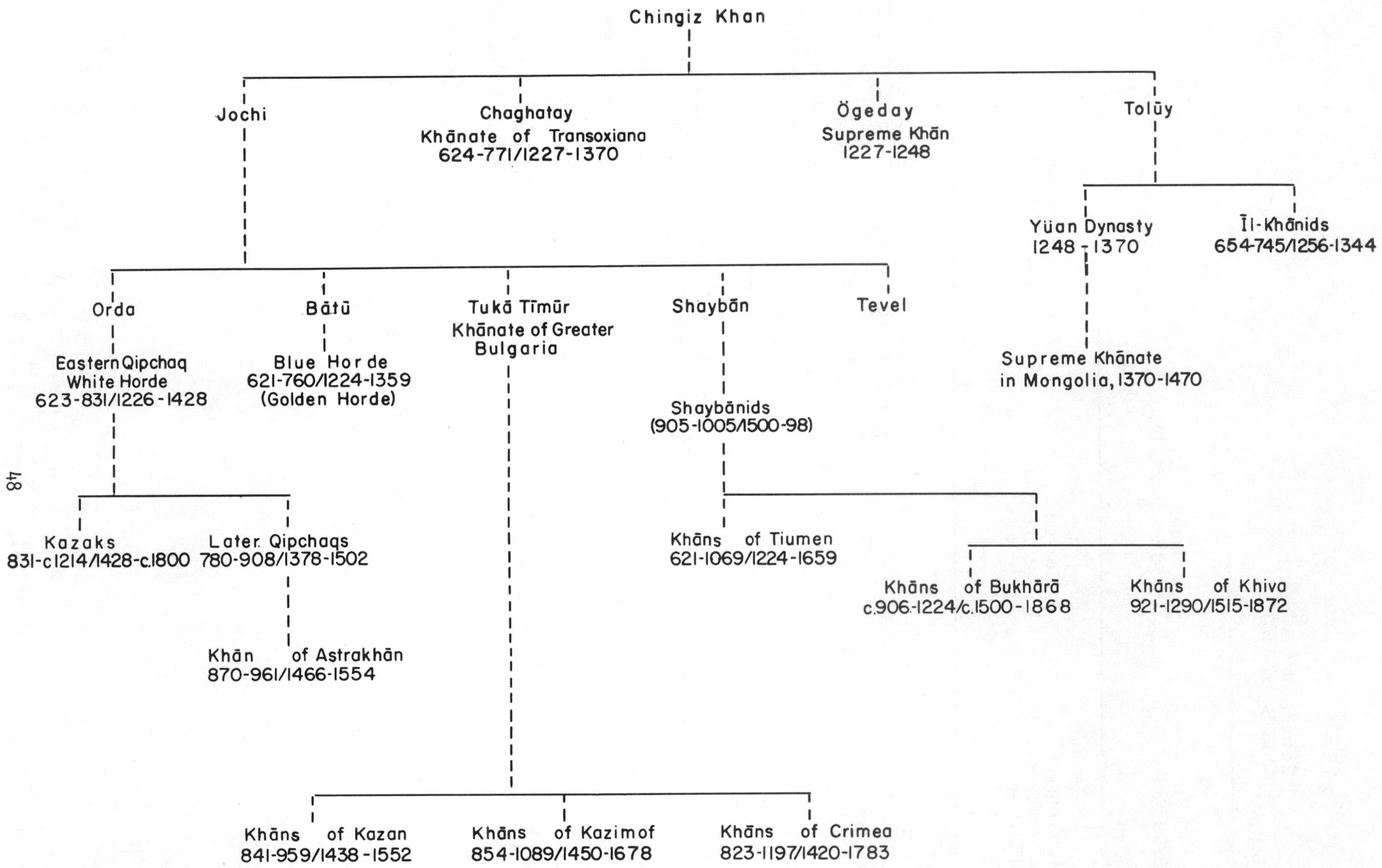
Chingiz Khan
Jochi
Chaghatay
Khānate of Transoxiana
624-771/1227-1370
Ögeday
Supreme Khān
1227-1248
Tolūy
Yüan Dynasty
1248 - 1370
Īl-Khānids
654-745/1256-1344
Supreme Khānate
in Mongolia, 1370-1470
Orda
Bātū
Tukā Tīmūr
Khānate of Greater
Bulgaria
Shaybān
Tevel
Eastern Qipchaq
White Horde
623-831/1226-1428
Blue Horde
621-760/1224-1359
(Golden Horde)
Shaybānids
(905-1005/1500-98)
Kazaks
831-c1214/1428-c.1800
Later. Qipchaqs
780-908/1378-1502
Khān of Astrakhān
870-961/1466-1554
Khāns of Tiumen
621-1069/1224-1659
Khāns of Bukhārā
c.906-1224/c.1500-1868
Khāns of Khiva
921-1290/1515-1872
Khāns of Kazan
841-959/1438-1552
Khāns of Kazimof
854-1089/1450-1678
Khāns of Crimea
823-1197/1420-1783

XX DESCENDANTS OF CHINGIZ KHĀN

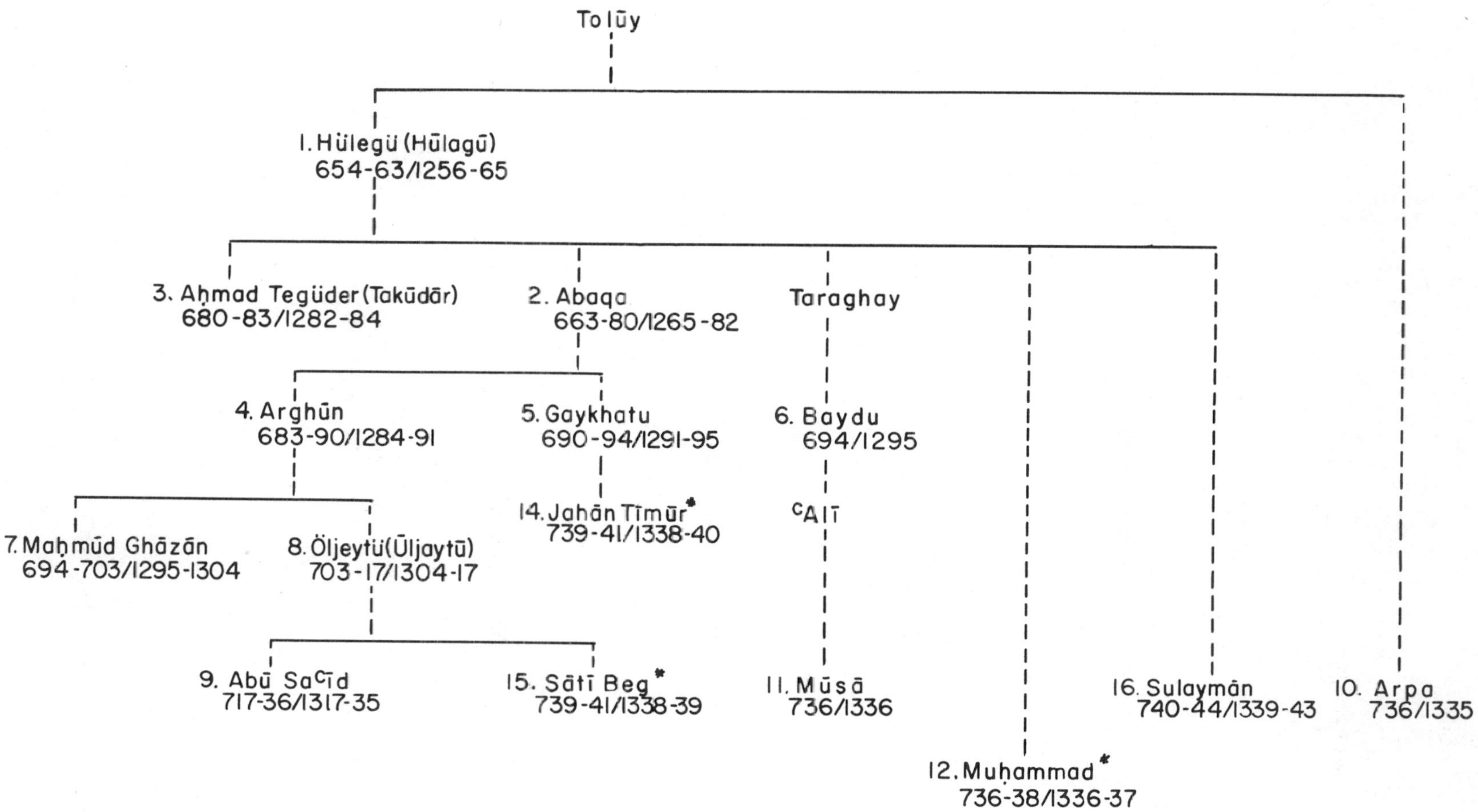

13. Tughiā Tīmūr* (738-52/1337-51)

* Nominated by other powers.

XXI ĪL-KHĀNIDS (654-754/1256-1353)
IRAN

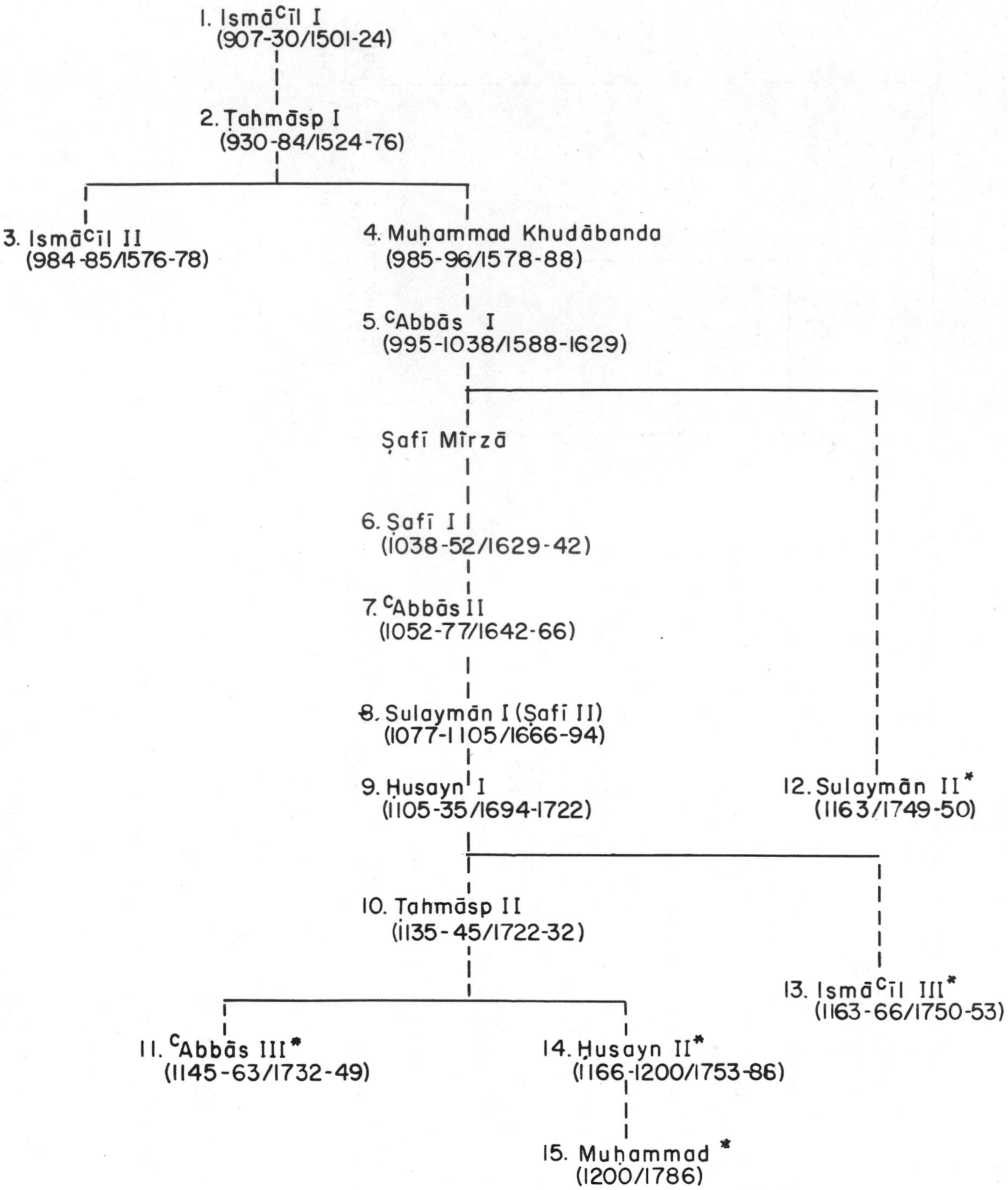

*Nominal rulers

XXII ṢAFAVIDS (907-1145/1501-1732)
IRAN

- Fatḥ ᶜAlī Khān (d. 1163/1750)
  - Muḥammad Ḥasan Khān (d. 1163/1750)
    - 1. Âghā Muḥammad (1193-1212/1779-97)
    - Ḥusayn Qulī Khān (d. 1193/1779)
      - 2. Fatḥ ᶜAlī Shāh (1212-50/1797-1834)
        - 3. Muḥammad (1250-64/1834-48)
          - 4. Nāṣir al-Dīn (1264-1313/1848-96)
            - 5. Muẓaffar al-Din (1313-24/1896-1907)
              - 6. Muḥammad ᶜAlī (1324-27/1907-09)
                - 7. Aḥmad (1327-42/1909-24)

XXIII QĀJĀRS (1193-1342/1779-1924)

IRAN

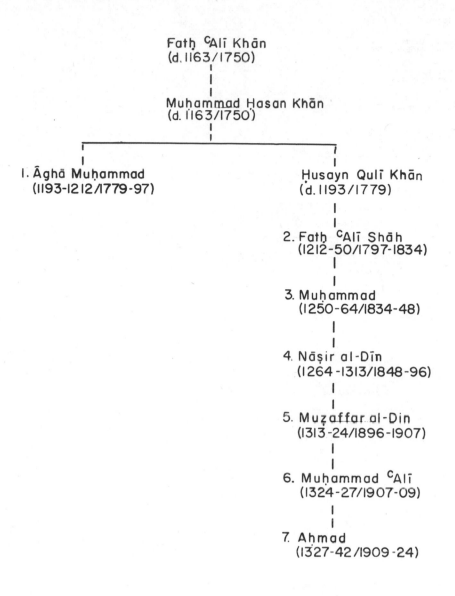

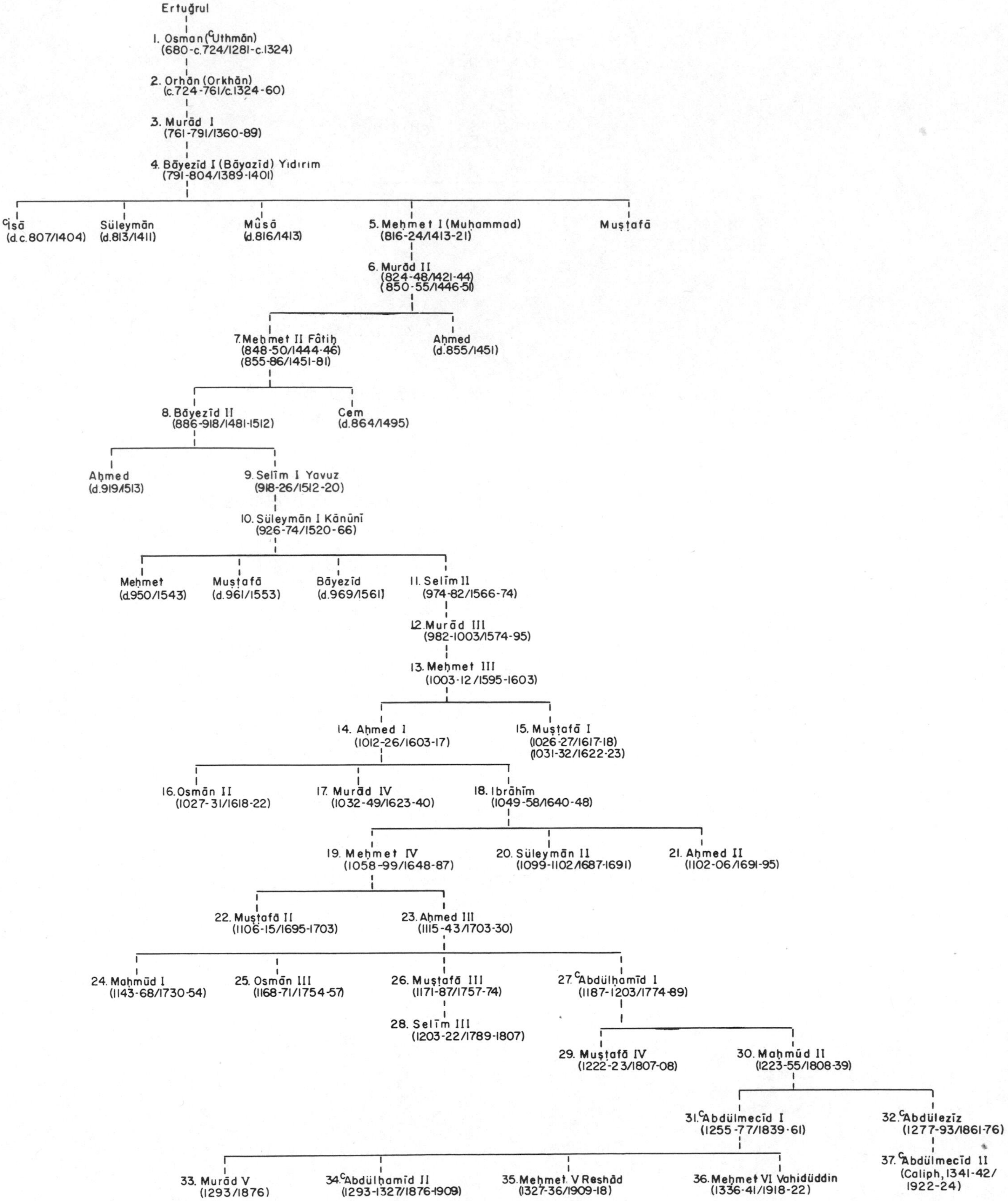
Ertuğrul
1. Osman (ᶜUthmān) (680-c.724/1281-c.1324)
2. Orhān (Orkhān) (c.724-761/c.1324-60)
3. Murād I (761-791/1360-89)
4. Bāyezīd I (Bāyazīd) Yıdırım (791-804/1389-1401)
ᶜIsā (d.c.807/1404)
Süleymān (d.813/1411)
Mûsā (d.816/1413)
5. Mehmet I (Muhammad) (816-24/1413-21)
Mustafā
6. Murād II (824-48/1421-44) (850-55/1446-51)
7. Mehmet II Fâtih (848-50/1444-46) (855-86/1451-81)
Ahmed (d.855/1451)
8. Bāyezīd II (886-918/1481-1512)
Cem (d.864/1495)
Ahmed (d.919/1513)
9. Selīm I Yavuz (918-26/1512-20)
10. Süleymān I Kānūnī (926-74/1520-66)
Mehmet (d.950/1543)
Mustafā (d.961/1553)
Bāyezīd (d.969/1561)
11. Selīm II (974-82/1566-74)
12. Murād III (982-1003/1574-95)
13. Mehmet III (1003-12/1595-1603)
14. Ahmed I (1012-26/1603-17)
15. Mustafā I (1026-27/1617-18) (1031-32/1622-23)
16. Osmān II (1027-31/1618-22)
17. Murād IV (1032-49/1623-40)
18. Ibrāhīm (1049-58/1640-48)
19. Mehmet IV (1058-99/1648-87)
20. Süleymān II (1099-1102/1687-1691)
21. Ahmed II (1102-06/1691-95)
22. Mustafā II (1106-15/1695-1703)
23. Ahmed III (1115-43/1703-30)
24. Mahmūd I (1143-68/1730-54)
25. Osmān III (1168-71/1754-57)
26. Mustafā III (1171-87/1757-74)
27. ᶜAbdülhamīd I (1187-1203/1774-89)
28. Selīm III (1203-22/1789-1807)
29. Mustafā IV (1222-23/1807-08)
30. Mahmūd II (1223-55/1808-39)
31. ᶜAbdülmecīd I (1255-77/1839-61)
32. ᶜAbdülezīz (1277-93/1861-76)
37. ᶜAbdülmecīd II (Caliph, 1341-42/1922-24)
33. Murād V (1293/1876)
34. ᶜAbdülhamīd II (1293-1327/1876-1909)
35. Mehmet V Reshād (1327-36/1909-18)
36. Mehmet VI Vahidüddin (1336-41/1918-22)

XXIV OTTOMANS (680-1342/1281-1924)

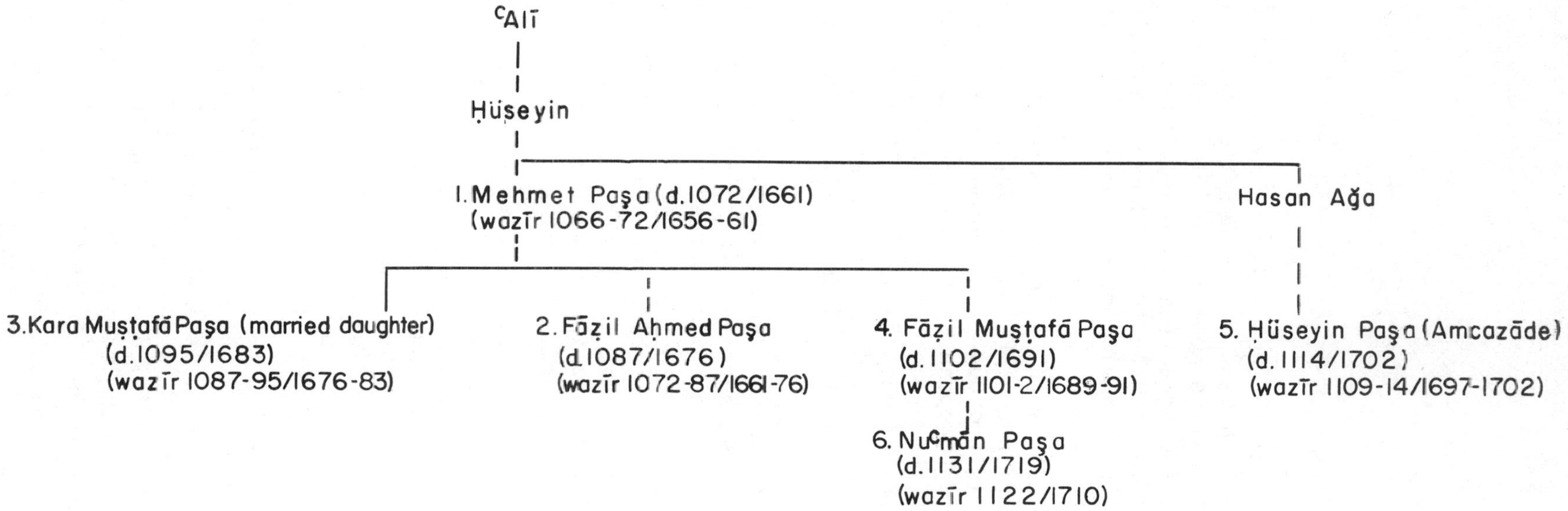
ᶜAlī
Ḥüseyin
1. Mehmet Paşa (d. 1072/1661)
(wazīr 1066-72/1656-61)
Hasan Ağa
3. Kara Muṣṭafā Paşa (married daughter)
(d. 1095/1683)
(wazīr 1087-95/1676-83)
2. Fāżil Aḥmed Paşa
(d. 1087/1676)
(wazīr 1072-87/1661-76)
4. Fāżil Muṣṭafā Paşa
(d. 1102/1691)
(wazīr 1101-2/1689-91)
6. Nuᶜmān Paşa
(d. 1131/1719)
(wazīr 1122/1710)
5. Ḥüseyin Paşa (Amcazāde)
(d. 1114/1702)
(wazīr 1109-14/1697-1702)

XXV KÖPRÜLÜ WAZĪRS

HISTORICAL ATLAS

The lack of an adequate historical atlas represents a major lacuna in Islamic Studies. Dr. R. Roolvink and others compiled the *Historical Atlas of the Muslim Peoples* (Amsterdam: Djambatan, 1957) which has almost 50 multi-colored maps covering the area from Spain to Indonesia and from the pre-Islamic Period to the Twentieth Century. Many of them concentrate on particular areas and specific chronological periods. However, the lack of an index is a serious weakness.

The weakness of Roolvink's work is the strength of Harry W. Hazard's *Atlas of Islamic History* (Princeton: Princeton University Press, 3rd Ed., 1954). His index is not only thorough, but in many cases includes the Arabic, Persian, Ottoman and European spelling of a place name. Each map is accompanied by a list of the dynasties and their dates for all the areas covered. The weakness is in the maps. The first 13 out of 18 cover a fixed area — Spain through Iran — and each deals with a century of changes. They are therefore limited in detail and cover a very long chronological period.

A more recent historical work covering the Arab world from Iraq and Arabia through Spain is Rolf Reichert's *A Historical and Regional Atlas of the Arab World*, Maps and Chronological Survey (Rio de Janiero: Sedegra Sociedade Editora e Grafica, Ltd., 1969; in English and Portuguese. The 68 black-and-white maps cover the Arabian Peninsula, Syria and Mesopotamia, Northeast Africa and Northwest Africa (Maghrib) on a century-by-century basis. Each map is accompanied by a text covering the major historical events, as well as 6 genealogy tables. An index is needed.

An example of an excellent historical atlas is the *Historical Atlas of Iran* published by Tehran University in 1971 under the editorship of Seyyid Hossein Naşr, Aḥmad Mostofi and Abbās Zaryab. Of the very large, colored maps, 20 are of use for students of Islamic Iran. Each map, with locations in Persian and English/French, includes all the major cities, many minor ones, general political lines, provinces and bodies of water. Each map is accompanied by a brief historical survey in Persian, French and English. All locations are indexed.

A second new major publication is the posthumous work of Donald E. Pitcher, *An Historical Geography of the Ottoman Empire From Earliest Times to the End of the Sixteenth Century* (Leiden: E.J. Brill, 1972). As the title indicates, the 36 multi-colored maps cover the years from the rise of the Ottomans to 1612. The political and provincial divisions are given in great detail. The work also includes an historical survey which stresses the dates of the territorial acquisitions and an index.

More surprising than the inadequacies of the historical atlases for the Medieval Period is the lack of a good collection of maps dealing with Twentieth Century political history. One textbook might include a map of the Sykes-Picot Agreement, while a second will show the San Remo Mandates, but no single work includes all the treaties, agreements and wars a student of Modern History could easily use. For a thorough discussion of all these resources, Medieval and Modern, one can consult Gerry A. Hale's "Maps and Atlases of the Middle East," *MESA Bulletin*, Vol. 3, No. 3 (October 1969), pp. 17-39.

Cost has been the major factor for limiting the number of maps included within this atlas, a number which could easily have been doubled under somewhat less inflationary circumstances. Therefore, only the first 13 maps cover the years to the Twentieth Century. The Muslim conquests and political changes in North Africa and Spain have not been included in order to limit the number of maps and areas covered.

The spelling of place names has usually followed the accepted English form rather than a transliterated one; e.g., Aleppo for Ḥalab, although the index includes these transliterated forms as cross-references. As indicated in the Introduction, line drawings have been used for financial reasons.

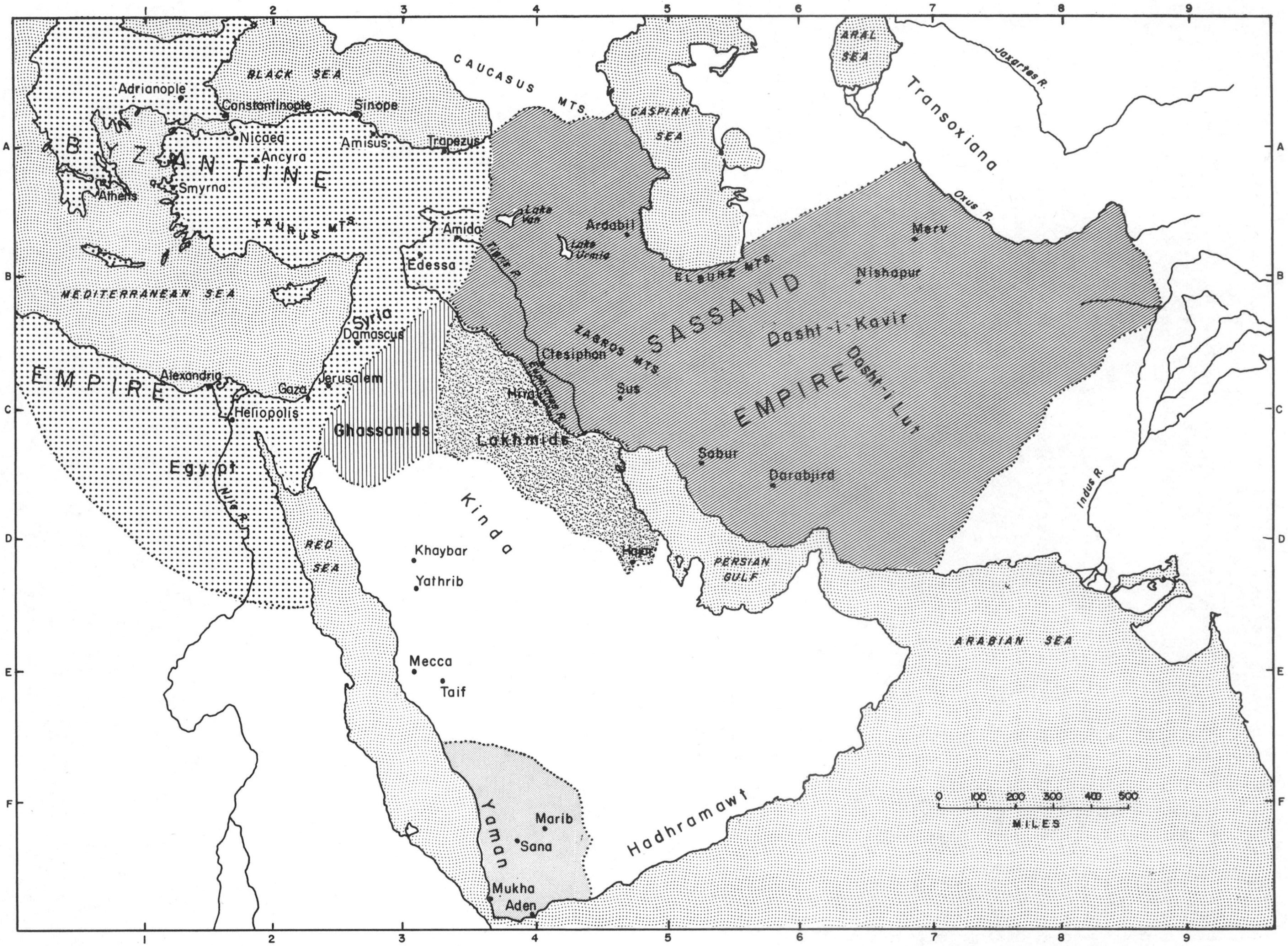

I EGYPT AND SOUTHWEST ASIA - CIRCA 600

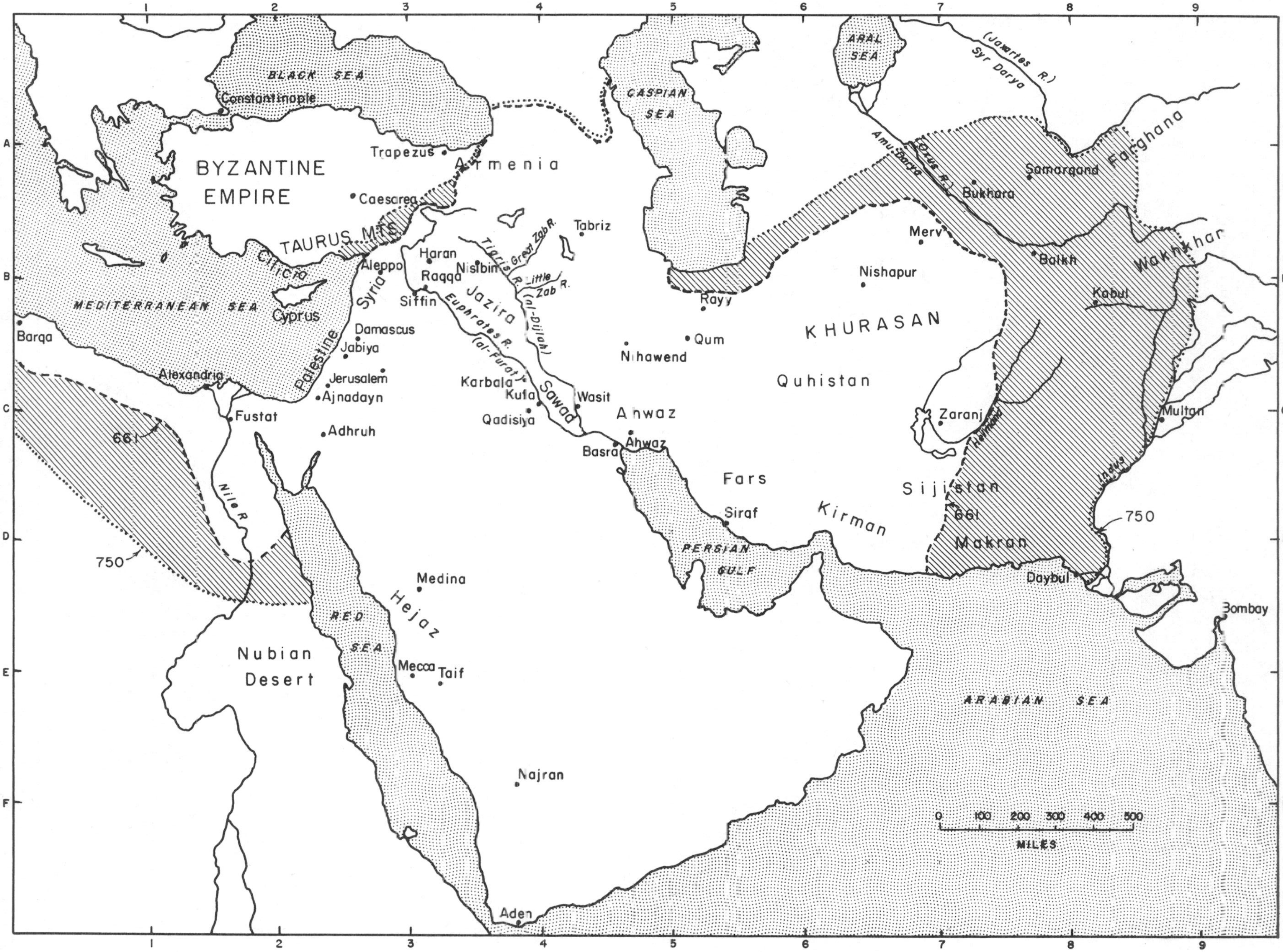

II CONQUESTS-RĀSHIDŪN AND ᶜUMAYYAD PERIODS

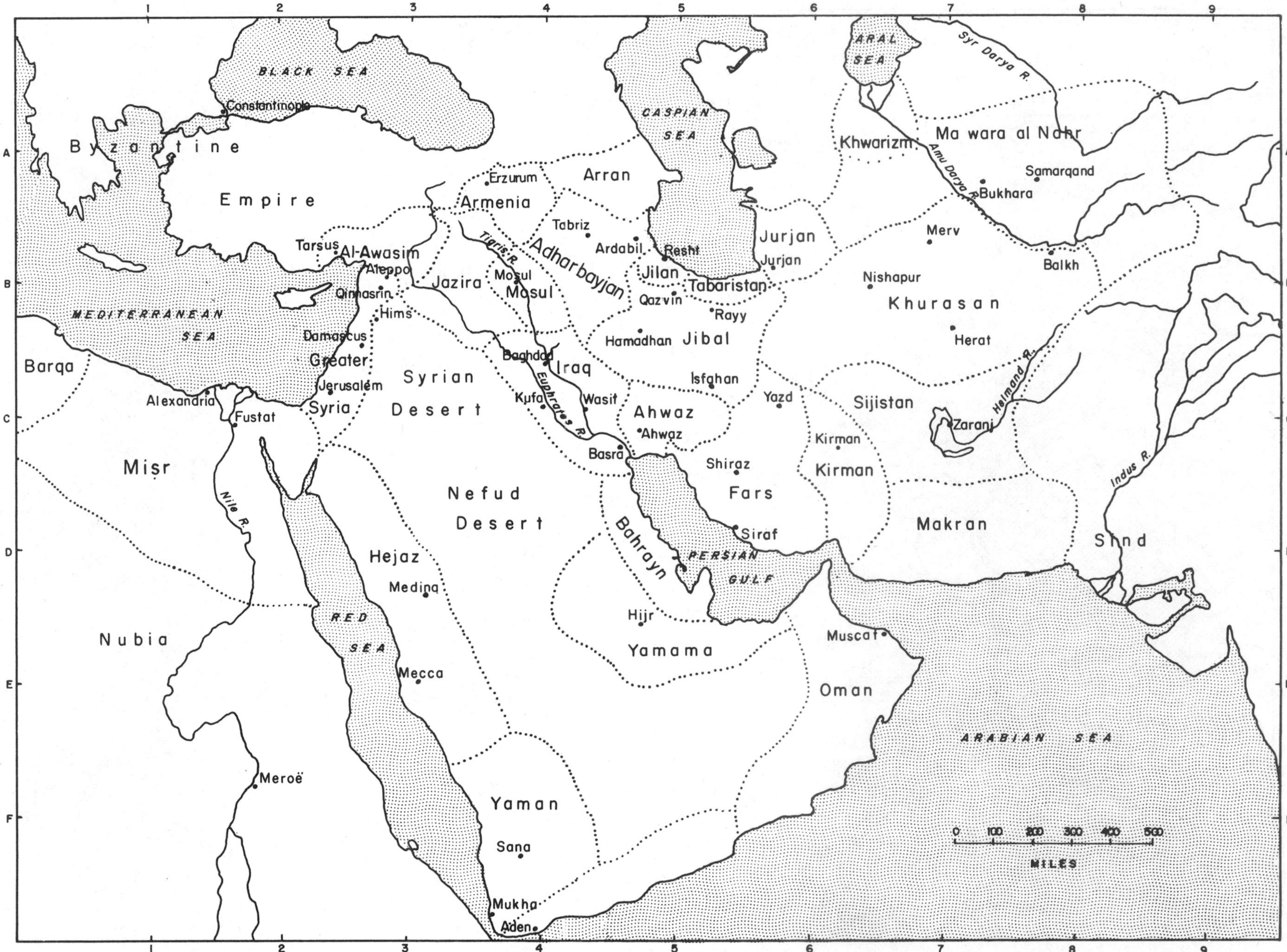

III ʿABBĀSID PROVINCES

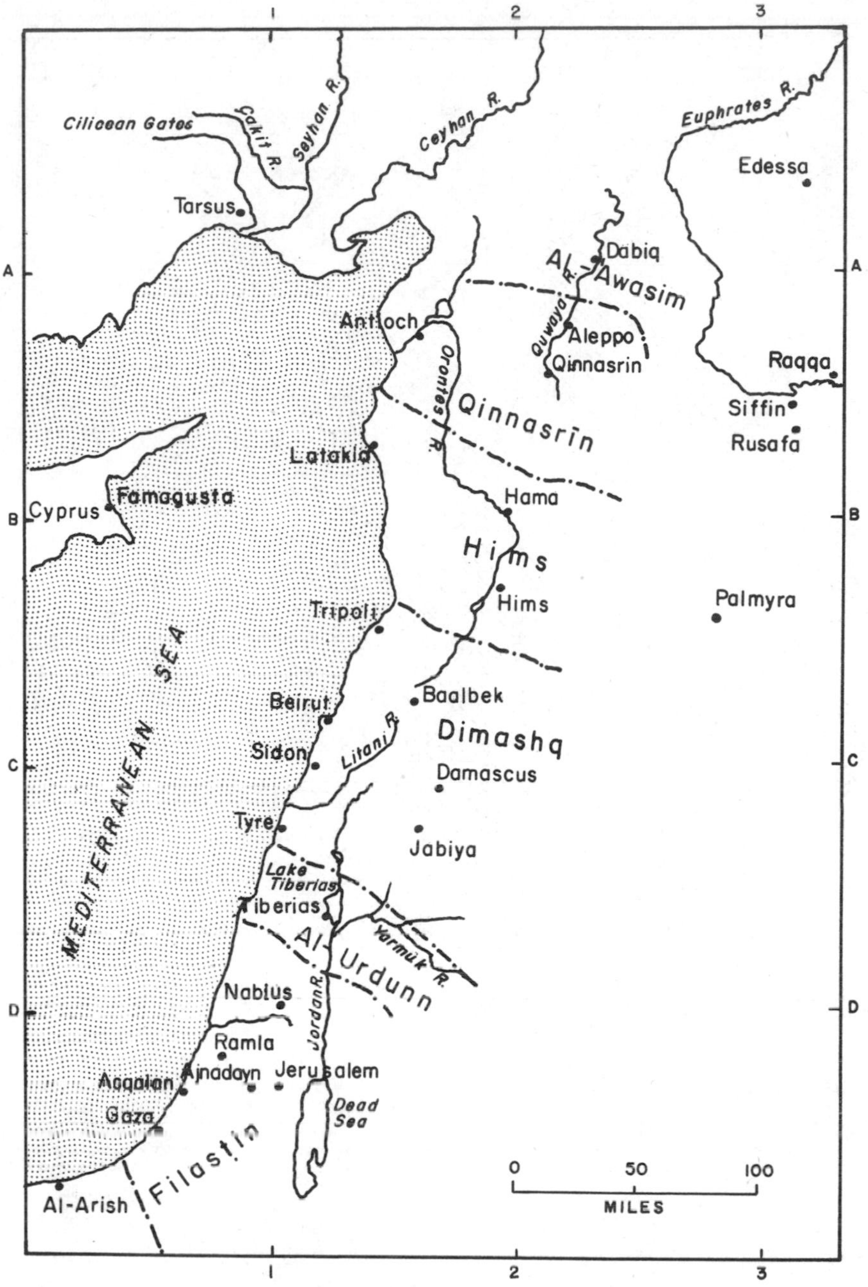

IV THE SYRIAN PROVINCES - ᶜABBĀSID PERIOD

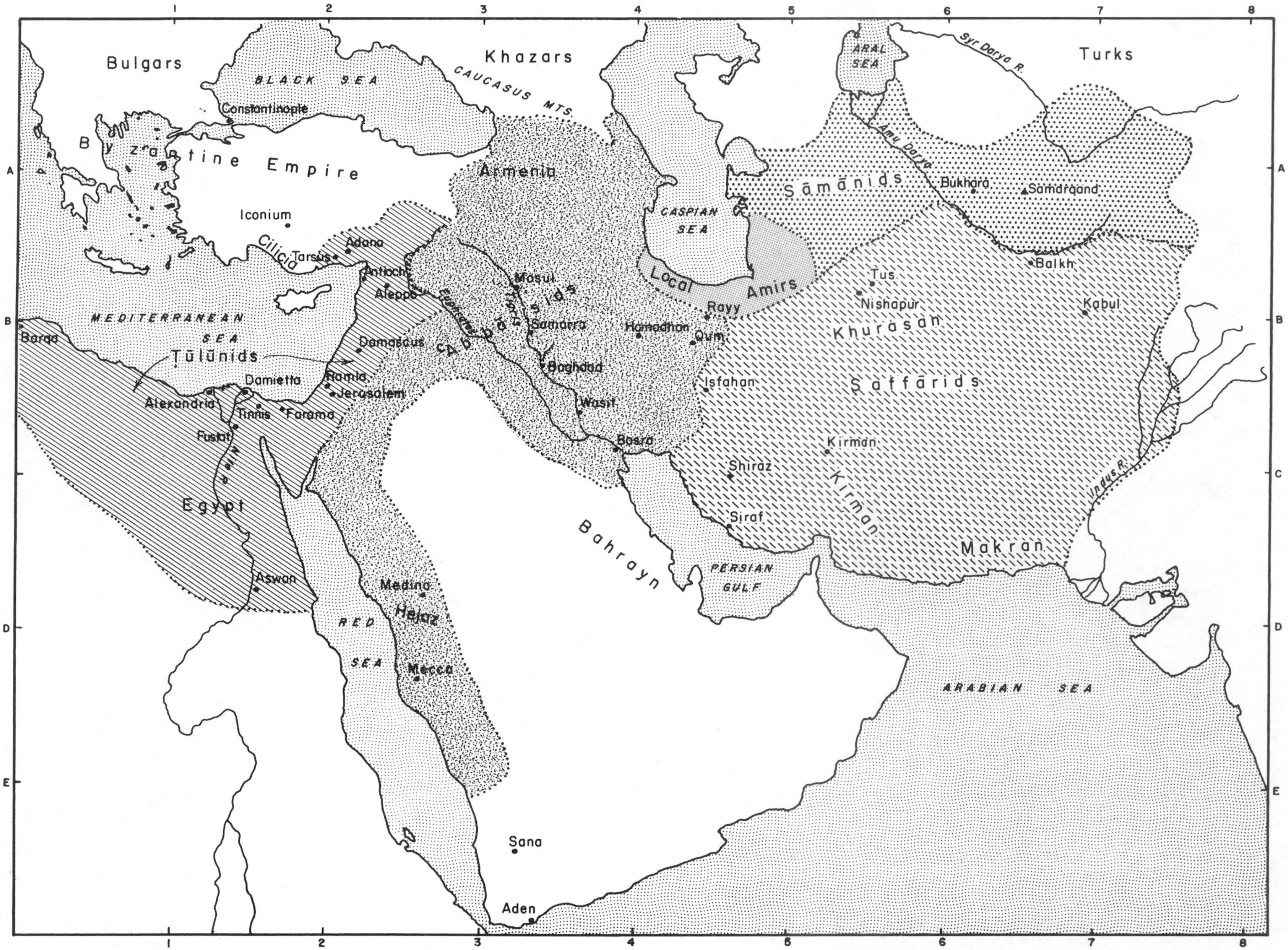

V EGYPT AND SOUTHWEST ASIA - LATE 9TH CENTURY

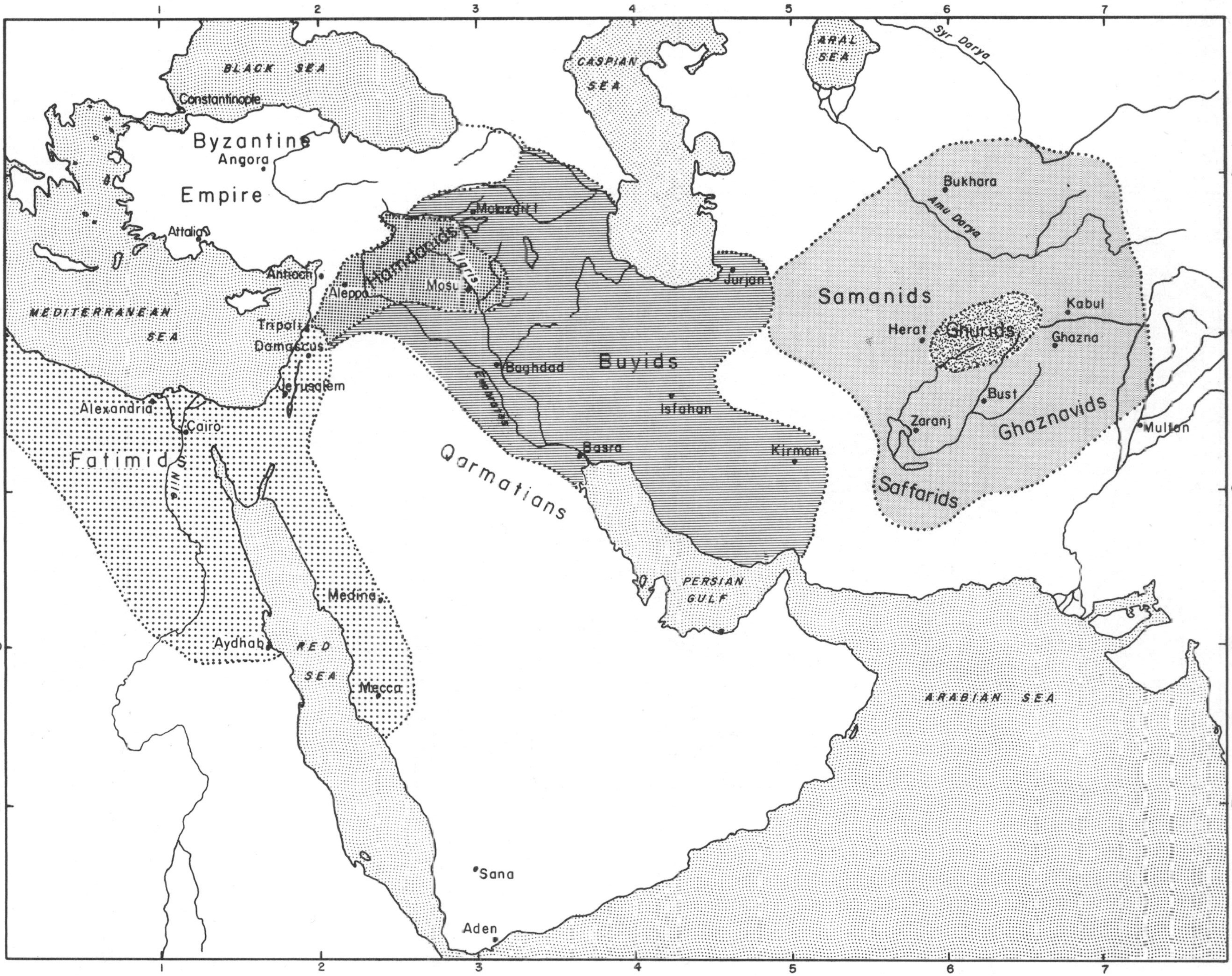

VI - EGYPT AND SOUTHWEST ASIA - LATE 10TH CENTURY

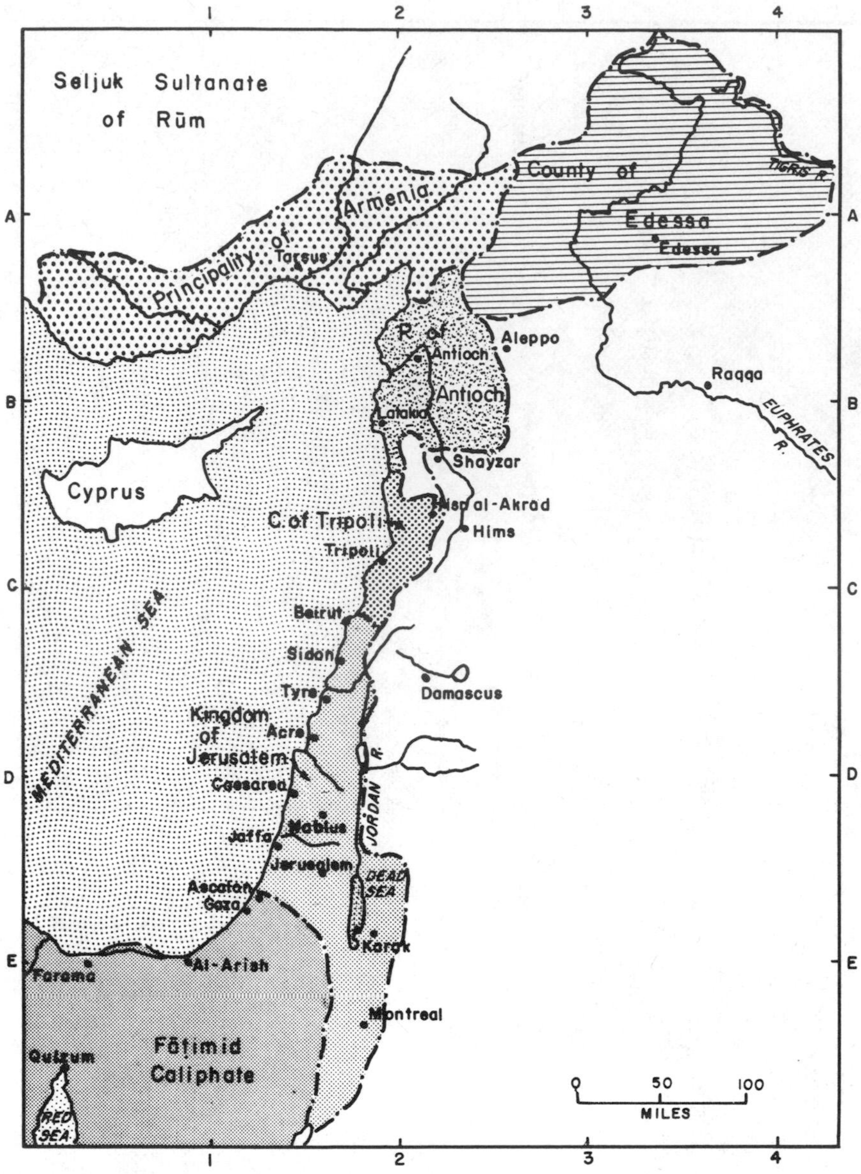
Seljuk Sultanate
of Rūm
Principality of
Armenia
Tarsus
County of
Edessa
Edessa
TIGRIS R.
P. of
Antioch
Antioch
Aleppo
Raqqa
EUPHRATES R.
Latakia
Shayzar
Cyprus
C. of Tripoli
Tripoli
Hims
Beirut
Sidon
Tyre
Damascus
MEDITERRANEAN SEA
Kingdom
of
Jerusalem
Acre
Caesarea
JORDAN R.
Nablus
Jaffa
Jerusalem
Ascalon
Gaza
DEAD SEA
Karak
Farama
Al-Arish
Montreal
Fāṭimid
Caliphate
Qulzum
RED SEA
0 50 100
MILES
1 2 3 4
A B C D E

VII CRUSADING STATES CIRCA 1130

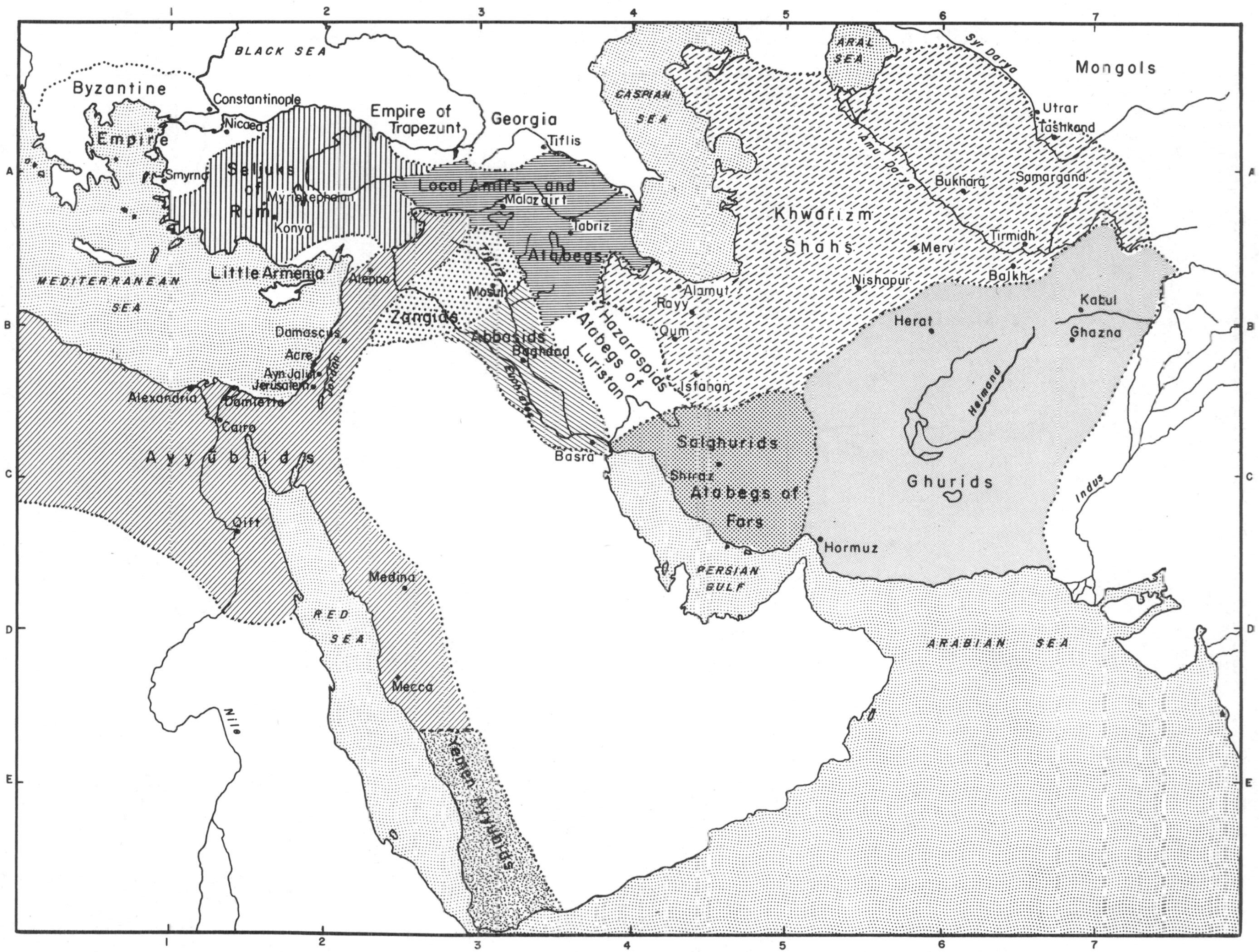

VIII - EGYPT AND SOUTHWEST ASIA - LATE 12TH CENTURY

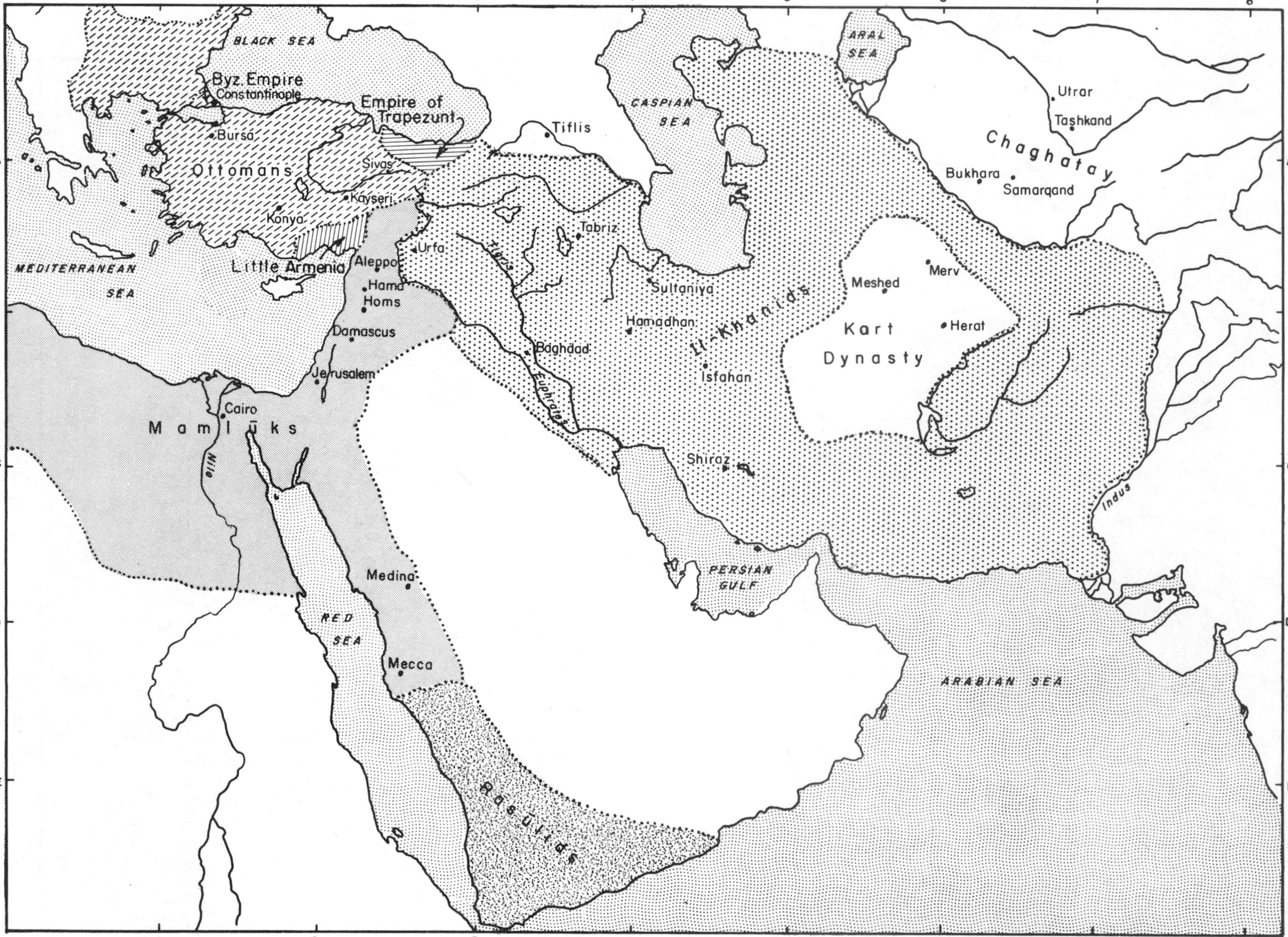

IX-EGYPT AND SOUTHWEST ASIA-EARLY 14TH CENTURY

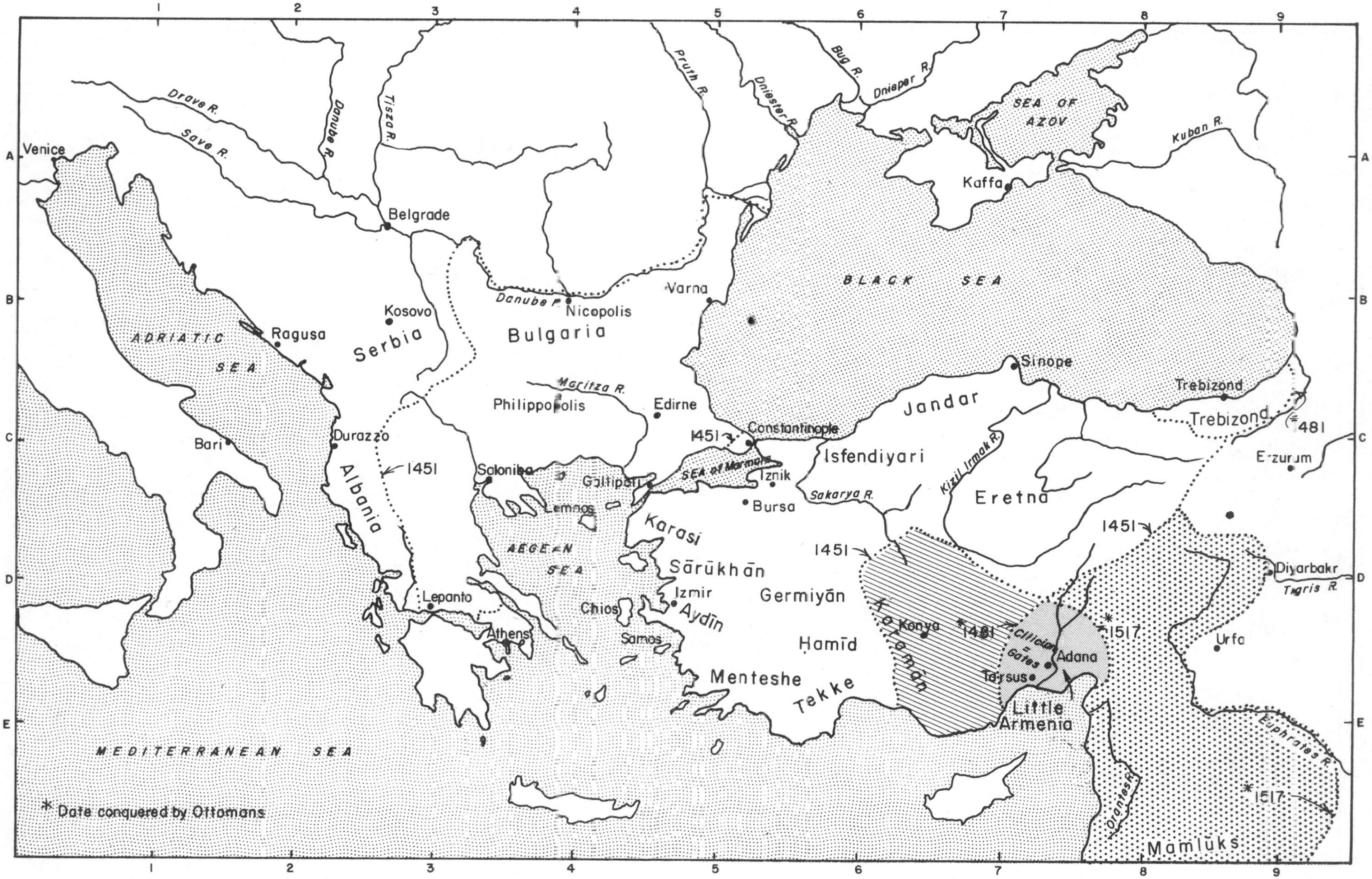

X · OTTOMAN CONQUESTS TO 1451

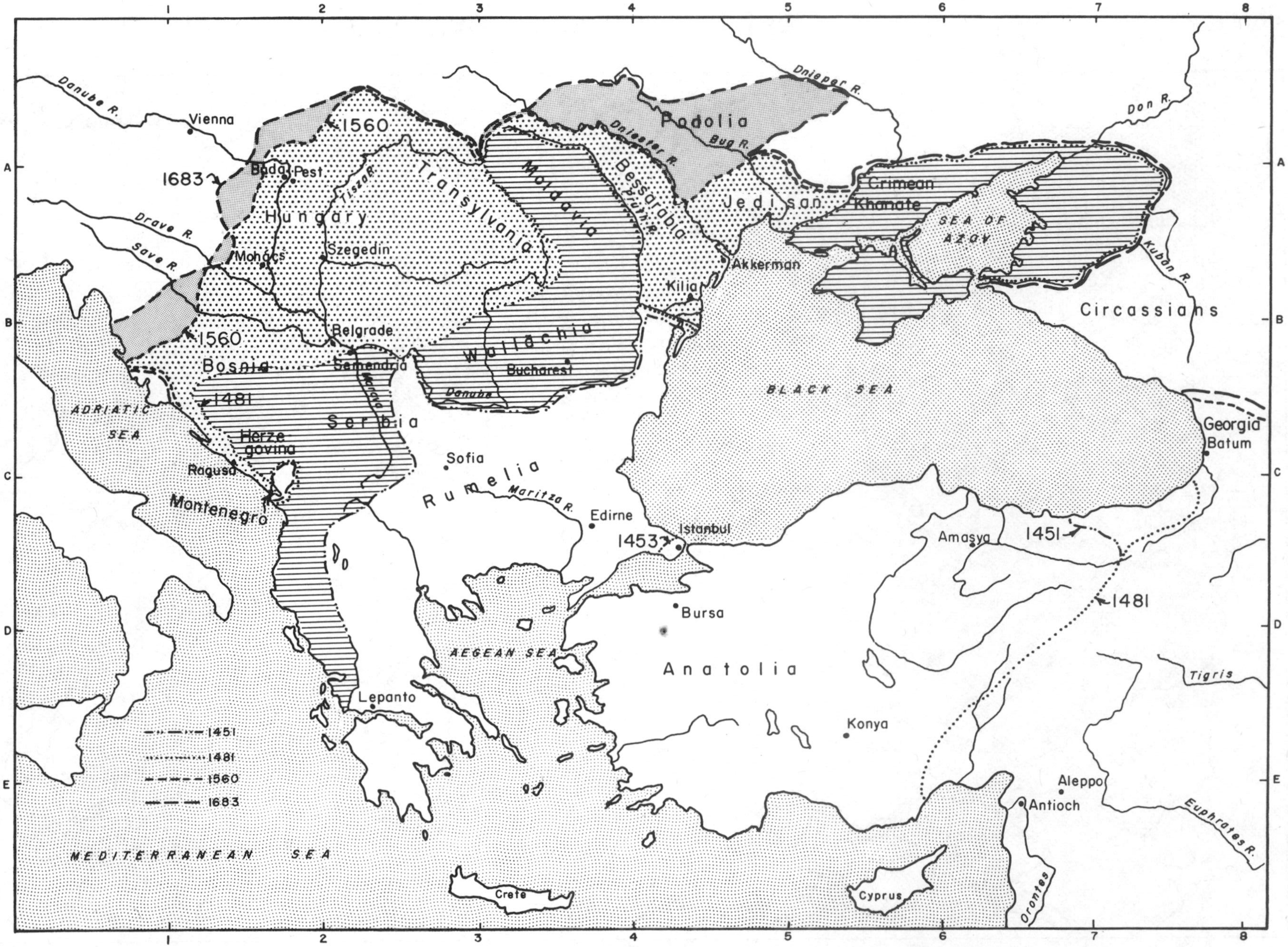

XI - OTTOMAN EMPIRE IN EUROPE AND ANATOLIA - 1451 - 1683

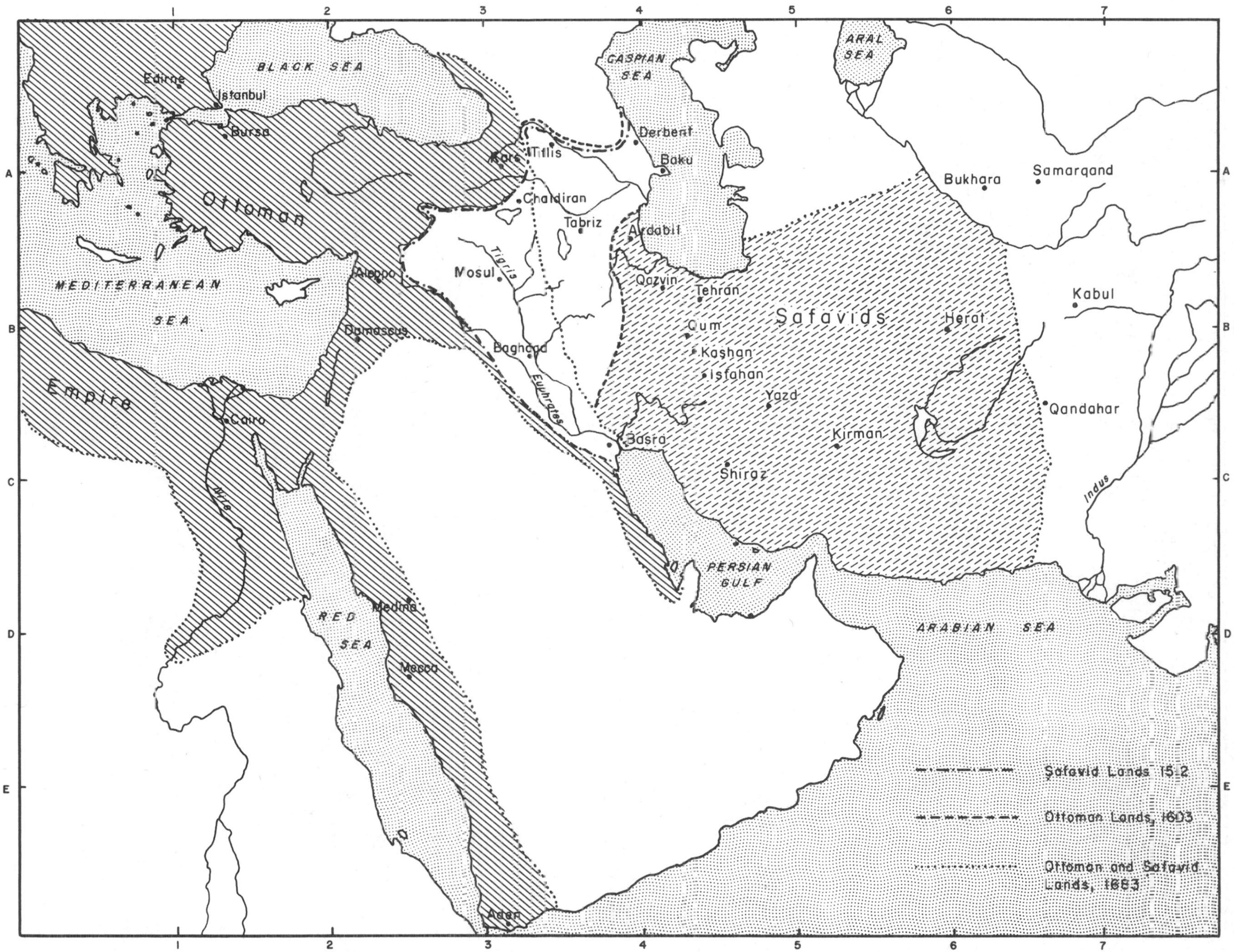

XII-EGYPT AND SOUTHWEST ASIA-17TH CENTURY

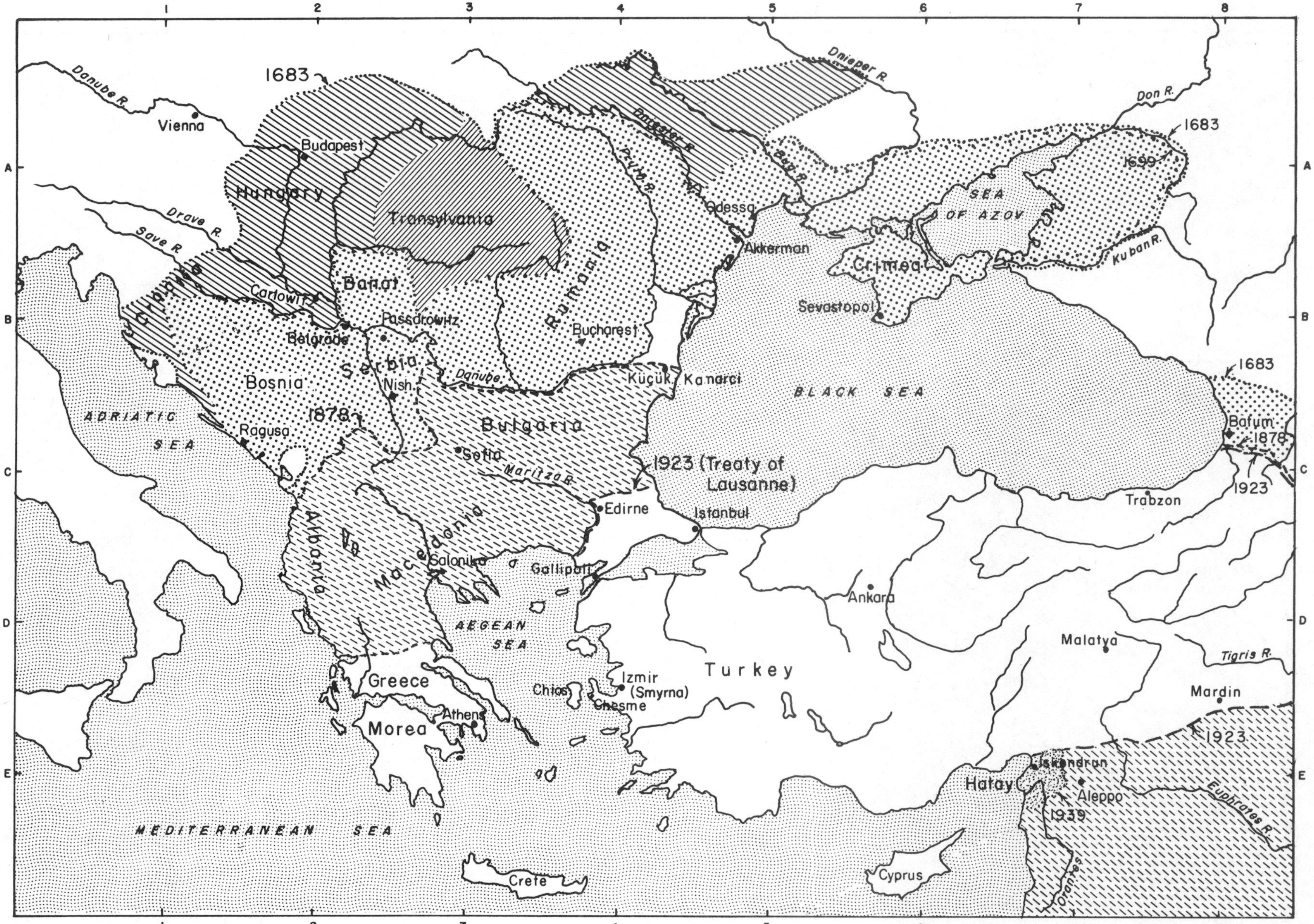

XIII - OTTOMAN EMPIRE IN EUROPE AND ANATOLIA, 1683 - 1923

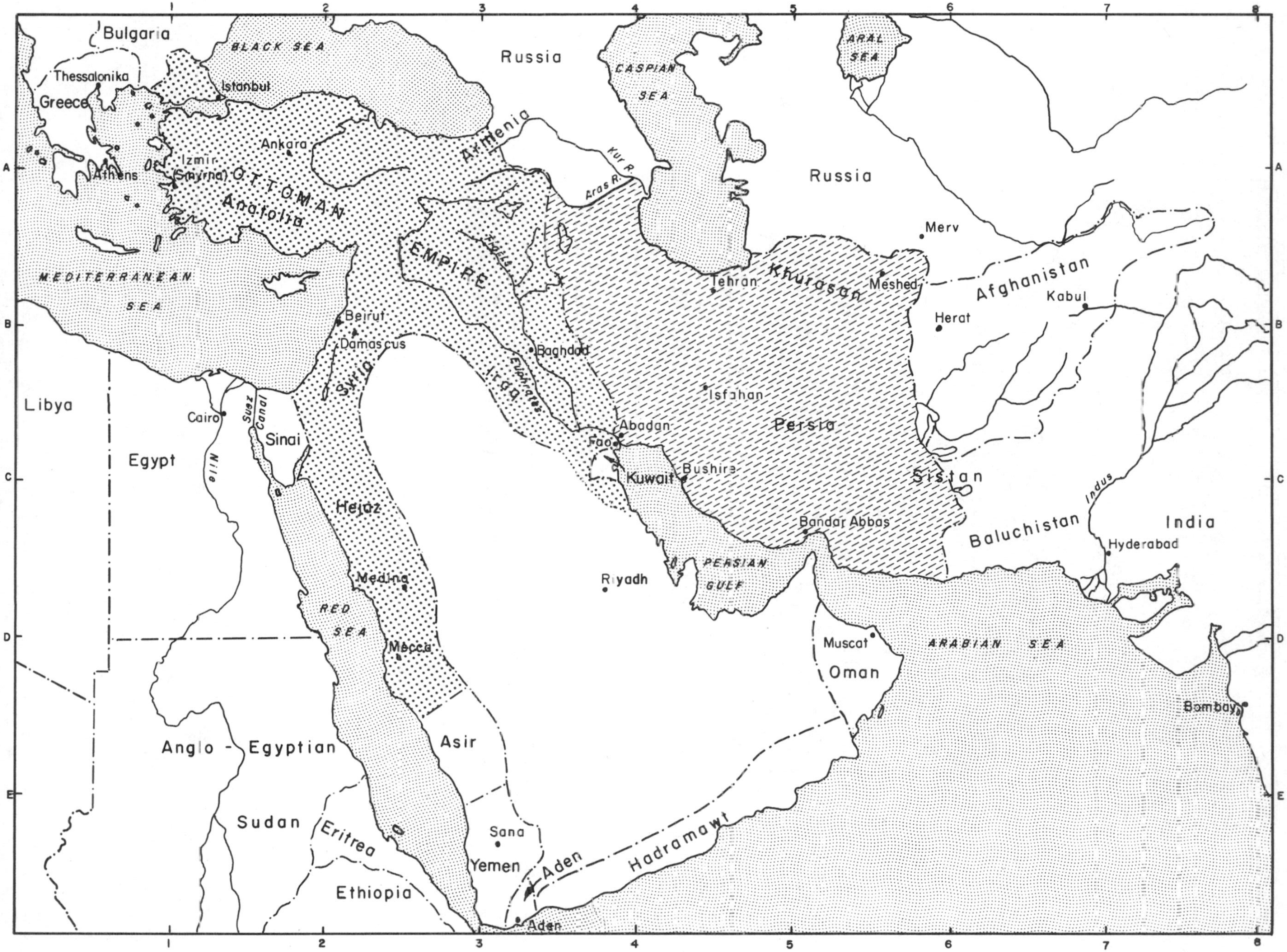

XIV - EGYPT AND SOUTHWEST ASIA, CIRCA 1914

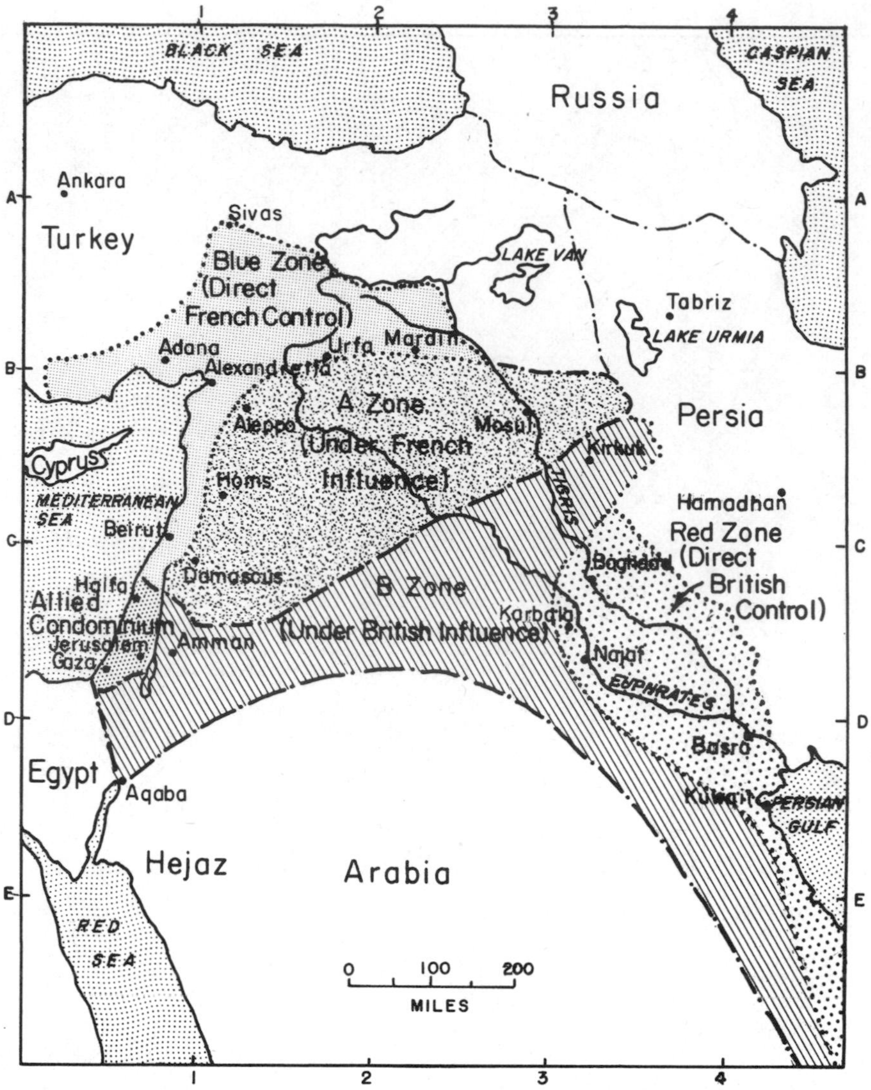

XV · THE SYKES-PICOT AGREEMENT - 1916

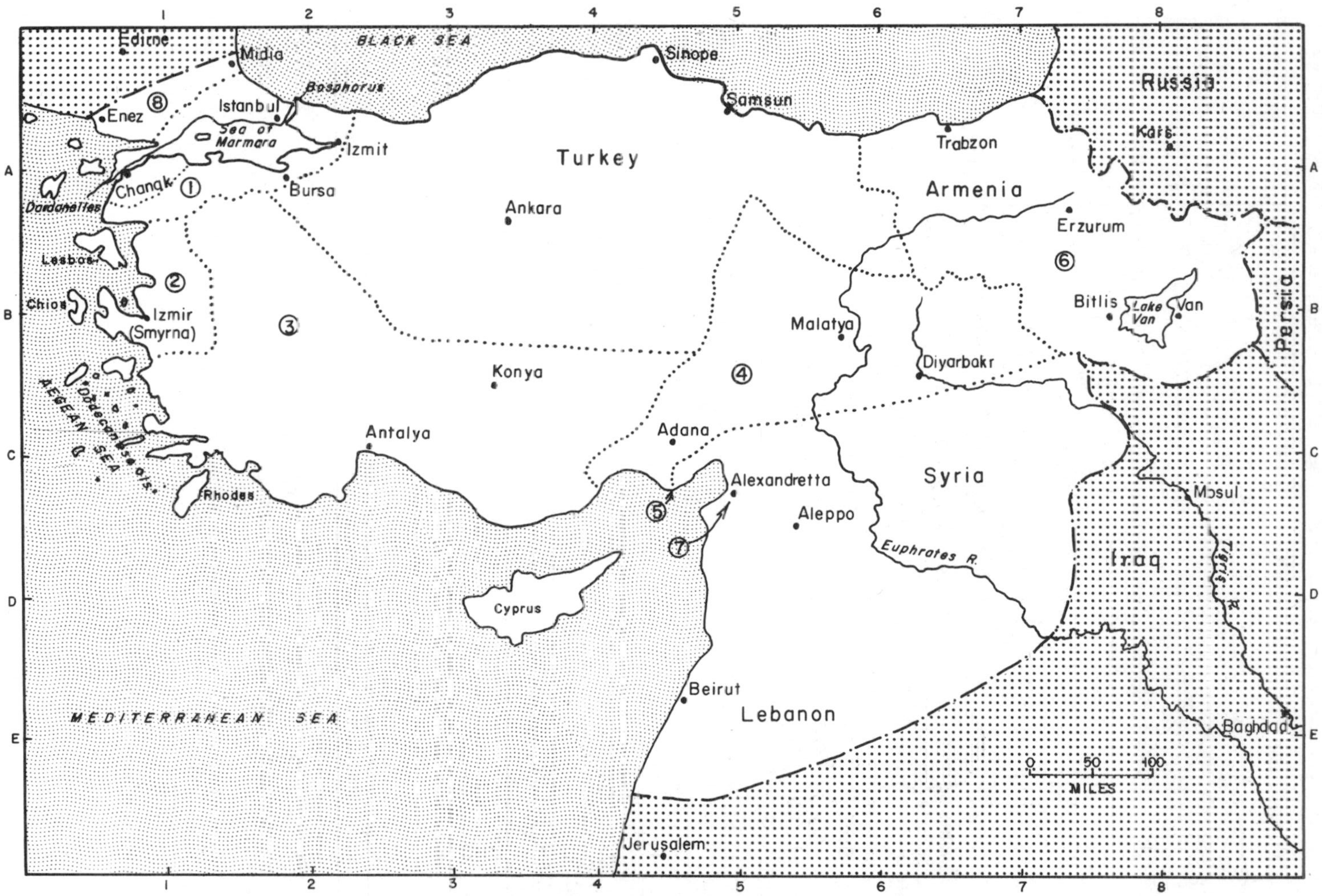

XVI-ALLIED PLANS FOR TURKEY, 1915 - 1920.

① International Zone by Treaty of Sèvres.

② Greek Zone by W. W. I promises.

③ Italian Zone by W. W. I promises and Treaty of Sèvres.

④ French Zone by W. W. I promises and Treaty of Sèvres.

⑤ Frontier by Treaty of Sèvres.

⑥ Russian Zone by Constantinople Agreement, then Armenian by Treaty of Sèvres.

⑦ Free Port.

⑧ Russian Zone by Constantinople Agreement.

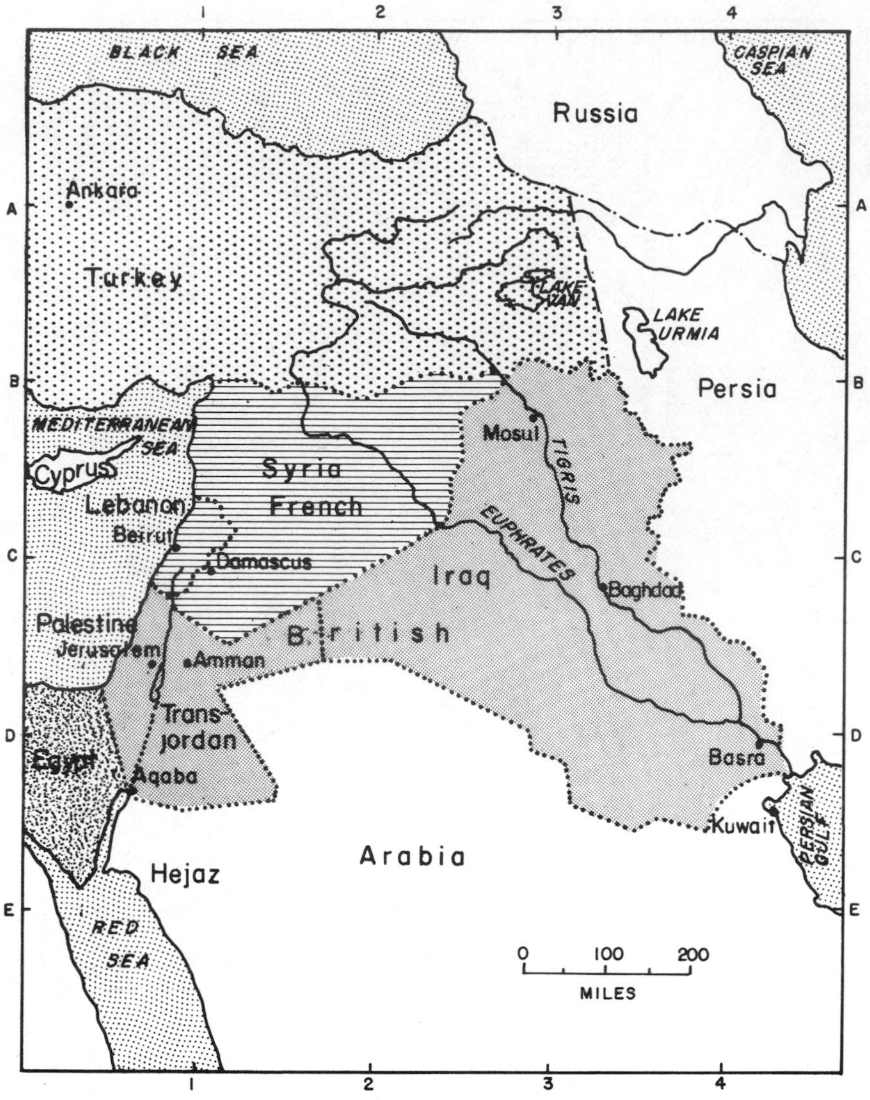

XVII - THE SAN REMO AGREEMENT

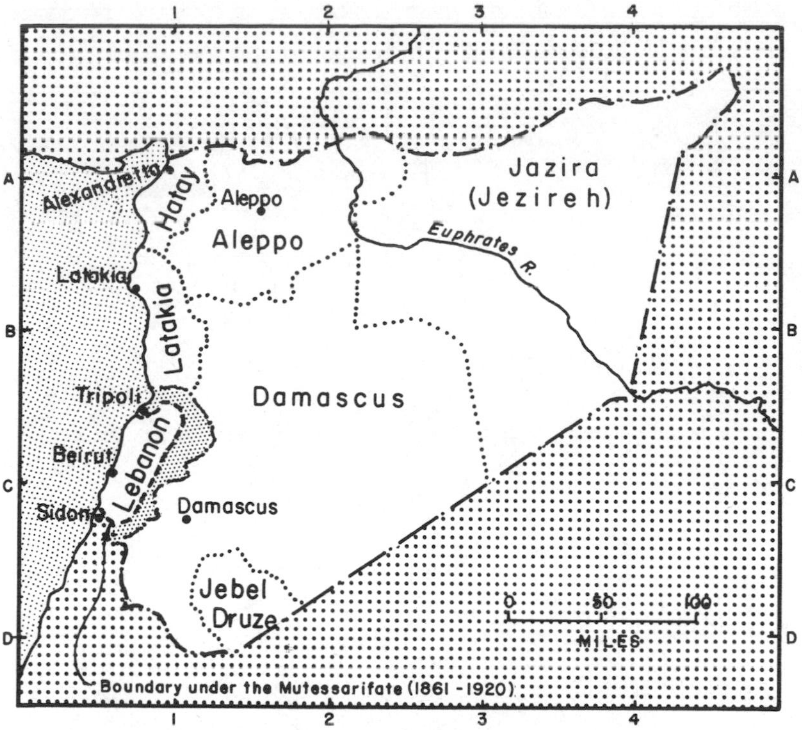

XVIII-SYRIA AND LEBANON
PROVINCES DURING FRENCH MANDATE

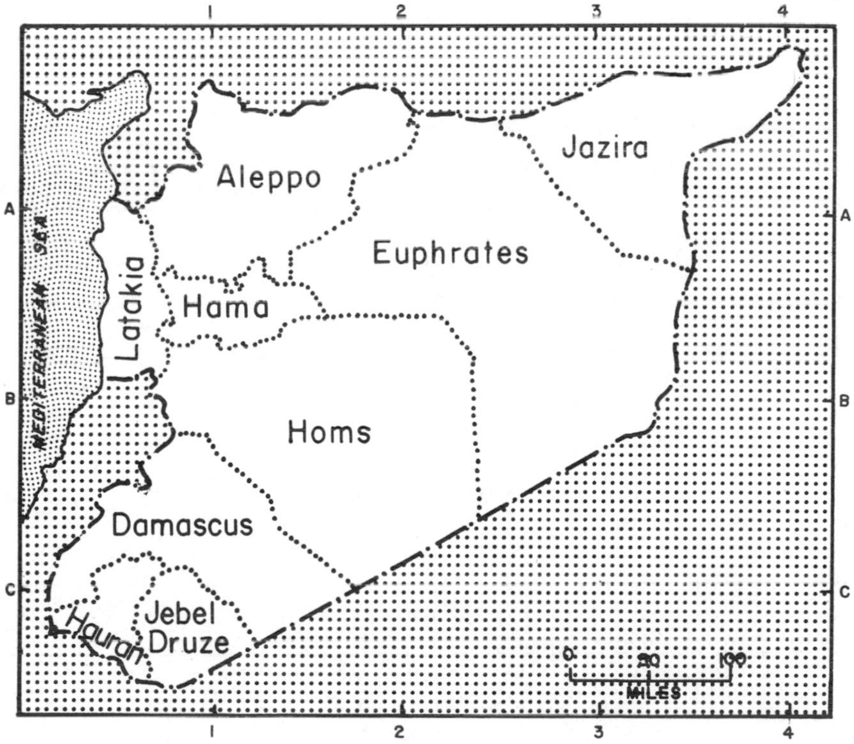

XIX-SYRIAN ADMINISTRATIVE PROVINCES
POST WWII

XX

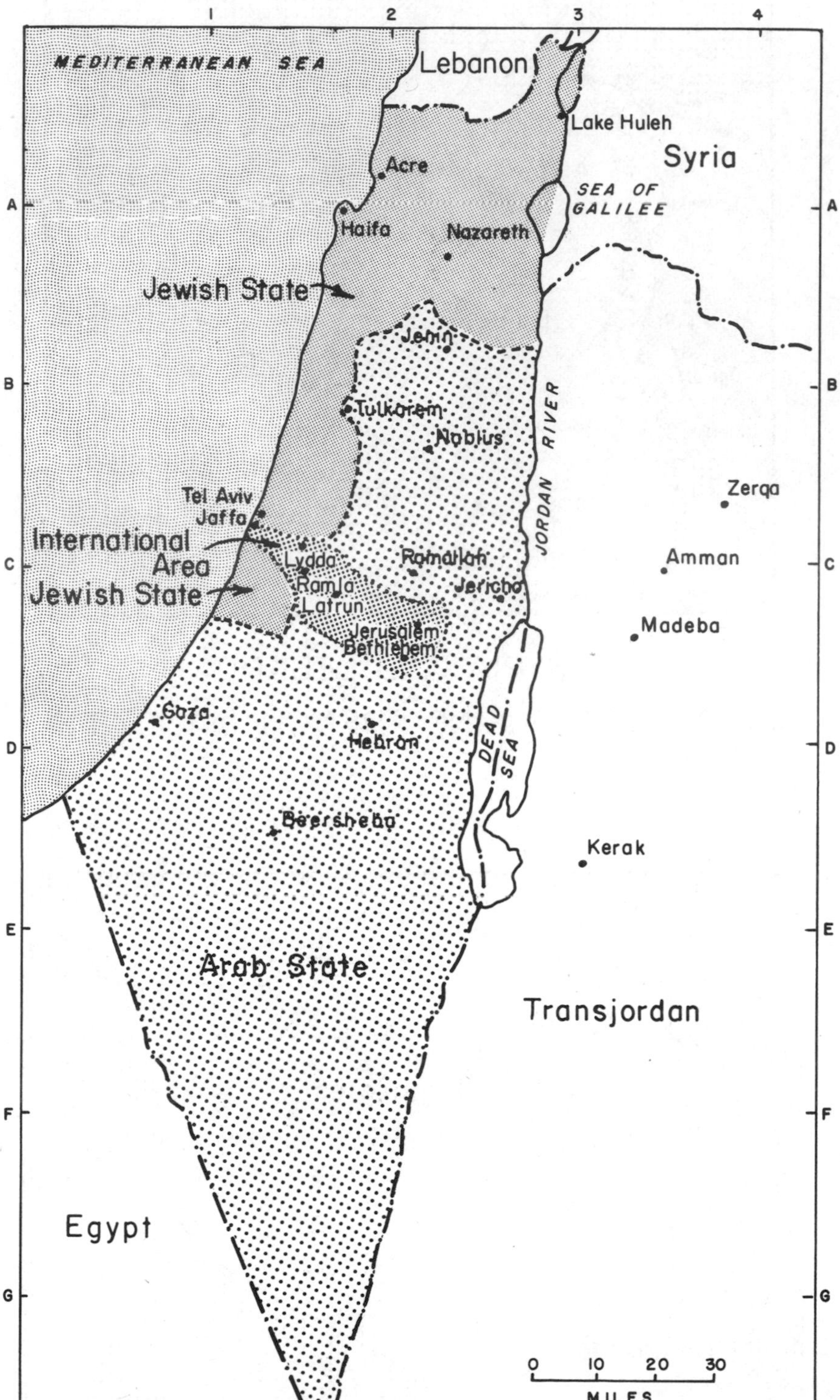

THE PEEL COMMISSION PARTITION PLAN, 1937.

XXI

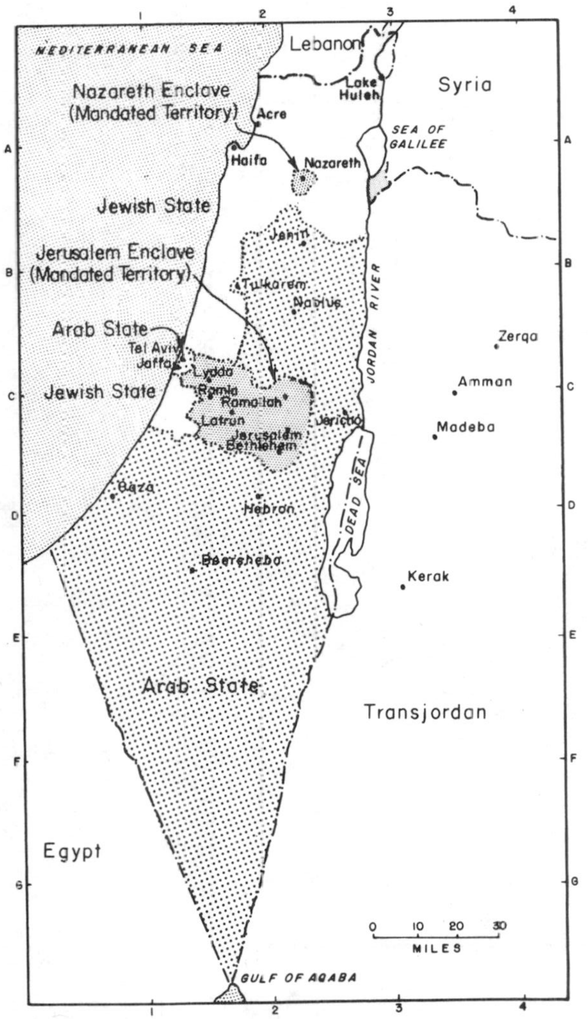

WOODHEAD COMMISSION PARTITION PLAN, 1938
PLAN A

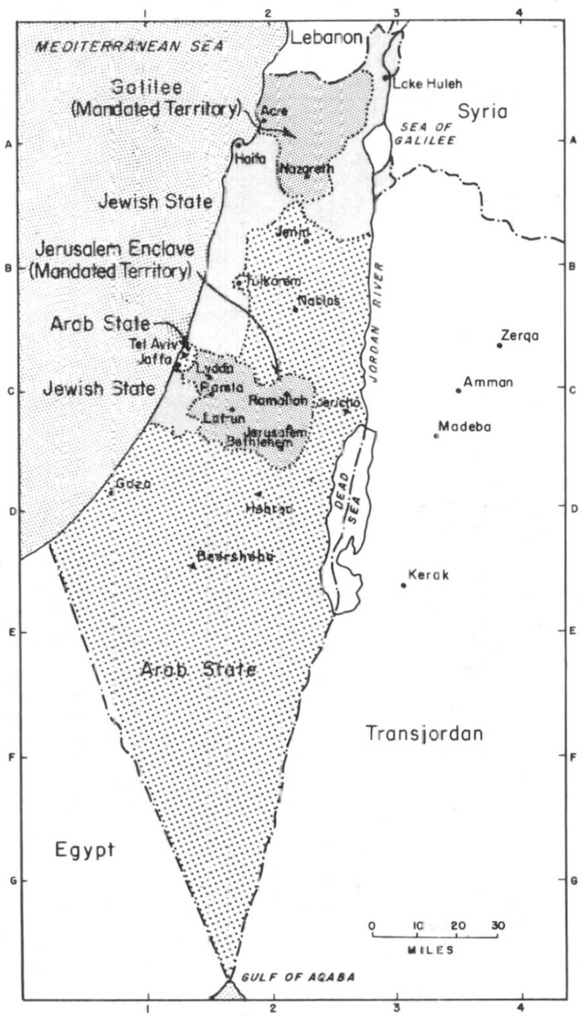

WOODHEAD COMMISSION PARTITION PLAN, 1938
PLAN B

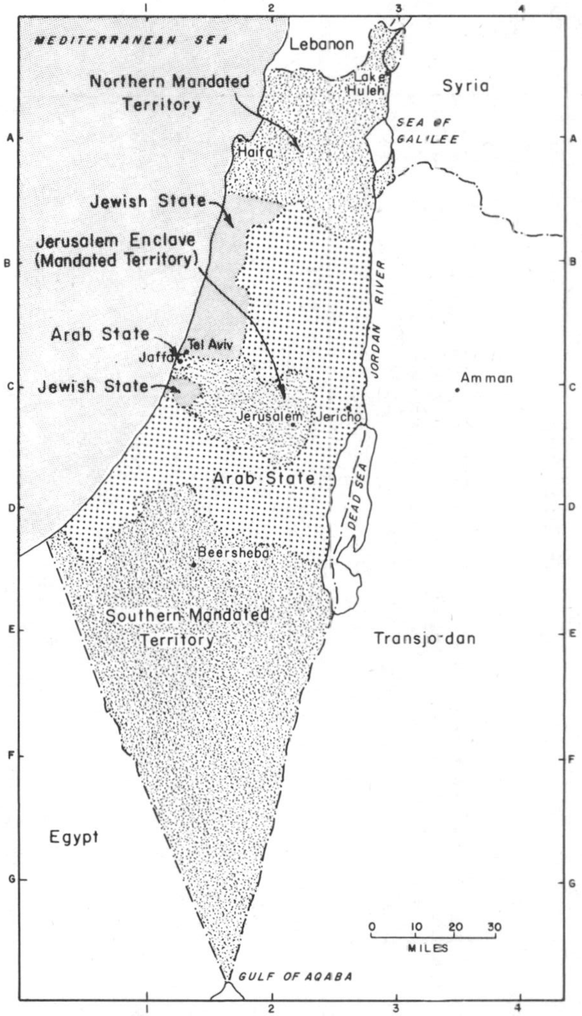

WOODHEAD COMMISSION PARTITION PLAN, 1938.
PLAN C

XXII

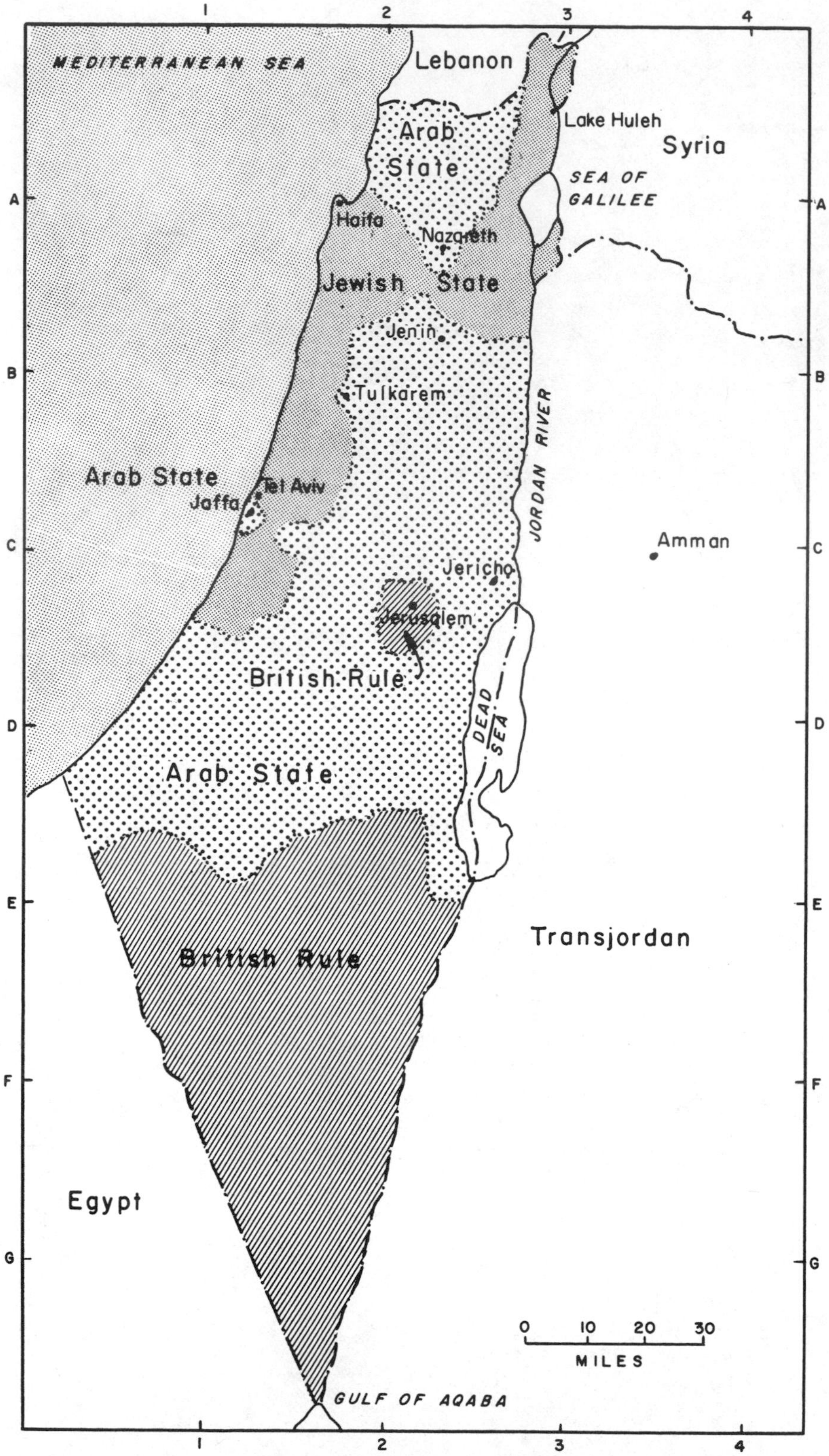

MORRISON-GRADY PARTITION PLAN, 1946

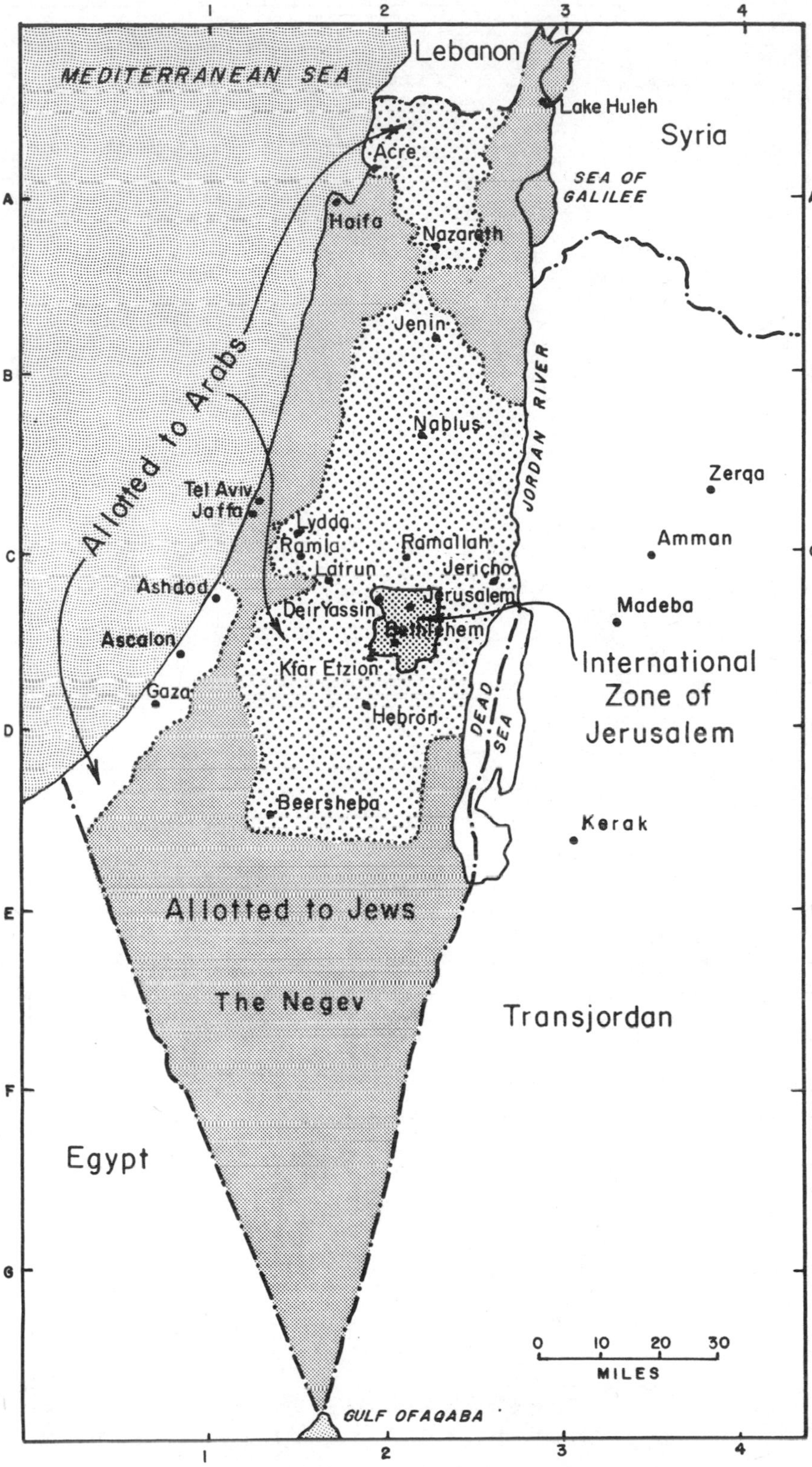

THE UNITED NATIONS PARTITION PLAN, NOVEMBER 29, 1947

XXIV

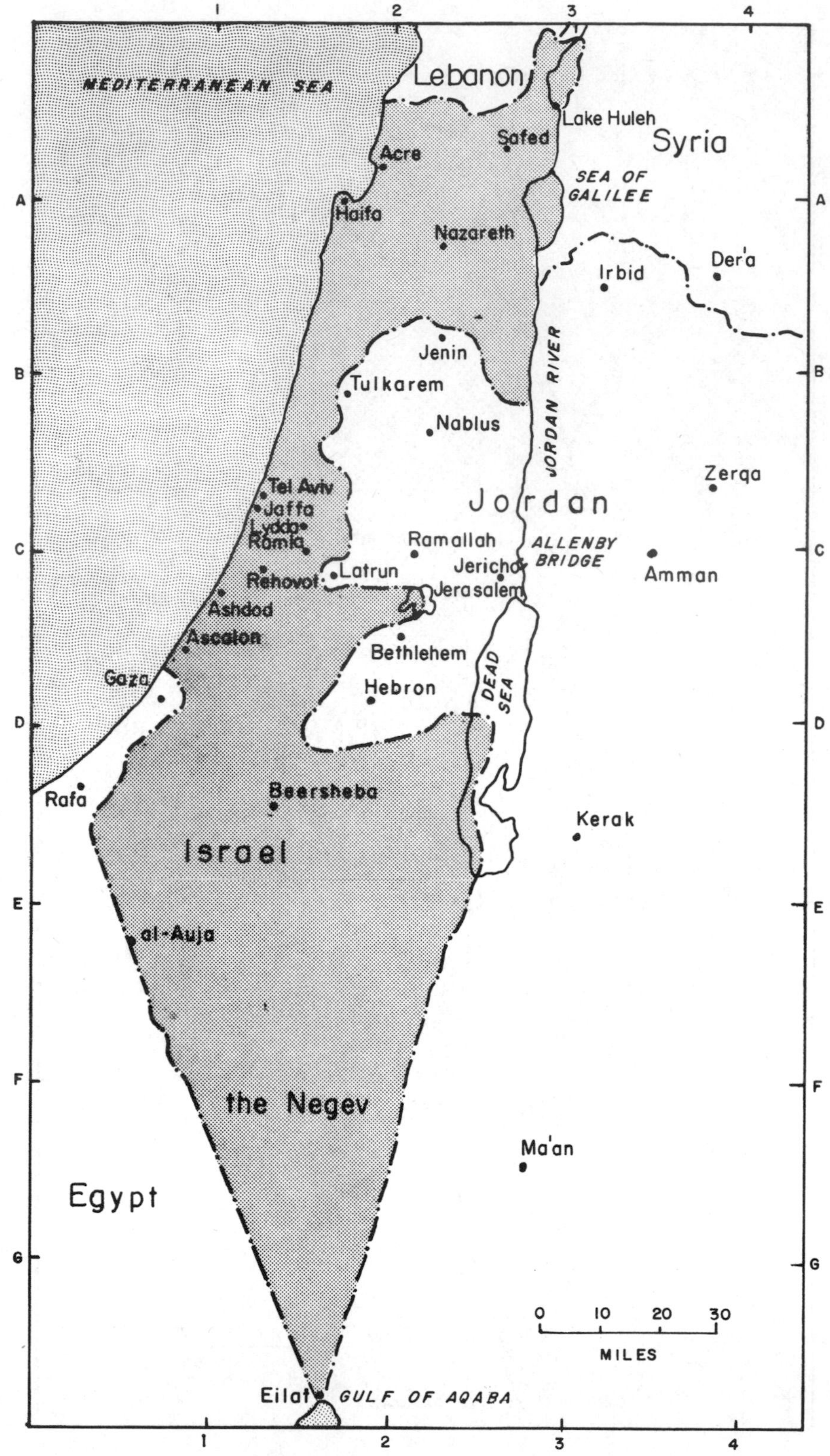

THE ISRAELI-ARAB ARMISTICE LINES-1949.

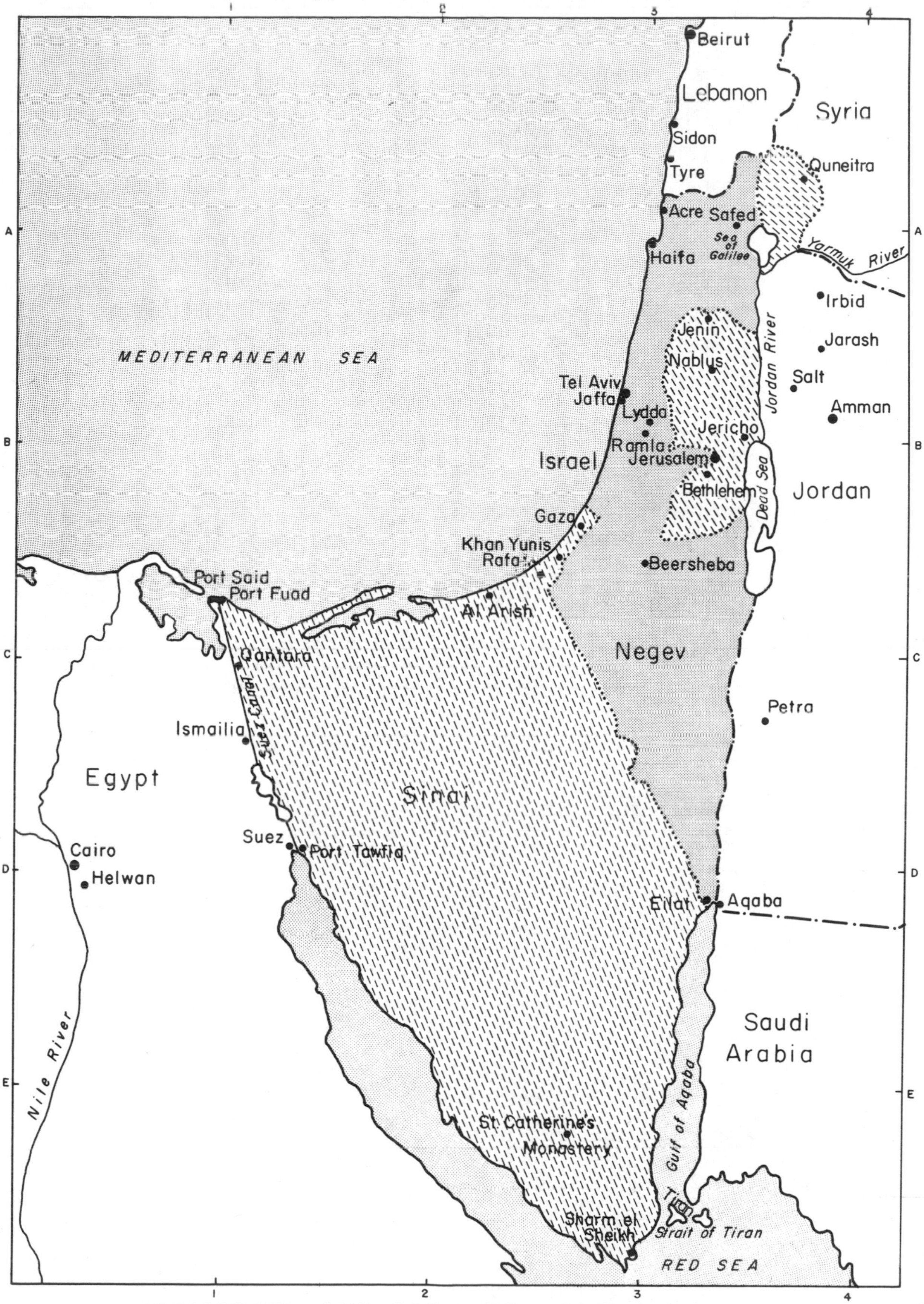

XXV-ISRAEL AND OCCUPIED LANDS-1967

SUEZ FRONT

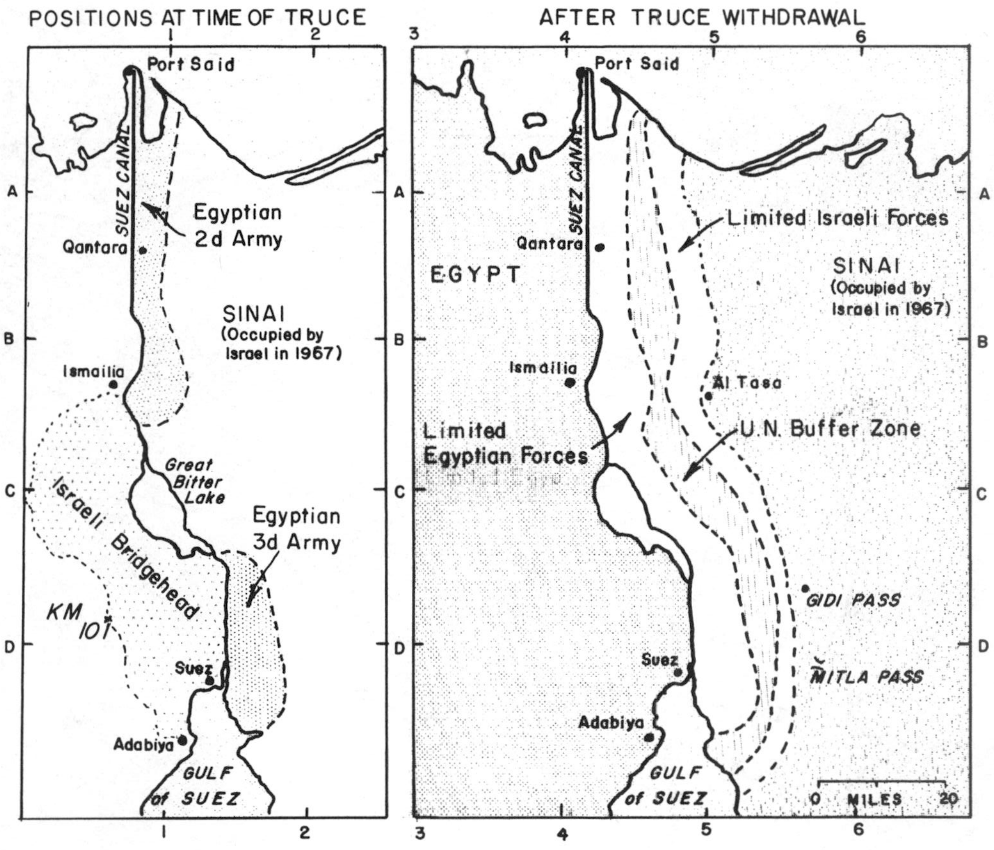

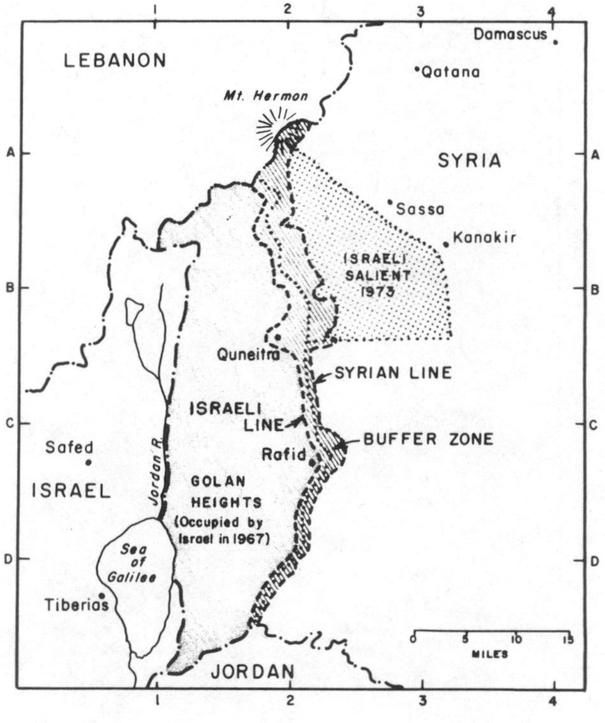

XXVI-ARAB-ISRAELI DISPUTE, 1973-74.

XXVII

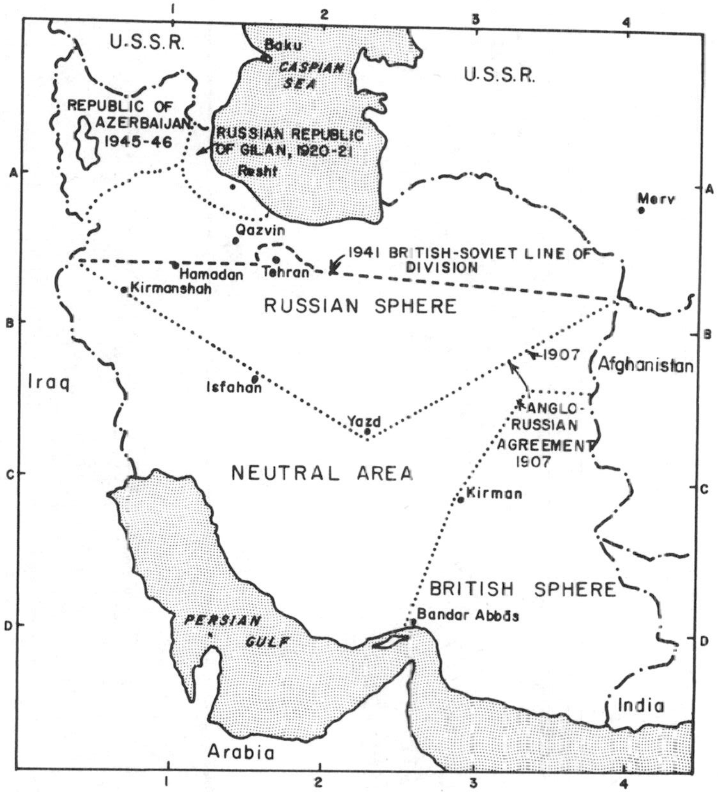

PROPOSED DIVISIONS OF IRAN, 1907-1946

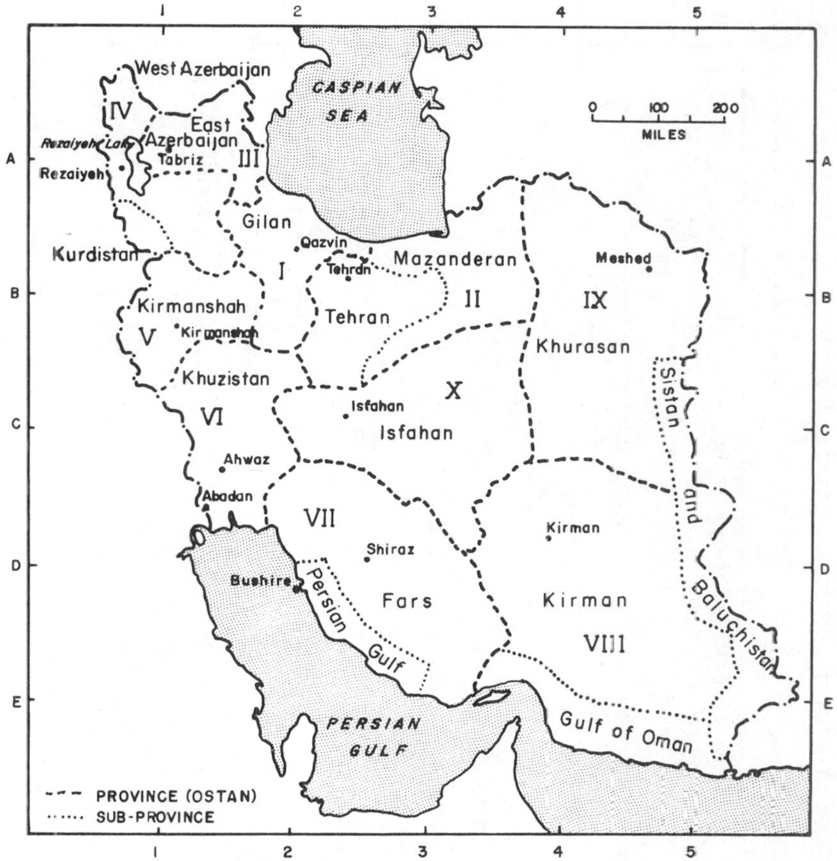

XXVIII-IRANIAN PROVINCES
POST WWII

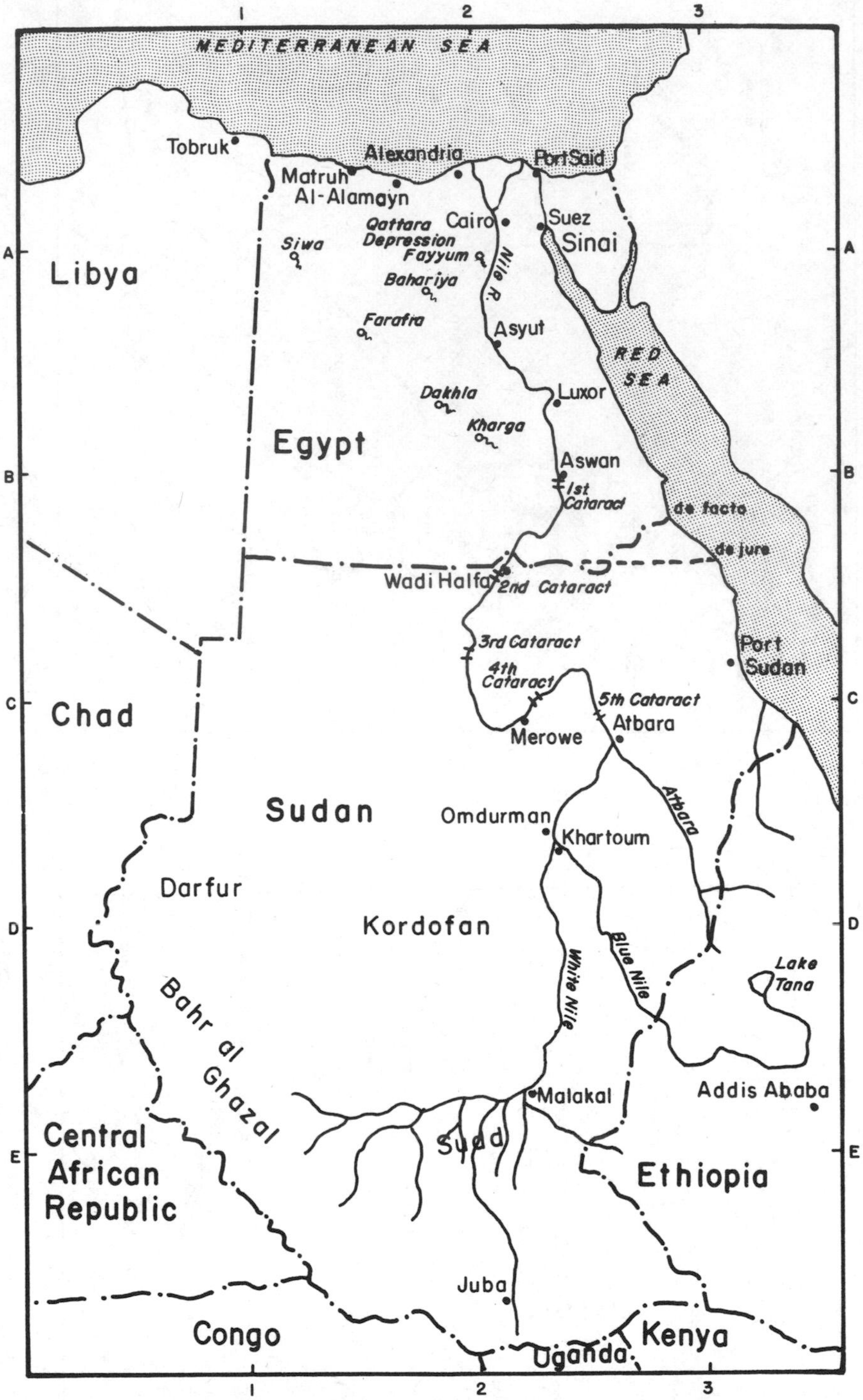

EGYPT AND SUDAN

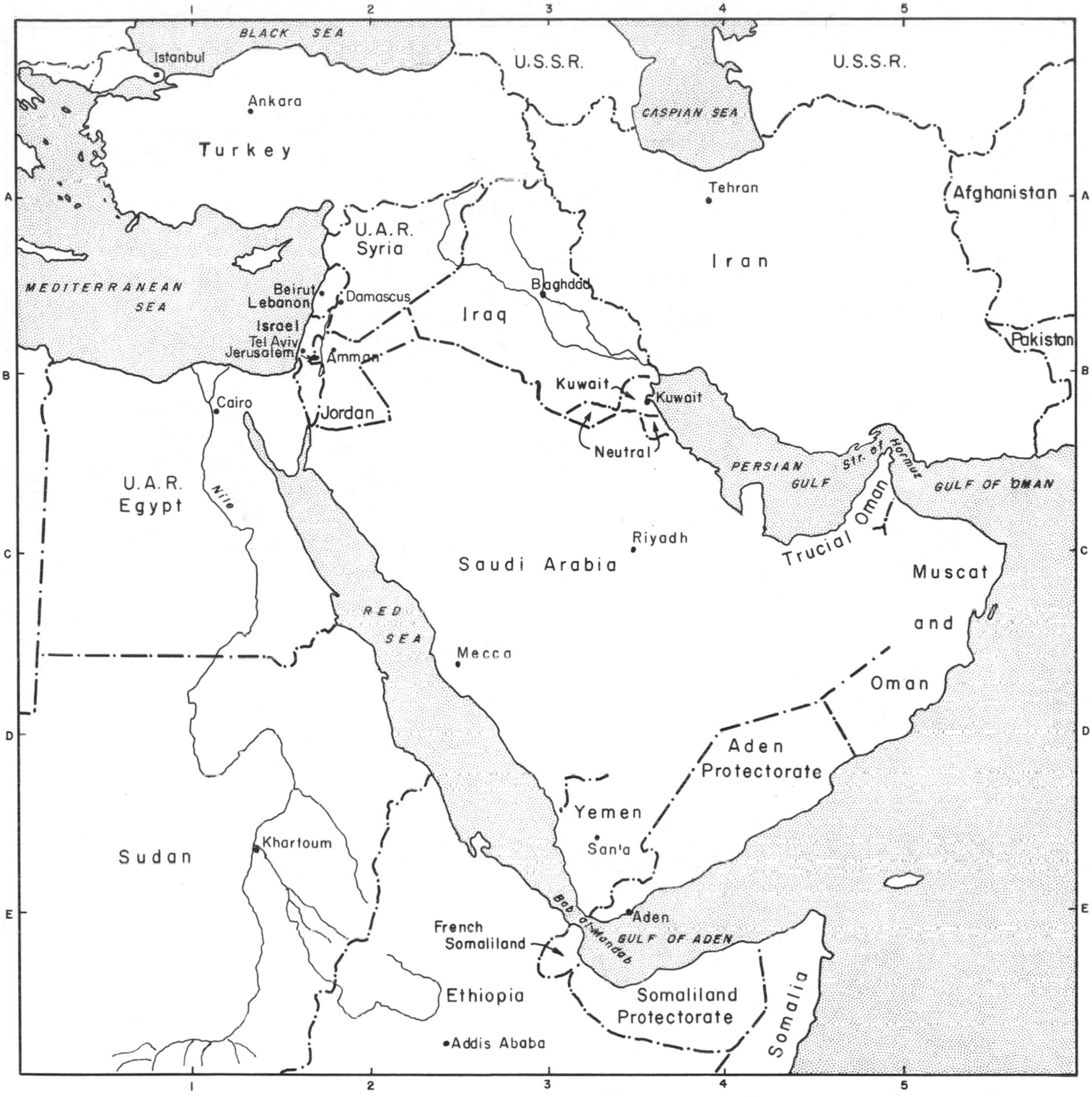

XXX - EGYPT AND SOUTHWEST ASIA - 1960

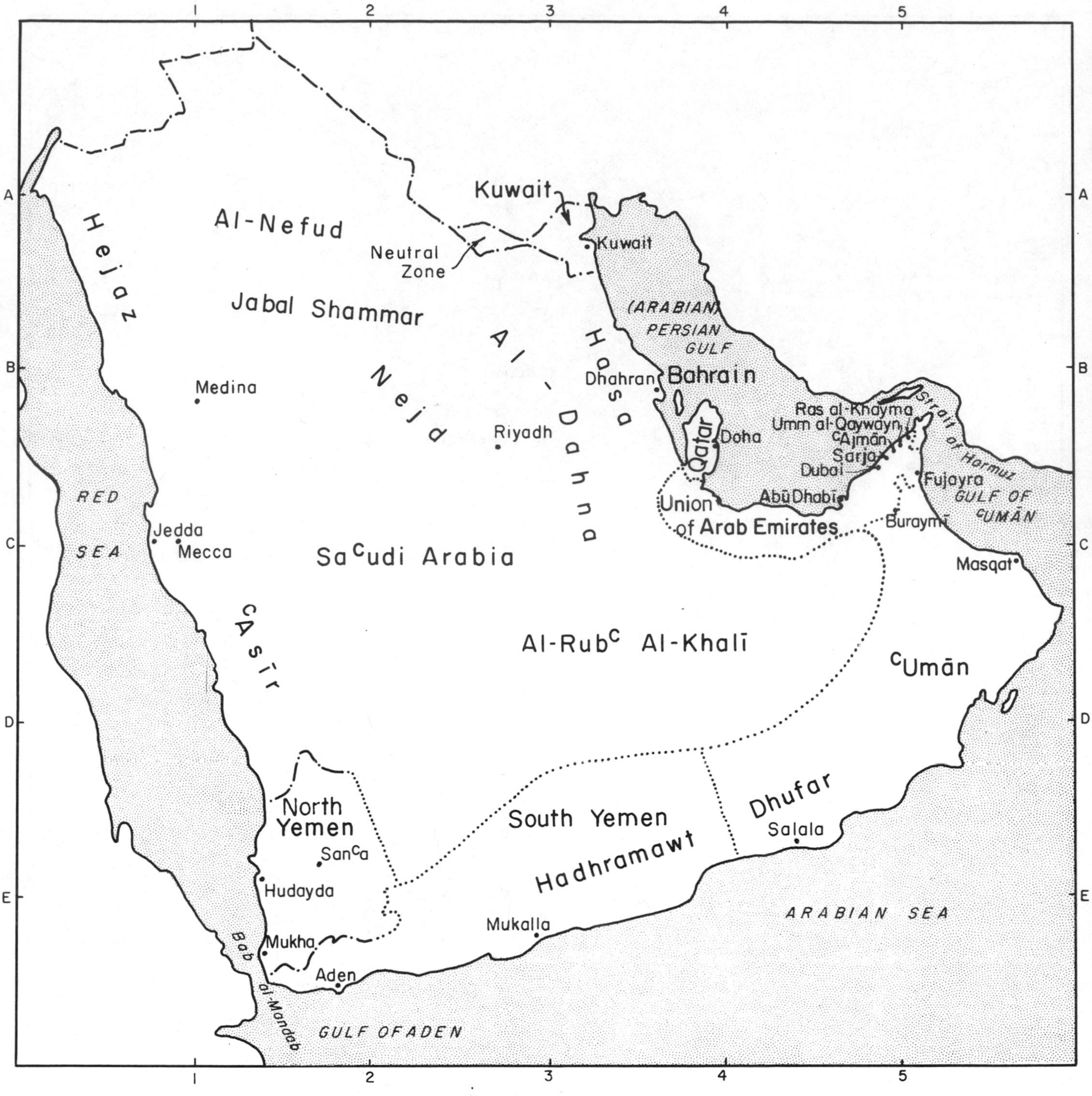

XXXI - ARABIAN PENINSULA, 1974.

C A L E N D A R S

The Islamic calendar, like many other calendars, is based on a lunar year of approximately 354 days, or about 11 days less than a solar year. In order to keep the lunar months in alignment with the major seasons, most users of a lunar calendar interpolate an extra or thirteenth month. The Muslim calendar has no extra month as a Qur'ānic revelation (sūra IX, verse 30) fixed the calendar year at twelve lunar months. The net result is that knowing the Muslim month and year in which an event took place does not indicate the corresponding season or specific month in the Gregorian Christian solar calendar. The only easy way to calculate the Christian equivalent for a Muslim date is to use a table such as the one that follows.

The Caliph ᶜUmār established the first year of the Muslim calendar as the year in which Muḥammad left Mecca for Medina. This departure or *hijra* became the name for the Muslim calendar (A.H. = *Anno Hejirae*) and 1/1/1 *hijra* was calculated as 14 July 622.

In order to calculate the approximate Christian date for a Muslim date, locate the Christian date for the first day of that Muslim year from the accompanying table and then add the appropriate number of months based upon the following chart of Muslim months:

Muḥarram	Jumādā l-ūlā	Ramaḍān
Ṣafar	Jumādā l-ākhira	Shawwāl
Rabīᶜ al-awwal	Rajab	Dhū-l-Qaᶜda
Rabīᶜ al-thānī	Shaᶜbān	Dhū-l-Ḥijja

In order to calculate the exact Christian day for a Muslim day, more elaborate tables than the one in this handbook must be used. The work by G.S.P. Freeman-Grenville, *The Muslim and Christian Calendars* (London: Oxford University Press, 1963), is available, has clear instructions and can be used for such purposes. A more detailed work which included other calendars, including the special Ottoman financial calendar, is E. Mahler, *Wustenfeld-Mahlersche Vergleichungs-Tabellen der mohammedanischen und christlichen Zeitrechnung* (Leipzig, 1926; 3rd Ed., Wiesbaden, 1961).

The best source for transforming the various calendars used by the Ottomans into Gregorian dates is Faik Resit Unat, *Hicri Tarihleri Milade Tarihe Cevirme Kilavuzu*, 3rd Ed. (Ankara, Turkey: Turk Tarih kurumu basimlvi, 1959).

A general survey of the types of calendars found in the Islamic world is H. Taqizadeh, "Various Eras and Calendars Used in the Countries of Islam," *BSOAS*, Vol. IX (1937-39), pp. 902-999; Vol. X (1940-42), pp. 107-132. The most comprehensive list of tables of the numerous pre-Ottoman Medieval calendars is found in V. Grummel, *La chronologie (Traite d'études byzantines)*, Vol. 1, ed. P. Lemerle (Paris, 1958). Among the calendars found in this work are Julian, Armenian, Coptic, Sassanian, Mongolian and Muslim calendars, plus data on comets, eclipses, earthquakes, etc. to 1453.

A few words of caution are necessary before using any table to calculate the exact Christian date for a given Muslim date (or *vice versa*). The Muslim calendar is based upon observation of the moon, not a fixed number of days. Therefore, although the tables and officially printed calendars say a new Muslim month begins on a particular Christian day, unless the ᶜulamā see the new moon, the month has not begun. This tradition persists today when the ᶜulamā, and not the government calendar, determine when the Muslim month of fasting, Ramaḍān, begins and ends. The net result is that a local calendar can be up to two days different from the calculated tables.

A second problem is that a Muslim month does not have to start on the same Christian day in two different cities. For example, the first day of Ramaḍān, 500 A.H. in Cairo, may or may not be the same day of the week in Baghdad.

Finally, the Muslim day begins at sunset. Therefore, when calculating the corresponding Christian date for a Muslim event held in the evening before midnight, it is necessary to subtract one day from the calculated Christian date. All of the preceding is a warning not to push an argument about the relationship between two very close pre-1800 events if it is based primarily on their respective Muslim (or corresponding Christian) dates — unless those dates have been very carefully checked.

1	16	July	622	51	18	Jan	671	101	24	July	719
2	5	July	623	52	8	Jan	672	102	12	July	720
3	24	June	624	53	27	Dec	672	103	1	July	721
4	13	June	625	54	16	Dec	673	104	21	June	722
5	2	June	626	55	6	Dec	674	105	10	June	723
6	23	May	627	56	25	Nov	675	106	29	May	724
7	11	May	628	57	14	Nov	676	107	19	May	725
8	1	May	629	58	3	Nov	677	108	8	May	726
9	20	Apr	630	59	23	Oct	678	109	28	Apr	727
10	9	Apr	631	60	13	Oct	679	110	16	Apr	728
11	29	Mar	632	61	1	Oct	680	111	5	Apr	729
12	18	Mar	633	62	20	Sept	681	112	26	Mar	730
13	7	Mar	634	63	10	Sept	682	113	15	Mar	731
14	25	Feb	635	64	30	Aug	683	114	3	Mar	732
15	14	Feb	636	65	18	Aug	684	115	21	Feb	733
16	2	Feb	637	66	8	Aug	685	116	10	Feb	734
17	23	Jan	638	67	28	July	686	117	31	Jan	725
18	12	Jan	639	68	18	July	687	118	20	Jan	736
19	2	Jan	640	69	6	July	688	119	8	Jan	737
20	21	Dec	640	70	25	June	689	120	29	Dec	737
21	10	Dec	641	71	15	June	690	121	18	Dec	738
22	30	Nov	642	72	4	June	691	122	7	Dec	739
23	19	Nov	643	73	23	May	692	123	26	Nov	740
24	7	Nov	644	74	13	May	693	124	15	Nov	741
24	28	Oct	645	75	2	May	694	125	4	Nov	742
26	17	Oct	646	76	21	Apr	695	126	25	Oct	743
27	7	Oct	647	77	10	Apr	969	127	13	Oct	744
28	25	Sept	648	78	30	Mar	697	128	3	Oct	745
29	14	Sept	649	79	20	Mar	698	129	22	Sept	746
30	4	Sept	650	80	9	Mar	699	130	11	Sept	747
31	24	Aug	651	81	26	Feb	700	131	31	Aug	748
32	12	Aug	652	82	15	Feb	701	132	20	Aug	749
33	2	Aug	653	83	4	Feb	702	133	9	Aug	750
34	22	July	654	84	24	Jan	703	134	30	July	751
35	11	July	655	85	14	Jan	704	135	18	July	752
36	30	June	656	86	2	Jan	705	136	7	July	753
37	19	June	657	87	23	Dec	705	137	27	June	754
38	9	June	658	88	12	Dec	706	138	16	June	755
39	29	May	659	89	1	Dec	707	139	5	June	756
40	17	May	660	90	20	Nov	708	140	25	May	757
41	7	May	661	91	9	Nov	709	141	14	May	578
42	26	Apr	662	92	29	Oct	710	142	4	May	759
42	15	Apr	663	93	19	Oct	711	143	22	Apr	760
44	4	Apr	664	94	7	Oct	712	144	11	Apr	761
45	24	Mar	665	95	26	Sept	713	145	1	Apr	762
46	13	Mar	666	96	16	Sept	714	146	21	Mar	763
47	3	Mar	667	97	5	Sept	715	147	10	Mar	764
48	20	Feb	668	98	25	Aug	716	148	27	Feb	765
49	9	Feb	669	99	14	Aug	717	149	16	Feb	766
50	29	Jan	670	100	3	Aug	718	150	6	Feb	767

151	26 Jan	768
152	14 Jan	769
153	4 Jan	770
154	24 Dec	770
155	13 Dec	771
156	2 Dec	772
157	21 Nov	773
158	11 Nov	774
159	31 Oct	775
160	19 Oct	776
161	9 Oct	777
162	28 Sept	778
163	17 Sept	779
164	6 Sept	780
165	26 Aug	781
166	15 Aug	782
167	5 Aug	783
168	24 July	784
169	14 July	785
170	3 July	786
171	22 June	787
172	11 June	788
173	31 May	789
174	20 May	790
175	10 May	791
176	28 Apr	792
177	18 Apr	793
178	7 Apr	794
179	27 Mar	795
180	16 Mar	796
181	5 Mar	797
182	22 Feb	798
183	12 Feb	799
184	1 Feb	800
185	20 Jan	801
186	10 Jan	802
187	30 Dec	802
188	20 Dec	803
189	8 Dec	804
190	27 Nov	805
191	17 Nov	806
192	6 Nov	807
193	25 Oct	808
194	15 Oct	809
195	4 Oct	810
196	23 Sept	811
197	12 Sept	812
198	1 Sept	813
199	22 Aug	814
200	11 Aug	815
201	30 July	816
202	20 July	817
203	9 July	818
204	28 June	819
205	17 June	820
206	6 June	821
207	27 May	822
208	16 May	823
209	4 May	824
210	24 Apr	825
211	13 Apr	826
212	2 Apr	827
213	22 Mar	828
214	11 Mar	829
215	25 Feb	830
216	18 Feb	831
217	7 Feb	832
218	27 Jan	833
219	16 Jan	834
220	5 Jan	835
221	26 Dec	835
222	14 Dec	836
223	3 Dec	837
224	23 Nov	838
225	12 Nov	839
226	31 Oct	840
227	21 Oct	841
228	10 Oct	842
229	30 Sept	843
230	18 Sept	844
231	7 Sept	845
232	28 Aug	846
233	17 Aug	847
234	5 Aug	848
235	26 July	849
236	15 July	850
237	5 July	851
238	23 June	852
239	12 June	853
240	2 June	854
241	22 May	855
242	10 May	856
243	30 Apr	857
244	19 Apr	858
245	8 Apr	859
246	28 Mar	860
247	17 Mar	861
248	7 Mar	862
249	24 Feb	863
250	13 Feb	864
251	2 Feb	865
252	22 Jan	866
253	11 Jan	867
254	1 Jan	868
255	20 Dec	868
256	9 Dec	869
257	29 Nov	780
258	18 Nov	871
259	7 Nov	872
260	27 Oct	873
261	16 Oct	874
262	6 Oct	875
263	24 Sept	876
264	13 Sept	877
265	3 Sept	878
266	23 Aug	879
267	12 Aug	880
268	1 Aug	881
269	21 July	882
270	11 July	883
271	29 June	884
272	18 June	885
273	8 June	886
274	28 May	887
275	16 May	888
276	6 May	889
277	25 Apr	890
278	15 Apr	891
279	3 Apr	892
280	23 Mar	893
281	13 Mar	894
282	2 Mar	895
283	19 Feb	896
284	8 Feb	897
285	28 Jan	898
286	17 Jan	899
287	7 Jan	900
288	26 Dec	900
289	16 Dec	901
290	5 Dec	902
291	24 Nov	903
292	13 Nov	904
293	2 Nov	905
294	22 Oct	906
295	12 Oct	907
296	30 Sept	908
297	20 Sept	909
298	9 Sept	910
299	29 Aug	911
300	18 Aug	912

301	7 Aug	913	351	9 Feb	962	401	15 Aug	1010
302	27 July	914	352	30 Jan	963	402	4 Aug	1011
303	17 July	915	353	19 Jan	964	403	23 July	1012
304	5 July	916	354	7 Jan	965	404	13 July	1013
305	24 June	917	355	28 Dec	965	405	3 July	1014
306	14 June	918	356	17 Dec	966	406	21 June	1015
307	3 June	919	357	7 Dec	967	407	10 June	1016
308	23 May	920	358	25 Nov	968	408	30 May	1017
309	12 May	921	359	14 Nov	969	409	20 May	1018
310	1 May	922	360	4 Nov	970	410	9 May	1019
311	21 Apr	923	361	24 Oct	971	411	27 Apr	1020
312	9 Apr	924	362	12 Oct	972	412	17 Apr	1021
313	29 Mar	925	363	2 Oct	973	413	6 Apr	1022
314	19 Mar	926	364	21 Sept	974	414	26 Mar	1023
315	8 Mar	927	365	10 Sept	975	415	15 Mar	1024
316	25 Feb	928	366	30 Aug	976	416	4 Mar	1025
317	14 Feb	929	367	19 Aug	977	417	22 Feb	1026
318	3 Feb	930	368	9 Aug	978	418	11 Feb	1027
319	24 Jan	931	369	29 July	979	419	31 Jan	1028
320	13 Jan	932	370	17 July	980	420	20 Jan	1029
321	1 Jan	933	371	7 July	981	421	9 Jan	1030
322	22 Dec	933	372	26 June	982	422	29 Dec	1030
323	11 Dec	934	373	15 June	983	423	19 Dec	1031
324	30 Nov	935	374	4 June	984	424	7 Dec	1032
325	19 Nov	936	375	24 May	985	425	26 Nov	1033
326	8 Nov	937	376	13 May	986	426	16 Nov	1034
327	29 Oct	938	377	3 May	987	427	5 Nov	1035
328	18 Oct	939	378	21 Apr	988	428	25 Oct	1036
329	6 Oct	940	379	11 Apr	989	429	14 Oct	1037
330	26 Sept	941	380	31 Mar	990	430	3 Oct	1038
331	15 Sept	942	381	20 Mar	991	431	23 Sept	1039
332	4 Sept	943	382	9 Mar	992	432	11 Sept	1040
333	24 Aug	944	383	26 Feb	993	433	31 Aug	1041
334	13 Aug	945	384	15 Feb	994	434	21 Aug	1042
335	2 Aug	946	385	5 Feb	995	435	10 Aug	1043
336	23 July	947	386	25 Jan	996	436	29 July	1044
337	11 July	948	387	14 Jan	997	437	19 July	1045
338	1 July	949	388	3 Jan	998	438	8 July	1046
339	20 June	950	389	23 Dec	998	439	28 June	1047
340	9 June	951	390	13 Dec	999	440	16 June	1048
341	29 May	952	391	1 Dec	1000	441	5 June	1049
342	18 May	953	392	20 Nov	1001	442	26 May	1050
343	7 May	954	393	10 Nov	1002	443	15 May	1051
344	27 Apr	955	394	30 Oct	1003	444	3 May	1052
345	15 Apr	956	395	18 Oct	1004	445	23 Apr	1053
346	4 Apr	957	396	8 Oct	1005	446	12 Apr	1054
347	25 Mar	958	397	27 Sept	1006	447	2 Apr	1055
348	14 Mar	959	398	17 Sept	1007	448	21 Mar	1056
349	3 Mar	960	399	5 Sept	1008	449	10 Mar	1057
350	20 Feb	961	400	25 Aug	1009	450	28 Feb	1058

451	17 Feb	1059	501	22 Aug	1107	551	25 Feb	1156
452	6 Feb	1060	502	11 Aug	1108	552	13 Feb	1157
453	26 Jan	1061	503	31 July	1109	553	2 Feb	1158
454	15 Jan	1062	504	20 July	1110	554	23 Jan	1159
455	4 Jan	1063	505	10 July	1111	555	12 Jan	1160
456	25 Dec	1063	506	28 June	1112	556	31 Dec	1160
457	13 Dec	1064	507	18 June	1113	557	21 Dec	1161
458	3 Dec	1065	508	7 June	1114	558	10 Dec	1162
459	22 Nov	1066	509	27 May	1115	559	30 Nov	1163
460	11 Nov	1067	510	16 May	1116	560	18 Nov	1164
461	31 Oct	1068	511	5 May	1117	561	7 Nov	1165
462	20 Oct	1069	512	24 Apr	1118	562	28 Oct	1166
463	9 Oct	1070	513	14 Apr	1119	563	17 Oct	1167
464	29 Sept	1071	514	2 Apr	1120	564	5 Oct	1168
465	17 Sept	1072	515	22 Mar	1121	565	25 Sept	1169
466	6 Sept	1073	516	12 Mar	1122	566	14 Sept	1170
467	27 Aug	1074	517	1 Mar	1123	567	4 Sept	1171
468	16 Aug	1075	518	19 Feb	1124	568	23 Aug	1172
469	5 Aug	1076	519	7 Feb	1125	569	12 Aug	1173
470	25 July	1077	520	27 Jan	1126	570	2 Aug	1174
471	14 July	1078	521	17 Jan	1127	571	22 July	1175
472	4 July	1079	522	6 Jan	1128	572	10 July	1176
473	22 June	1080	523	25 Dec	1128	573	30 June	1177
474	11 June	1081	524	15 Dec	1129	574	19 June	1178
475	1 June	1082	525	4 Dec	1130	575	8 June	1179
476	21 May	1083	526	23 Nov	1131	576	28 May	1180
477	10 May	1084	527	12 Nov	1132	577	17 May	1181
478	29 Apr	1085	528	1 Nov	1133	578	7 May	1182
479	18 Apr	1086	529	22 Oct	1134	579	26 Apr	1183
480	8 Apr	1087	530	11 Oct	1135	580	14 Apr	1184
481	27 Mar	1088	531	29 Sept	1136	581	4 Apr	1185
482	16 Mar	1089	532	19 Sept	1137	582	24 Mar	1186
483	6 Mar	1090	533	8 Sept	1138	583	13 Mar	1187
484	23 Feb	1091	534	28 Aug	1139	584	2 Mar	1188
485	12 Feb	1092	535	17 Aug	1140	585	19 Feb	1189
486	1 Feb	1093	536	6 Aug	1141	586	8 Feb	1190
487	21 Jan	1094	537	27 July	1142	587	29 Jan	1191
488	11 Jan	1095	538	16 July	1143	588	18 Jan	1192
489	31 Dec	1095	539	4 July	1144	589	7 Jan	1193
490	19 Dec	1096	540	24 June	1145	590	27 Dec	1193
491	9 Dec	1097	541	13 June	1146	591	16 Dec	1194
492	28 Nov	1098	542	2 June	1147	592	6 Dec	1195
493	17 Nov	1099	543	22 May	1148	593	24 Nov	1196
494	6 Nov	1100	544	11 May	1149	594	13 Nov	1197
495	26 Oct	1101	545	30 Apr	1150	595	3 Nov	1198
496	15 Oct	1102	546	20 Apr	1151	596	23 Oct	1199
497	5 Oct	1103	547	8 Apr	1152	597	12 Oct	1200
498	23 Sept	1104	548	27 Mar	1153	598	1 Oct	1201
499	13 Sept	1105	549	18 Mar	1154	599	20 Sept	1202
500	2 Sept	1106	550	7 Mar	1155	600	10 Sept	1203

601	29 Aug	1204	651	3 Mar	1253	701	5 Sept	1301
602	18 Aug	1205	652	21 Feb	1254	702	26 Aug	1302
603	8 Aug	1206	653	10 Feb	1255	703	15 Aug	1303
604	28 July	1207	654	30 Jan	1256	704	4 Aug	1304
605	16 July	1208	655	19 Jan	1257	705	24 July	1305
606	6 July	1209	656	8 Jan	1258	706	13 July	1306
607	25 June	1210	657	29 Dec	1258	707	3 July	1307
608	15 June	1211	658	18 Dec	1259	708	21 June	1308
609	3 June	1212	659	6 Dec	1260	709	11 June	1309
610	23 May	1213	660	26 Nov	1261	710	31 May	1310
611	13 May	1214	661	15 Nov	1262	711	20 May	1311
612	2 May	1215	662	4 Nov	1263	712	9 May	1312
613	20 Apr	1216	663	24 Oct	1264	713	28 Apr	1313
614	10 Apr	1217	664	13 Oct	1265	714	17 Apr	1314
615	30 Mar	1218	665	2 Oct	1266	715	7 Apr	1315
616	19 Mar	1219	666	22 Sept	1267	716	26 Mar	1316
617	8 Mar	1220	667	10 Sept	1268	717	16 Mar	1317
618	25 Feb	1221	668	31 Aug	1269	718	5 Mar	1318
619	15 Feb	1222	669	20 Aug	1270	719	22 Feb	1319
620	4 Feb	1223	670	9 Aug	1271	720	12 Feb	1320
621	24 Jan	1224	671	29 July	1272	721	31 Jan	1321
622	13 Jan	1225	672	18 July	1273	722	20 Jan	1322
623	2 Jan	1226	673	7 July	1274	723	10 Jan	1323
624	22 Dec	1226	674	27 June	1275	724	30 Dec	1323
625	12 Dec	1227	675	15 June	1276	725	18 Dec	1324
626	30 Nov	1228	676	4 June	1277	726	8 Dec	1325
627	20 Nov	1229	677	25 May	1278	727	27 Nov	1326
628	9 Nov	1230	678	14 May	1279	728	17 Nov	1327
629	29 Oct	1231	679	3 May	1280	729	5 Nov	1328
630	18 Oct	1232	680	22 Apr	1281	730	25 Oct	1329
631	7 Oct	1233	681	11 Apr	1282	731	15 Oct	1330
632	26 Sept	1234	682	1 Apr	1823	732	4 Oct	1331
633	16 Sept	1235	683	20 Mar	1284	733	22 Sept	1332
634	4 Sept	1236	684	9 Mar	1285	734	12 Sept	1333
635	24 Aug	1237	685	27 Feb	1286	735	1 Sept	1334
636	14 Aug	1238	686	16 Feb	1287	736	21 Aug	1335
637	3 Aug	1239	687	6 Feb	1288	737	10 Aug	1336
638	23 July	1240	688	25 Jan	1289	738	30 July	1337
639	12 July	1241	689	14 Jan	1290	739	20 July	1338
640	1 July	1242	690	4 Jan	1291	740	9 July	1339
641	21 June	1243	691	24 Dec	1921	741	27 June	1340
642	9 June	1244	692	12 Dec	1292	742	17 June	1341
643	29 May	1245	693	2 Dec	1293	743	6 June	1342
644	19 May	1246	694	21 Nov	1294	744	26 May	1343
645	8 May	1247	695	10 Nov	1295	745	15 May	1344
646	26 Apr	1248	696	30 Oct	1296	746	4 May	1345
647	16 Apr	1249	697	19 Oct	1297	747	24 Apr	1346
648	5 Apr	1250	698	9 Oct	1298	748	13 Apr	1347
649	26 Mar	1251	699	28 Sept	1299	749	1 Apr	1348
650	14 Mar	1252	700	16 Sept	1300	750	22 Mar	1349

751	11 Mar	1350	801	13 Sept	1398	851	19 Mar	1447
752	28 Feb	1351	802	3 Sept	1399	852	7 Mar	1448
753	18 Feb	1352	803	22 Aug	1400	853	24 Feb	1449
754	6 Feb	1353	804	11 Aug	1401	854	14 Feb	1450
755	26 Jan	1354	805	1 Aug	1402	855	3 Feb	1451
756	16 Jan	1355	806	21 July	1403	856	23 Jan	1452
757	5 Jan	1356	807	10 July	1404	857	12 Jan	1453
758	25 Dec	1356	808	29 June	1405	858	1 Jan	1454
759	15 Dec	1357	809	18 June	1406	859	22 Dec	1454
760	3 Dec	1358	810	8 June	1407	860	11 Dec	1455
761	23 Nov	1359	811	27 May	1408	861	29 Nov	1456
762	11 Nov	1360	812	16 May	1409	862	19 Nov	1457
763	31 Oct	1361	813	6 May	1410	863	8 Nov	1458
764	21 Oct	1362	814	25 Apr	1411	864	28 Oct	1459
765	10 Oct	1363	815	13 Apr	1412	865	17 Oct	1460
766	28 Sept	1364	816	3 Apr	1413	866	6 Oct	1461
767	18 Sept	1365	817	23 Mar	1414	867	26 Sept	1462
768	7 Sept	1366	818	13 Mar	1415	868	15 Sept	1463
769	28 Aug	1367	819	1 Mar	1416	869	3 Sept	1464
770	16 Aug	1368	820	18 Feb	1417	870	23 Aug	1465
771	5 Aug	1369	821	8 Feb	1418	871	13 Aug	1466
772	26 July	1370	822	28 Jan	1419	872	2 Aug	1467
773	15 July	1371	823	17 Jan	1420	873	22 July	1468
774	3 July	1372	824	6 Jan	1421	874	11 July	1469
775	23 June	1373	825	26 Dec	1421	875	30 June	1470
776	12 June	1374	826	15 Dec	1422	876	20 June	1471
777	2 June	1375	827	5 Dec	1423	877	8 June	1472
778	21 May	1376	828	23 Nov	1424	878	29 May	1473
779	10 May	1377	829	13 Nov	1425	879	18 May	1474
780	30 Apr	1378	830	2 Nov	1426	880	7 May	1475
781	19 Apr	1379	831	22 Oct	1427	881	26 Apr	1476
782	7 Apr	1380	832	11 Oct	1428	882	15 Apr	1477
783	28 Mar	1381	833	30 Sept	1429	883	4 Apr	1478
784	17 Mar	1382	834	19 Sept	1430	884	25 Mar	1479
785	6 Mar	1383	835	9 Sept	1431	885	13 Mar	1480
786	24 Feb	1384	836	28 Aug	1432	886	2 Mar	1481
787	12 Feb	1385	837	18 Aug	1433	887	20 Feb	1482
788	2 Feb	1386	838	7 Aug	1434	888	9 Feb	1483
789	22 Jan	1387	839	27 July	1435	889	30 Jan	1484
790	11 Jan	1388	840	16 July	1436	890	18 Jan	1485
791	31 Dec	1388	841	5 July	1437	891	7 Jan	1486
792	20 Dec	1389	842	24 June	1438	892	28 Dec	1486
793	9 Dec	1390	843	14 June	1439	893	17 Dec	1487
794	29 Nov	1391	844	2 June	1440	894	5 Dec	1488
795	17 Nov	1392	845	22 May	1441	895	25 Nov	1489
796	6 Nov	1393	846	12 May	1442	896	14 Nov	1490
797	27 Oct	1394	847	1 May	1443	897	4 Nov	1491
798	16 Oct	1395	848	20 Apr	1444	898	23 Oct	1492
799	5 Oct	1396	849	9 Apr	1445	899	12 Oct	1493
800	24 Sept	1397	850	29 Mar	1446	900	2 Oct	1494

901	21	Sept	1495	951	25	Mar	1544	1001	8	Oct	1592
902	9	Sept	1496	952	15	Mar	1545	1002	27	Sept	1593
903	30	Aug	1497	953	4	Mar	1546	1003	16	Sept	1594
904	19	Aug	1498	954	21	Feb	1547	1004	6	Sept	1595
905	8	Aug	1499	955	11	Feb	1548	1005	28	Aug	1596
906	28	July	1500	956	30	Jan	1549	1006	14	Aug	1597
907	17	July	1501	957	20	Jan	1550	1007	4	Aug	1598
908	7	July	1502	958	9	Jan	1551	1008	24	July	1599
909	26	June	1503	959	29	Dec	1551	1009	13	July	1600
910	14	June	1504	960	18	Dec	1552	1010	2	July	1601
911	4	June	1505	961	7	Dec	1553	1011	21	June	1602
912	24	May	1506	962	26	Nov	1554	1012	11	June	1603
913	13	May	1507	963	16	Nov	1555	1013	30	May	1604
914	2	May	1508	964	4	Nov	1556	1014	19	May	1605
915	21	Apr	1509	965	24	Oct	1557	1015	9	May	1606
916	10	Apr	1510	966	14	Oct	1558	1016	28	Apr	1607
917	31	Mar	1511	967	3	Oct	1559	1017	17	Apr	1608
918	19	Mar	1512	968	22	Sept	1560	1018	6	Apr	1609
919	9	Mar	1513	969	11	Sept	1561	1019	26	Mar	1610
920	26	Feb	1514	970	31	Aug	1562	1020	16	Mar	1611
921	15	Feb	1515	971	21	Aug	1563	1021	4	Mar	1612
922	5	Feb	1516	972	9	Aug	1564	1022	21	Feb	1613
923	24	Jan	1517	973	29	July	1565	1023	11	Feb	1614
924	13	Jan	1518	974	19	July	1566	1024	31	Jan	1615
925	3	Jan	1519	975	8	July	1567	1025	20	Jan	1616
926	23	Dec	1519	976	26	June	1568	1026	9	Jan	1617
927	12	Dec	1520	977	16	June	1569	1027	29	Dec	1617
928	1	Dec	1521	978	5	June	1570	1028	19	Dec	1618
929	20	Nov	1522	979	26	May	1571	1029	8	Dec	1619
930	10	Nov	1523	980	14	May	1572	1030	26	Nov	1620
931	29	Oct	1524	981	3	May	1573	1031	16	Nov	1621
932	18	Oct	1525	982	23	Apr	1574	1032	5	Nov	1622
933	8	Oct	1526	983	12	Apr	1575	1033	25	Oct	1623
934	27	Oct	1527	984	31	Mar	1576	1034	14	Oct	1624
935	15	Sept	1528	985	21	Mar	1577	1035	3	Oct	1625
937	5	Sept	1529	986	10	Mar	1578	1036	22	Sept	1626
937	25	Aug	1530	987	28	Feb	1579	1037	12	Sept	1627
938	15	Aug	1531	988	17	Feb	1580	1038	31	Aug	1638
939	3	Aug	1532	989	5	Feb	1581	1039	21	Aug	1629
940	23	July	1533	990	26	Jan	1582	1040	10	Aug	1630
941	13	July	1534	991	25	Jan	1583	1041	30	July	1631
942	2	July	1535	992	14	Jan	1584	1042	19	July	1632
943	20	June	1536	993	3	Jan	1585	1043	8	July	1633
944	10	June	1537	994	23	Dec	1585	1044	27	June	1634
945	30	May	1538	995	12	Dec	1586	1045	17	June	1635
946	19	May	1539	996	2	Dec	1587	1046	5	June	1636
947	8	May	1540	997	20	Nov	1588	1047	26	May	1637
948	27	Apr	1541	998	10	Nov	1589	1048	15	May	1638
949	17	Apr	1542	999	30	Oct	1590	1049	4	May	1639
950	6	Apr	1543	1000	19	Oct	1591	1050	23	Apr	1640

1051	12 Apr	1641	1101	15 Oct	1689	1151	21 Apr	1738
1052	1 Apr	1642	1102	5 Oct	1690	1152	10 Apr	1739
1053	22 Mar	1643	1103	24 Sept	1671	1153	29 Mar	1740
1054	10 Mar	1644	1104	12 Sept	1692	1154	19 Mar	1741
1055	27 Feb	1645	1105	2 Sept	1693	1155	8 Mar	1742
1056	17 Feb	1646	1106	22 Aug	1694	1156	25 Feb	1743
1057	6 Feb	1647	1107	12 Aug	1695	1157	15 Feb	1744
1058	27 Jan	1648	1108	31 July	1696	1158	3 Feb	1745
1059	15 Jan	1649	1109	20 July	1697	1159	24 Jan	1746
1060	4 Jan	1650	1110	10 July	1698	1160	13 Jan	1747
1061	25 Dec	1650	1111	29 June	1699	1161	2 Jan	1748
1062	14 Dec	1651	1112	18 June	1700	1162	22 Dec	1748
1063	2 Dec	1652	1113	8 June	1701	1163	11 Dec	1749
1064	22 Nov	1653	1114	28 May	1702	1164	30 Nov	1750
1065	11 Nov	1654	1115	17 May	1703	1165	20 Nov	1751
1066	31 Oct	1655	1116	6 May	1704	1166	8 Nov	1752
1067	20 Oct	1656	1117	25 Apr	1705	1167	29 Oct	1753
1068	9 Oct	1657	1118	15 Apr	1706	1168	18 Oct	1754
1069	29 Sept	1658	1119	4 Apr	1707	1169	7 Oct	1755
1070	18 Sept	1659	1120	23 Mar	1708	1170	26 Sept	1756
1071	6 Sept	1660	1121	13 Mar	1709	1171	15 Sept	1757
1072	27 Aug	1661	1122	2 Mar	1710	1172	4 Sept	1758
1073	16 Aug	1662	1123	19 Feb	1711	1173	25 Aug	1759
1073	5 Aug	1663	1124	9 Feb	1712	1174	13 Aug	1760
1074	25 July	1664	1125	28 Jan	1713	1175	2 Aug	1761
1075	14 July	1665	1126	17 Jan	1714	1176	23 July	1762
1077	4 July	1666	1127	7 Jan	1715	1177	12 July	1763
1078	23 June	1667	1128	27 Dec	1715	1178	1 July	1764
1079	11 June	1668	1129	16 Dec	1716	1179	20 June	1765
1080	1 June	1669	1130	5 Dec	1717	1180	9 June	1766
1081	21 May	1670	1131	24 Nov	1718	1181	30 May	1767
1082	10 May	1671	1132	14 Nov	1719	1182	18 May	1768
1083	29 Apr	1672	1133	2 Nov	1720	1183	7 May	1769
1084	18 Apr	1673	1134	22 **Oct**	1721	1184	27 Apr	1770
1085	7 Apr	1674	1135	12 Oct	1733	1185	16 Apr	1771
1086	28 Mar	1675	1136	1 Oct	1723	1186	4 Apr	1772
1087	16 Mar	1676	1137	20 Sept	1724	1187	25 Mar	1773
1088	6 Mar	1677	1138	9 Sept	1725	1188	14 Mar	1774
1089	23 Feb	1678	1139	29 Aug	1726	1189	4 Mar	1775
1090	12 Feb	1679	1140	19 Aug	1727	1190	21 Feb	1776
1091	2 Feb	1680	1141	7 Aug	1728	1191	19 Feb	1777
1092	21 Jan	1681	1142	27 July	1729	1192	30 Jan	1778
1093	10 Jan	1682	1143	17 July	1730	1193	19 Jan	1779
1094	31 Dec	1682	1144	6 July	1731	1194	8 Jan	1780
1095	20 Dec	1683	1145	24 June	1732	1195	28 Dec	1780
1096	8 Dec	1684	1146	14 June	1733	1196	17 Dec	1781
1097	28 Nov	1685	1147	3 June	1734	1197	7 Dec	1782
1098	17 **Nov**	1686	1148	24 May	1735	1198	26 Nov	1783
1099	7 Nov	1687	1149	12 May	1736	1199	14 Nov	1784
1100	26 Oct	1688	1150	1 May	1737	1200	4 Nov	1785

1201	24 Oct	1786
1202	13 Oct	1878
1203	2 Oct	1788
1204	21 Sept	1789
1205	10 Sept	1790
1206	31 Aug	1791
1207	19 Aug	1792
1208	9 Aug	1793
1209	29 July	1794
1210	18 July	1795
1211	7 July	1796
1212	26 June	1797
1213	15 June	1798
1214	5 June	1799
1215	25 May	1800
1216	14 May	1801
1217	4 May	1802
1218	23 Apr	1803
1219	12 Apr	1804
1220	1 Apr	1805
1221	21 Mar	1806
1222	11 Mar	1807
1223	28 Feb	1808
1224	16 Feb	1809
1225	6 Feb	1810
1226	26 Jan	1811
1227	16 Jan	1812
1228	4 Jan	1813
1229	24 Dec	1813
1230	14 Dec	1814
1231	3 Dec	1815
1232	21 Nov	1816
1233	11 Nov	1817
1234	31 Oct	1818
1235	20 Oct	1819
1236	9 Oct	1820
1237	28 Sept	1821
1238	18 Sept	1822
1239	7 Sept	1823
1240	26 Aug	1824
1241	16 Aug	1825
1242	5 Aug	1826
1243	25 July	1827
1244	14 July	1828
1245	3 July	1829
1246	22 June	1830
1247	12 June	1831
1248	31 May	1832
1249	21 May	1833
1250	10 May	1834
1251	29 Apr	1835
1252	18 Apr	1836
1253	7 Apr	1837
1254	27 Mar	1838
1255	17 Mar	1839
1256	5 Mar	1840
1257	23 Feb	1841
1258	12 Feb	1842
1259	1 Feb	1843
1260	22 Jan	1844
1261	10 Jan	1845
1262	30 Dec	1845
1263	20 Dec	1846
1264	9 Dec	1847
1265	27 Nov	1848
1266	17 Nov	1849
1267	6 Nov	1850
1268	27 Oct	1851
1269	15 Oct	1852
1270	4 Oct	1853
1271	24 Sept	1854
1272	13 Sept	1855
1273	1 Sept	1856
1274	22 Aug	1857
1275	11 Aug	1858
1276	31 July	1859
1277	20 July	1860
1278	9 July	1861
1279	29 June	1862
1280	18 June	1863
1281	6 June	1864
1282	27 May	1865
1283	16 May	1866
1284	5 May	1867
1285	24 Apr	1868
1286	13 Apr	1869
1287	3 Apr	1870
1288	23 Mar	1871
1289	11 Mar	1872
1290	1 Mar	1873
1291	18 Feb	1874
1292	7 Feb	1875
1293	28 Jan	1876
1294	16 Jan	1877
1295	5 Jan	1878
1296	26 Dec	1878
1297	15 Dec	1879
1298	4 Dec	1880
1299	23 Nov	1881
1300	12 Nov	1882
1301	2 Nov	1883
1302	21 Oct	1884
1303	10 Oct	1885
1304	30 Sept	1886
1305	19 Sept	1887
1306	7 Sept	1888
1307	28 Aug	1889
1308	17 Aug	1890
1309	7 Aug	1891
1310	26 July	1892
1311	15 July	1893
1312	5 July	1894
1313	24 June	1895
1314	12 June	1896
1315	2 June	1897
1316	22 May	1898
1317	12 May	1899
1318	1 May	1900
1319	20 May	1901
1320	10 Apr	1902
1321	30 Mar	1903
1322	18 Mar	1904
1323	8 Mar	1905
1324	25 Feb	1906
1325	14 Feb	1907
1326	4 Feb	1908
1327	23 Jan	1909
1238	13 Jan	1910
1329	2 Jan	1911
1330	22 Dec	1911
1331	11 Dec	1912
1332	30 Nov	1913
1333	19 Nov	1914
1334	9 Nov	1915
1335	28 Oct	1916
1336	17 Oct	1917
1337	7 Oct	1918
1338	26 Sept	1919
1339	15 Sept	1920
1340	4 Sept	1921
1341	24 Aug	1922
1342	14 Aug	1923
1343	2 Aug	1924
1344	22 July	1925
1345	12 July	1926
1346	1 July	1927
1347	20 June	1928
1348	9 June	1929
1349	29 May	1930
1350	19 May	1931

1351	7	May	1932
1352	26	Apr	1933
1353	16	Apr	1934
1354	5	Apr	1935
1355	24	Mar	1936
1356	14	Mar	1937
1357	3	Mar	1938
1358	21	Feb	1939
1359	10	Feb	1940
1360	29	Jan	1941
1361	19	Jan	1942
1362	8	Jan	1943
1363	28	Dec	1943
1364	17	Dec	1944
1365	6	Dec	1945
1366	25	Nov	1946
1367	15	Nov	1947
1368	3	Nov	1948
1369	24	Oct	1949
1370	13	Oct	1950
1371	2	Oct	1951
1372	21	Sept	1952
1373	10	Sept	1953
1374	30	Aug	1954
1375	20	Aug	1955
1376	8	Aug	1956
1377	29	July	1957
1378	18	July	1958
1379	7	July	1959
1380	25	June	1960
1381	14	June	1961
1382	4	June	1962
1383	25	May	1963
1384	13	May	1964
1385	2	May	1965
1386	22	Apr	1966
1387	11	Apr	1967
1388	31	May	1968
1389	20	Mar	1969
1390	9	Mar	1970
1391	27	Feb	1971
1392	16	Feb	1972
1393	4	Feb	1973
1394	25	Jan	1974
1395	14	Jan	1975
1396	3	Jan	1976
1397	23	Dec	1976
1398	12	Dec	1977
1399	2	Dec	1978
1400	21	Nov	1979
1401	9	Nov	1980
1402	30	Oct	1981
1403	19	Oct	1982
1404	8	Oct	1983
1405	27	Sept	1984
1406	16	Sept	1985
1407	6	Sept	1986
1408	26	Aug	1987
1409	14	Aug	1988
1410	4	Aug	1989
1411	24	July	1990
1412	13	July	1991
1413	2	July	1992
1414	21	June	1993
1415	10	June	1994
1416	31	May	1995
1417	19	May	1996
1418	9	May	1997
1419	28	Apr	1998
1420	17	Apr	1999
1421	6	Apr	2000

SELECTED GLOSSARY

A = Arabic   E = English   H = Hebrew   P = Persian   T = Turkish

(A) ^{c}abd	1. Ordinary word for "slave": ghulām (q.v.) , kul (q.v.) and mamlūk (q.v.). 2. When used with one of the names of Allāh, in the sense of servant; e.g., ^{c}abd al-Raḥmān.
(A) abū	The "kunya" (q.v.) part of a name when used in a construct: "The father of ..."
(A) adab	Until ^{c}Abbāsid Period, it meant necessary general culture for a gentleman; then associated with more narrowly defined specific knowledge needed for a given office or social function. *Belles-lettres.*
(T) agha; ağa	Most common usage is as an Ottoman title, usually translated as "chief," " senior" or "master" and used for medium-level and some high-level officials of Janissary Corps, Sultan's palace service and local officials.
(A) ahl	Family, intimates, people, household; often used in conjunction with other words as follows:
(A) ahl al-bayt	"The people of the house": Usually means the family of the Prophet.
(A) ahl al-dhimma or ahl al-kitāb (q.v.)	"People of the indefinitely renewed contract": Christians, Jews, etc. who have a revealed Book, entered into special relationship with Muslim community. They are permitted religious freedom in return for payment of the jizya (q.v.) and political neutrality.
(A) ahl al-kitāb or ahl al-dhimma (q.v.)	"People of the Book": those who possess a revealed Book and enter into special relationship with the Muslim community.
(A) ahl al-Sunna	"The people of the Sunna (Sunnī)" (q.v.) Muslims.
(T) aqçe; akçe	The Ottoman silver coin of varying weight, fineness and value; known in West as aspre or asper.
(E) Alawite	Name given by French for an extreme Shī^{c}ite (q.v.) group, the Nuṣayrīs (q.v.); found in modern Syria and have played a critical role in post-1945 Syrian

	politics. cAlawī is used by Sunnī's (q.v.) probably with a pejorative meaning.
(A) cālim	One learned in the Islamic sciences. culamā' (plural).
(H) aliya	A wave or period of Jewish immigration to Palestine and Israel; first aliya covered years 1882 to 1903.
(A) Allāh	God.
(A) cāmil	"Agent" who could hold various posts including that of provincial governor, but by 4th/10th Century, it usually meant a finance officer, especially in control of the Kharāj (q.v.)
(A) amīr	Commander, governor, prince: Under the cAbbāsids, the title was held by governors and some military commanders whose power varied in time and place.
(A) amīr al-Mu'minīn	"Commander of the Believers": title adopted by Caliph cUmar b. al-Khaṭṭāb and succeeding caliphs.
(A) amīr al-umarā'	"Commander of the Commanders": title granted to powerful military leaders in Baghdad from 324/936.
(A) amṣār (plural)	A fortified military camp established by Muslims such as Fusṭāṭ, al-Baṣra and al-Kūfa.
(A) al-Anṣār	"The helpers." Term used to designate the Medinans who supported Muḥammad.
(A) caṣabīya	Term made famous by historian Ibn Khaldūn, implying a group solidarity, an *"esprit de corps."*
(E) assassin	Westernized form of "ḥashshāshīn," one who might have used hashish; applied to Medieval Nizārī Shīcites of Persia and Syria who used assassination as a weapon.
(E) Assyrian	See Nestorian.
(T) atabeǧ; atabey	"Father-Prince." A Seljuk term for an advisor and guardian to Seljuk prince; some atabegs were able to establish their own bases of power and dynastic rule such as the Zangids.
(A) acyān	"Notable persons": originally most important inhabitants of an area, but by 17th Century A.D. under Ottomans, meant local notables with virtual control over their districts; often officially recognized by the Sublime Porte (q.v.).
(E) Ashkenazim	Jews of European origin, but primarily those from area of Eastern Europe called the Pale of Settlement and Yiddish speaking.
(A) Bahā'īs	Adherents of a religion founded in 13th/19th Century Iran by Bahā' Allāh and disseminated to Europe and the United States.
(A) banū	Refers to a family, tribe or people when followed

	by the name of that group's eponymous ancestor.
(A) barīd	Postal service, specifically the Medieval postal and intelligence service.
(A) Ba^{c}th	"Renaissance": A major Arab Socialist political party founded in Syria, having at various times controlled the governments of Syria and Iraq.
(A) bāṭinī	Devotee of esoteric interpretation of sacred texts, particularly associated with Ismā^{c}īlīs (q.v.). The sect appears as bāṭinīya (A) or batinites (E).
(A) bayt al-māl	Generally refers to a Muslim state treasury whose main sources of revenue were the jizya (q.v.) and kharāj (q.v.).
(E) Bedouin	From "badw"; refers to pastoral nomads whose language and culture are Arabic.
(T) beg; bey	Turkish title usually translated as "lord," but also as "chief," "master" or even "mister"; found among Turkish peoples or in areas they ruled.
(A) bid^{c}a	"Innovation": A belief or practice not found in the sunna (q.v.) and which the traditionalists would consider unacceptable.
(E) caliph (A) khalīfa	"Successor": The title implied continuation by its holder of Muḥammad's religious and political leadership over the Muslim community, but without direct divine revelation.
(E) Copt; (A) Qibṭ	A monophysite (q.v.) Christian in Egypt.
(A) dā^{c}ī	"He who summons": Refers to propagandists for particular dissenting sects, specifically original ^{c}Abbāsid Movement and Ismā^{c}īlīs (q.v.).
(A) Dār al-Ḥarb	"The Abode of War": Territories not under Muslim political control where jihāds (q.v.) take place.
(A) Dār al-Islām	"The Abode of Islam": Territories in which the sharī^{c}a (q.v.) prevails.
(A) dawla	The state or dynasty; also used as second part of a laqab (q.v.).
(T) defter (P) daftar	A register or account book used by administrative officials.
(T) defterdār (P) daftardār	Keeper of the defter (account book); also head of the treasury.
(T) derebey	"Valley lord": Local Anatolian rulers who in the 18th Century A.D. were virtually independent of the central Ottoman government.
(T) dervish; (A) darwīsh	Usually refers to member of a ṣūfī (q.v.) order.
(E) devshirme (T) devşirme	Term for Ottoman system of collecting subject Christian boys for training, conversion and even-

	tual use in palace, Janissary Corps and other branches of government.
(A) dhimmī	See: ahl al-dhimma.
(A) Dhū-l-Ḥijja	Twelfth month of Muslim year in which every Muslim is to make the pilgrimage to Mecca if physically and financial able - Ḥajj (q.v.).
(H) Diaspora	Dispersion of Jews from Palestine following destruction of Second Temple in 70 A.D. All Jews outside Israel comprise the Diaspora.
(A) dihqān	Arabized form of Persian term for "head of a village"; historically referred to lower Sassanian feudal nobility and descendants under Muslim rule.
(A) dīn	Religion, faith; also found as part of a compound laqab (q.v.).
(A) dīnār	Muslim gold coin of varying weight, fineness and value.
(A) dirham	Muslim silver coin of varying weight, fineness and value.
(A) dīwān	1) Collection of poetry or prose; 2) A register; 3) A government department.
(E) Druze	Religious group found chiefly in Greater Syria, whose faith derives from Fāṭimid Ismā^{c}īlī doctrines and identifies al-Ḥākim as the final Imām.
(P) emir	See: amīr.
(P) emirate	See: amīrate.
(A) faqīh fuqahā (plural)	Specialist in sharī^{c}a (q.v.), particularly its derivative details; that is, a jurist.
(E) al-Fatah (A) Fatḥ	Palestinian fidā'īyīn (q.v.) group founded by Yāṣir ^{c}Arafāt which has been undertaking operations since 1965.
(A) Fātiḥa	The opening sūra (q.v.) of the Qur^{c}ān (q.v.) and a critical component in prayer.
(A) fatwā; (T) fetvā	Opinion on legal question issued by a muftī (q.v.).
(A) fallāḥ; (E) fellah; fallaḥīn (plural)	Peasant; used most often when speaking of the Egyptian agricultural population.
(A) fidā'ī	One who sacrifices his life.
(A) fidā'īyīn (E) fedayeen	Religious and political organizations in which members risk their own lives to achieve their goals. Term associated with such religious groups as the Assassins; in modern times with various Palestinian organizations.
(A) fiqh	Jurisprudence, the science of sharī^{c}a (q.v.).

(A) fitna	Rebellion or civil strife; Fitna of Ibn al-Zubayr (A.D.683-693) was very important in Islamic history.
(A) ghāzī	Refers to one who took part in raids against infidels; later became a title of honor.
(P) ghulām	Male slave, particularly military or palace slaves.
(A) ḥadīth	Tradition relating to what Prophet Muḥammad said and did; one of four principal sources of the sharīᶜa (q.v.).
(A) ḥāfiẓ	One who has learned the Qur'ān by heart; also a traditionist.
(H) haganah	"Defense": Military arm of Jewish Agency which became the foundation for the modern Israeli army.
(A) ḥājib	"Chamberlain": Actual power of the individual with this title varied among Medieval Islamic states; this office-holder in Islamic Spain ranked above the wazir.
(A) ḥajj	Formal pilgrimage to Mecca and its environs during first 2 weeks of Dhū l-Ḥijja (q.v.); obligatory for every healthy Muslim over age of puberty who can afford it.
(A) ḥājj	Title held by one who has made this "Greater Pilgrimage."
(A) ḥakam	An arbitrator or judge.
(T) han	See: khān.
(A) Ḥanafī	Follower of Sunnī maḏhhab (q.v.) or school of law named after Abū Ḥanīfa.
(A) Ḥanbalī	Follower of Sunnī madhhab (q.v.) or school of law named after Aḥmad ibn Ḥanbal.
(A) ḥanīf	A pre-Islamic Arab monotheist.
(A) ḥarām	Forbidden, particularly in a legal sense.
(A) ḥaram	Sacred, usually associated with areas around Mecca and Medina, as well as Jerusalem.
(T) harem (A) ḥarīm	Primarily, restricted areas of a Muslim's home, particularly the women's quarters; originally it meant "women."
(A) ḥashīshīya	Name given to Syrian followers of Nizārī Ismāᶜīlī (q.v.).
(A) hijra (E) hegira	Emigration or "departure from friends" of Muḥammad when he went from Mecca to Medina in 622 A.D. Name now applied to Muslim calendar that begins 622 A.D.
(A) ḥisba	1) Functions of person supervising business and public morality, the muḥtasib (q.v.). 2) Duty of every Muslim to fulfill obligations in sharīᶜa (q.v.).

(H) histadrut	General Federation of Labor, founded in Palestine in 1920 by Jewish workers, is involved in traditional trade union activities, cooperative economic ventures, social, educational, cultural and welfare services.
(A) ^{c}Īd al-Aḍḥā	"Sacrificial feast" celebrated on 10th of Dhū-l-Ḥijja; also called al-^{c}Īd al-Kabīr and büyük bayram (the major festival).
(A) ^{c}Īd al-Fiṭr	Festival on 1st of Shawwāl marking end of month of fasting, Ramaḍān (q.v.); also called al-^{c}Īd al-Ṣaghīr and küçük bayram (the minor festival).
(A) ijāza	Certificate given on completion of a critical text reading, which conveys to recipient (in personal attendance) authority to expound the text to others.
(A) ijmā^{c}	Consensus of scholarly community of Believers on a religious regulation; one of the principal sources of the sharī^{c}a (q.v.).
(A) ijtihād	Use of individual reasoning to determine a specific Islamic rule; term has shifted meaning over time, varying from a very general to an extremely restricted application of personal reasoning.
(A) al-Ikhwān al-Muslimūn	"The Muslim Brethren": Very important politico-religious movement in modern Egypt founded by Ḥasan al-Bannā', stressing fundamentals of Islam as a guide for all activities.
(T) iltizam	Ottoman system of tax farming where the iltizam holder, the multazim, paid a fixed fee to government for right to collect local taxes, usually from peasants, but also applied to urban taxes. It was prevalent in the Arab provinces.
(A) Imām	1) Leader of prayer of whole community of Believers; as such was a title of caliphs. 2) For Ismā^{c}īlī (q.v.) and Ithnā ^{c}asharī (q.v.). Shī^{c}ī the Imām is the necessary, divinely guided, infallible, sinless political and religious leader.
(A) iqṭā^{c}	Medieval administrative grant whereby land revenues, but not ownership, were turned over to a muqta^{c} (q.v.) in return for service, usually military. This system of tax farming has often been mistranslated as "fief."
(A) ^{c}irḍ	Honor, particularly of a family or lineage; usually related to virtue of female members of a family.
(H) Irgun	Irgun Zvai Leumi (National Military Organization); established in 1937 by Jews in Palestine as military organization whose goal was establishment of a Jewish state by any means, but not under the Jewish Agency control.

(A) Islām	Submission, that is, submission to Allāh and accepting Muḥammad as His Prophet; to be a Muslim.
(A) ism	Proper name of a Muslim; for example, Muḥammad.
(A) Ismāᶜīlī (E) Ismailites	Member of a Shīᶜite sect who believes that an infallible Imāmate passed from ᶜAlī to his descendants through a Seventh Imām, Ismāᶜīl, and to his descendants. Fāṭimids and Assassins were Ismāᶜīlīs. Also a sect called Ismailites or Seveners.
(A) isnād	Chain of transmitters, particularly applied to those who passed on the Ḥadīths (q.v.) until they were collected.
(A) istiḥsān	Act of reaching a personal opinion on a legal question without the strict use of analogy.
(A) istiṣlāh	Act of reaching a legal decision by taking the public welfare into account.
(A) Ithnā ᶜasharī	Member of a Shīᶜite sect who believes there were 12 successive Imāms descending from ᶜAlī, the last of whom disappeared but will one day return. Usually translated as the Twelvers.
(A) Jāhilīya	The period of Arab history before Islām, translated as the "Days of Ignorance."
(A) jāmiᶜ	Usually the major or "Friday" mosque in a city.
(E) Janissary	A corruption of the Turkish yeni cheri (new troops), referring to the Ottoman infantry recruited through the devshirme (q.v.).
(A) jazīra	An island: Can refer to Arabian Peninsula, the land in northern Iraq and Syria between the Tigris and Euphrates Rivers, or a province in modern Syria.
(A) jihād	The Holy War whose goal is either the expansion or defense if Islām.
(A) jinn	Creatures created from smokeless flame who can appear in different forms and carry out all types of activities.
(A) jizya	Poll or head tax leveled on dhimmīs (q.v.) living in Muslim lands.
(A) jund	A military troop, military settlement and later a district or province, especially in Syria.
(A) kaᶜba	Name of sacred "cube-shaped" building in Mecca containing the Black Stone, a meteorite, which along with the building, is regarded as holy. Muslims pray toward the Kaᶜba.
(A) kadi	See: qāḍī.
(A) kāfir	An unbeliever or infidel.
(T) kānūn	Laws issued by Ottoman sultans based on their right

of ^{c}urf (q.v.) custom, as opposed to laws based on the sharī^{c}a (q.v.).

(T) kānūnnāme — Collection of kānūns (q.v.).

(A) kātib — A secretary.

(A) khalīfa — See: caliph.

(T) khān — 1) Title implying authority used in post-Mongol Iran for rulers and local governors, but eventually a polite title for males. 2) Large building for travelers and/or merchandise.

(A) kharāj — The specific meaning has varied, but as a general rule for the pre-Ottoman Period, it referred to the land tax as opposed to jizya (q.v.).

(A) khārijī
(E) kharijites — Minor Muslim sect, usually in political opposition to a Sunni or Shī^{c}ī ruler, who believed that equality of all believers applied to those qualified for office of caliph, as well as all other offices. The sect appears as kharijites.

(A) khaṭīb — The one who gives the khuṭba (q.v.).

(P) khedive — Ancient Persian title acquired in 1867, for a high price, by Ismā^{c}īl, Governor of Egypt; held by his family members until 1914 when they took title of sulṭān.

(A) al-Khulafā' al-Rāshidūn — "The Rightly Guided" Caliphs: The term refers to period from 632-661 A.D. when Abū Bakr, ^{c}Umar, ^{c}Uthmān and ^{c}Alī were the first 4 caliphs.

(A) khuṭba — Sermon given at the Friday noon prayer by a khaṭīb (q.v.); sermon used for disseminating political information, as well as a religious instruction vehicle. One symbol of political sovereignty of a ruler was mentioning that ruler's name in the khuṭba.

(H) kibbutz
kibbutzim (plural) — Collective, communal, agricultural units established in Palestine and Israel by Jews.

(E) kibla — See: qibla.

(A) al-Kitāb — "The Book," that is, the Qur'ān (q.v.); Koran (E).

(H) Knesset — Israeli parliament.

(E) Koran — See: Qur'ān.

(T) Kuds — See: al-Quds.

(T) kul — A slave, particularly one in the service of the Ottoman government.

(A) kunya — Patronymic part of a Muslim name, Abū —— (father of); may refer to an actual son or be an honorific title. Also Umm —— (mother of).

(A) Kurd — Person identified with a linguistic (Kurdish) cultural group whose traditional home has been northern Iraq, southeastern Turkey and northwestern Iran. Most Kurds have b̲een engaged in nomadic occupations and are Sunnī Muslims.

(A) laqab	Honorific part of a Muslim name, many times as a compound ending in — al-Dīn or — al-Dawla, such as Ṣalāḥ al-Dīn (Saladin).
(A) madhhab	Refers to the accepted Sunnī legal "school" or "rite" which today number four: Ḥanafī, Ḥanbalī, Mālikī and Shāfiʿī.
(A) Madīna (E) Medina	Specifically known as Madīnat al-Rasūl, City of the Prophet, it refers to pre-Islamic oasis of Yathrib in Arabia where Muḥammad established his new politico-religious community.
(A) madrasa	Muslim school, originally a Sunnī (q.v.) school for teaching sharīʿa (q.v.); term later applied to most secondary schools that taught the Islamic sciences.
(A) maghrib	West: Term came to mean general area of Libya, Tunisia, Algeria and Morocco. Al-Maghrib is the Arabic name of Morocco.
(A) mahdī	"The Guided One." It usually refers to one who is divinely guided, a Messiah.
(A) majlis	An assembly; and today, a parliament.
(A) malik	"King": Title held by modern monarchs, but relatively rare in earlier times.
(A) Mālikī	Follower of the Sunnī (q.v.) madhhab; named after Mālik ibn Anas.
(A) mamlūk	"One possessed": Technically meant a slave, but came to refer to a male, white (usually Turkish) who formed an elite cavalry corps. They were manumitted after being trained and instructed in Islām. The height of their power was when they controlled Egypt, 1260-1517 A.D.
(H) Mapai	Major Israeli political party, Labor and Socialist, which has dominated Israeli governments.
(A) maqṣūra	Enclosed portion of a mosque where a monarch could pray separated from the rest of the congregation.
(E) Maronite	Christian church, primarily found in Lebanon, that has been in communion with Roman Catholicism since the 17th Century. The President of Lebanon is always a Maronite.
(A) masjid	A mosque.
(A) mawlā mawālī (plural)	A client: Means by which a non-kin individual could be brought into a tribe; one system by which non-Arabs were brought into the early Muslim system.

(A) Mawlid al-Nabī	Muḥammad's birthday, celebrated on Rabī^{c} I, 12.
(E) Melchite (E) Melkite	A church that broke from Greek Orthodoxy; entered into communion with Roman Catholic Church; also called Greek Catholic.
(A) miḥna	Court of inquiry, particularly associated with the Mu^{c}tazilite (q.v.) position of some of the early ^{c}Abbāsid caliphs.
(A) miḥrāb	Niche in the qibla (q.v.) wall of a mosque. One interpretation is that it indicates the direction of prayer, as well as where Muḥammad stood when he led the prayers.
(T) millet	Referred to non-Muslim, internally autonomous religious communities in Ottoman Empire. The three major millets were: Armenian Orthodox, Greek Orthodox and Jewish.
(E) minaret (A) manāra	The tower of a mosque from which the muezzin (q.v.) gives the call to prayer.
(A) minbar	The pulpit in a mosque from which the khuṭba (q.v.) is given.
(A) mīrī	Government or publicly-owned property.
(E) Monophysite	Member of an Eastern Church who believes Christ has a single nature.
(A) mudīr	Director or administrator.
(A) mu'adhdhin (E) muezzin	The one who calls the faithful to prayer five times daily.
(A) muftī	A person trained in the sharī^{c}a (q.v.) who gives a non-binding legal opinion, a fatwā (q.v.), in response to questions submitted to him.
(A) Muhājirūn	Meccan emigrants who joined Muḥammad in Medina.
(A) Muḥarram	First month of Muslim year. On the 10th of the month of Shī^{c}ites (q.v.) mourn the martyrdom of Ḥusayn, ^{c}Alī's son, at Karbala in 61/680.
(A) muḥtasib	Market inspector who was also in charge of enforcing public morality. See also: ḥisba.
(A) mujtahid	Individual who exercised personal interpretation of the sharī^{c}a to form a legal opinion. Shī^{c}ites (q.v.) permit their ^{c}ulamā' (q.v.) this role, while for most periods, it was denied to Sunnī ^{c}ulamā'. See also: ijtihād.
(A) mukhtār	The head of a village.
(A) mulk; (A) milk	Private property.
(P) mullā; mollā	Member of the ^{c}ulamā', but particularly applied to Shī^{c}ite ^{c}ulamā' (q.v.) of Iran.

(T) multezim (A) multazim	Holder of an iltizam (q.v.).
(A) Munāfiqūn	Medinan group who rejected Muḥammad; translated as "hypocrites."
(A) Muslim	"One who submits": The official name for those who accepted Islām.
(A) Mu^{c}tazilī	A member of a particular school of Islamic rational thought strongly influenced by Hellenism. The sect is called Mutazilite.
(A) nabī	A prophet, while al-Nabī or al-Nabī al-Ummī refers to Muḥammad.
(A) nasab	The part of a Muslim name that refers to his or her lineage; that is, ibn or bint (son or daughter) of an immediate or distant relative.
(A) naṣrānī;naṣārā (pl.)	A Christian.
(E) Nestorian	Christian who believes that Christ has two separate natures, a divine and a human one. Members were found in Iraq, Iran and Syria.
(A) nisba	The adjectival part of a Muslim name which can denote family origin, profession, etc.
(A) Nuṣayrī	Follower of an extreme Shī^{c}ite group in Syria who believes ^{c}Alī is the incarnation of the diety. See: Alawite.
(T) Osmanli	An Ottoman; that is, one who was a Muslim, knowledgeable of Ottoman ways and originally, in theory, a slave of the sulṭān.
(P) Pahlavi	1) Name of the present ruling dynasty of Iran. 2) Name for pre-Islamic form of Middle Persian.
(T) paşa (E) pasha	Turkish title of very high rank, normally military, under the Ottomans; was held by Ottoman officials into the 20th Century.
(P) pīr	A title for the head of a ṣūfī (q.v.) order; also means: elder, veteran.
(E) Porte	See: Sublime Porte.
(A) qāḍī	Muslim judge learned in the sharī^{c}a (q.v.) whose decisions were legally binding.
(A) qānūn	See: kānūn
(A) qibla	The direction of prayer; also refers to the wall of any mosque facing the Ka^{c}ba (q.v.) in Mecca which has the miḥrāb (q.v.).
(A) qirā'a	Certificate in which it is stated that the student himself read the text aloud before the holder of the ijāza (q.v.). Recitation of the Qu'rān.

(A) qiyās	Process of juridical reasoning by analogy that is accepted by Sunnī madhhabs as one of the sources of the sharī^{c}a (q.v.).
(A) al-Quds	The Holy, in particular, the Muslim name for Jerusalem.
(A) al-Qur'ān (E) Koran	"The Book," considered divine, containing God's revelations as revealed in Arabic to Prophet Muḥammad, and the basis for the Islamic way of life.
(A) Quraysh	Name of major Meccan family of Muḥammad's time. Medieval Muslim political theorists believed that a caliph, to be legitimate, had to be descended from the Quraysh through the male line.
(A) ra'īs (T) reis	Chief, leader, etc. Sometimes used as part of a compound name.
(A) Ramaḍān	Ninth month of Muslim year when Muslims are to fast from dawn to sunset.
(A) rasūl	Messenger, but also used to refer to prophets as "messengers of God."
(A) ra'y	Personal opinion: Muslim juridical term implying personal speculation; sometimes used synonymously with ijtihād (q.v.).
(A) ra^{c}āya (T) reaya (E) rayah	A flock: In the Ottoman Empire it initially meant all non-Osmanli, but eventually came to refer only to non-Muslim taxpayers.
(E) razzia	A Bedouin raid or ghazw raid.
(A) ribāṭ	A ṣūfī (q.v.) hospice; fortified military hospice.
(A) Ridda	Apostacy, in particular, refers to breaking away from Islām of a number of tribes just before and immediately following the death of Muḥammad.
(A) Rūm	First the Byzantine (Roman) Empire, then Anatolia, particularly under Seljuk rule.
(T) Rumeli	Ottoman territories in Europe.
(H) Sabra	1) Jew born in Palestine or Israel since the late 19th Century A.D. 2) Cactus fruit with prickly exterior and sweet interior.
(A) ṣaḥn	The courtyard of a mosque.
(A) ṣalāt	Ritual prayer to be performed by Muslims five times a day.
(A) samā^{c}	Certificate stating that a student attended a reading presided over by one holding an ijāza (q.v.).
(T) sancak (E) sanjak	Ottoman military or administrative district. The number of sanjaks varied greatly.
(A) sāqiya	Water wheel used for raising water into an irri-

gation canal or ditch.

(E) Saracen — A Muslim, usually referring to an Arab.

(P) saray
(E) seraglio — A palace; later the seat of government; for Europeans, the women's quarters of the palace or ḥarīm (q.v.).

(P) sardār — Military commander: Title was even held by Englishmen when Commanders-in-Chief of the Egyptian army.

(A) ṣawm — "Fasting" or "abstinence." Al-ṣawm is the legal, prescribed fast during month of Ramaḍān (q.v.).

(A) sayyid — Master, lord, etc., but became an honorific title for Muḥammad's descendants; used today for "mister."

(E) Sephardim — Technically a Jew whose ancestors came from Spain, knew the "Spanish" Jewish rite and possibly spoke Ladino. Term has been used for all Mediterranean or "Oriental" Jews.

(A) shādūf — Means of raising irrigation water with a counterweight.

(A) shāfiᶜī — Follower of the Sunnī madhhab (q.v.) named after Shāfiᶜi

(P) shāh — King: Title used by a number of Persian dynasties.

(A) shahādah — Bearing witness to Muslim creed that "there is no God but Allāh; Muḥammad is His Prophet."

(A) sharīᶜa — Islamic law generally said to be based on Qur'ān (q.v.), Ḥadīth (q.v.), Qiyās (q.v.) and Ijmāᶜ (q.v.).

(A) sharīf — Title meaning "highborn" or "noble"; came to be applied to descendants of ᶜAlī's son, Ḥasan.

(A) shaykh; (T) şeyh
(E) sheikh — "Old Man": Head of a tribe; leader of a village; head of a ṣūfī order.

(A) Shaykh al-Islām
(T) şeyhülislam — Title of the leading religious figure aside from the caliph in a Muslim state. Under the Mamlūks he was a qāḍī (q.v.), while eventually the Ottomans appointed the muftī (q.v.) of Istanbul to the office.

(A) shayṭān — The devil, Satan.

(A) Shīᶜa — "Party" or group of Muslims who believe that the caliphate should have gone to ᶜAlī and his descendants. They have further divided into many groups, including the Ithnā ᶜasharī (q.v.) and Ismāᶜīlīs (q.v.).

(A) Shīᶜī; (E) Shīᶜite — Follower of the Shīᶜa; sect is called Shīᶜite.

(A) shurṭa — Police.

(P) sipāhī — Cavalryman in Ottoman Empire, usually holding a timar (q.v.).

(A) sīra — Biography, but particularly associated with the

	biography of Muḥammad.
(E) Sublime Porte	European translation of phrase Bāb-ī ᶜĀlī, High Gate; term stood for the Ottoman Grand Wazir office, and eventually the Ottoman government.
(A) ṣūfī	A Muslim mystic.
(A) sulṭān	Title which came to mean "supreme secular power," primarily associated with rulers of Turkish origin.
(A) sunna	The customary procedure for living, which came to mean "the way and customs of Muḥammad."
(A) sunnī	"One who follows the way of Muḥammad," in particular those who accept one of the 4 madhhabs (q.v.) as opposed to Shīᶜī sects. Sometimes mistranslated as "orthodox," although the majority sect among Muslims.
(A) sūq	Market.
(A) sūra	A chapter in the Qur'ān (q.v.).
(A) tafsīr	Qur'ānic exegesis.
(T) Tanzimat	"Reordering" or "reorganization." Term used to describe period of modernization and Westernization in the Ottoman Empire, 1839-1878.
(A) taqīya	Act by which an individual hides his true beliefs, practiced by Ismāᶜīlīs (q.v.) and other sects at various times.
(A) taqlīd	Imitation in sense of complete acceptance and following of the sharīᶜa (q.v.) as expounded in the various madhhabs.
(A) ṭarīqa	Term applied to ṣūfī (q.v.) orders, as well as the "path" followed by ṣūfis to reach gnosis.
(T) tekke	Building in which ṣūfī members of an order perform their rituals.
(T) timar	Ottoman grant of income from a tax source, usually land, in return for service, in particular for the Ottoman cavalry, the sipāhīs.
(T) timarci (E) timariot	The holder of a timar.
(P) Tūdeh	A Leftist, and then the Communist Party of Iran.
(T) tughra	Official signature of Ottoman sulṭāns in the form of an elaborate cartouche.
(T) turkman (E) turkoman	A Turkish-speaking nomad.
(A) ᶜulamā' (E) ulema	Plural of ᶜālim (q.v.); refers to those learned in Islām; sometimes translated as the "Muslim clergy."
(A) ᶜumda	Head or chief of a village, particularly used in Egypt.

(A) 'umma	A nation or people; used in terms of modern nationalism, as well as Muḥammad's new Islamic community at Medina.
(A) ᶜurf	Custom or customary practice having a very limited and restricted role as a sharīᶜa (q.v.) source.
(T) vali; (A) wālī	Governor, particularly of a vilayet (q.v.).
(T) vilayet (A) wilāya	An Ottoman administrative unit of varying size and number.
(A) wādī	A valley, river or dry river bed.
(A) wafd	Delegation: Name of a major Egyptian political party founded by Saᶜd Zaghlūl.
(A) waqf	Endowment deed, whereby revenues from a particular source are permanently allocated for a pious purpose such as the building of a mosque.
(A) wazīr; (T) vezir (E) vizier	Advisor to a ruler who, under the early ᶜAbbāsids and other dynasties, was the equivalent of a Prime Minister.
(H) yishuv	Name for the Jewish community in Palestine before 1948.
(A) zakāt	Obligatory alms tax on all Muslims.
(T) zeamet	Ottoman timar with an annual revenue between 20,000 and 100,000 aqçe (q.v.).

C H R O N O L O G Y

The selecting for this chronological list is based upon the author's teaching experience. For example, only some of the previously listed dynasties and rulers are included, in addition to a number of battles, treaties, etc.

For the events before 1947, no scholarly work has a chronology significantly more detailed than the following list, although a number of books do include chronologies. Beginning with its first issue in 1947, the *Middle East Journal* devoted a section to a very detailed chronology of current events. It is the best source for contemporary affairs, although the individual names, treaties and conferences are not indexed. Annual events can be found listed in greater detail in the *Middle East Record,* edited by Daniel Dishon (Tel Aviv: Israel Universities Press), which has published volumes for 1965 through 1968. There are also various standard annual references which can be used.

570	Traditional date for birth of Muḥammad.
602	End of Lakhmid dynasty at Ḥīra.
610	Muḥammad receives first revelation.
615	Emigration of some Muslims from Mecca to Abyssinia.
622	Hijra. Beginning of Muslim calendar.
	Sept. 24: Muḥammad's arrival at Yathrib (Medina)(Madīna)).
624	Muḥammad's victory at Badr.
625	Muḥammad's temporary defeat at Uḥud.
627	Battle of the Khandaq (Trench) at Medina. Meccans repulsed.
628	Agreement at al-Ḥudaybiya between Muḥammad and Meccans.
630	Pilgrimage to Mecca.
630-631	"Year of Delegations" of Arab tribal leaders to Muḥammad.
632	June 8: Death of Muḥammad.
632-634	Reign of Caliph Abū Bakr.
633	End of al-Ridda Wars. Defeat of Musaylima by Khālid b. al-Walīd.
634	July: Defeat of Byzantines at Ajnadayn.
	Aug.: Death of Abū Bakr.
634-644	Reign of Caliph ᶜUmar.
635	Occupation of Damascus by Khālid b. al-Walīd.
	Expulsion by ᶜUmar of Jews from Khaybar and Christians from Najrān.
636	May: Defeat of Sassanians at Qādisīya.
	Aug.: Defeat of Byzantines at Yarmūk.
638	Muslim conquest of Jerusalem.
640	Jan.: ᶜAmr b. al-ᶜĀṣ enters Egypt.
640	Establishment of Kufa (al-Kūfa) and Basra (al-Baṣra) as garrison bases (amṣār).
641	ᶜAmr b. al-ᶜĀṣ captures Babylon. Fusṭāṭ founded.
642	Defeat of Sassanians at Nihawend and fall of Persia.

644	Nov.: Murder of cUmar by a Persian Christian slave.
644-656	Reign of Caliph cUthmān.
646	Final capture of Alexandria, previously held from 642-645.
649	Conquest of Cyprus by Mucāwiya, Governor of Syria.
651	Yazdigird III, last Sassanian ruler, murdered at Merv.
656	June: Assassination of cUthmān by Muslims.
656-661	Reign of Caliph cAlī. First Civil War.
656	Dec. 9: Battle of the Camel near Basra; cAlī defeats al-Zubayr, Talha and cĀ'isha.
ca. 658	Battle of Ṣiffīn between cAlī and Mucāwiya.
ca. 659	Arbitration at Adhruḥ.
ca. 659	Massacre by cAlī of Kharijites at Nahrawān Canal.
661	Jan. 24: cAlī murdered by a Kharijite. al-Ḥasan b. cAlī renounces claim to caliphate.
661-750	Umayyad Dynasty.
661-680	Reign of Caliph Mucāwiya I.
662-675	Ziyād ibn Abīhi, Governor of Basra; then Kufa as well.
667	Arabs cross Amū Darya (Oxus).
670	Establishment of Qayrawān. cUqba b. Nāfic (d.683) active in North Africa.
674-679	Siege of Constantinople fails.
680-683	Reign of Caliph Yazīd I.
680	Oct. 10: (10th Muharram A.H. 61) al-Ḥusayn b. cAlī martyred at Karbalā'.
683-692	Fitna of Ibn al-Zubayr (Second Civil War).
683-684	Reign of Caliph Mucāwiya II.
684-685	Reign of Caliph Marwān I.
684	July: Battle of Marj Rāhiṭ. Victory of Kalb over Qays.
685-705	Reign of Caliph cAbd al-Malik.
685-687	Revolt of Mukhtār at al-Kūfa.
692	al-Ḥajjāj b. Yūsuf ends Fitna of Ibn al-Zubayr; occupies Mecca.
694-714	al-Ḥajjāj b. Yūsuf, Governor of Iraq.
705-715	Reign of Caliph Walīd I.
705	Umayyad Mosque of Damascus built.
ca. 705	Wāsiṭ founded as a garrison city.
711	Ṭāriq, subordinate of Mūsā b. Nuṣayr, invades Spain.
711-713	Conquest of Sind and Transoxiana.
714	Death of al-Ḥajjāj.
717-718	Siege of Constantinople under Maslama fails.
717-720	Reign of Caliph cUmar II.
717	First Muslim expedition across Pyrenees.
720-759	Occupation of Narbonne.
720-724	Reign of Caliph Yazīd II.
724-743	Reign of Caliph Hishām.
732	Battle of Tours (Poitiers). Charles Martel defeats Muslims.
739-742	Anti-Arab Berber revolt in North Africa.
740	Failure of Shīcite revolt and death of Zayd.
745-750	Reign of Caliph Marwān II.
747	June: cAbbāsid revolt begun by Abū Muslim near Merv. Third Civil War.
749	Sept.: cAbbāsid troops take Kufa.

749	Nov.: Abū-l-^{c}Abbās (posthumously called al-Saffāḥ), proclaimed Caliph at Kufa.
750	Feb.: Marwān defeated at Battle of Greater Zāb.
750	June: Massacre of most members of Umayyad family by ^{c}Abbāsids.
750-1258	^{c}Abbāsid Dynasty.
750-754	Reign of Caliph Abū-l-^{c}Abbās al-Saffāḥ.
754-775	Reign of Caliph Abū Ja^{c}far al-Manṣūr.
755-1031	Umayyad Dynasty of Spain.
755-788	^{c}Abd al-Raḥmān I in Cordoba.
755	Assassination of Abū Muslim by order of al-Manṣūr.
757	Death of scholar Ibn al-Muqaffa^{c}.
762	Founding of Baghdad (Madīnat al-Salām).
762	Unsuccessful Shī^{c}ite revolt at Medina led by Muḥammad b. ^{c}Abdullāh, "The Pure Soul."
763	Death of Shī^{c}ite Ibrāhīm b. ^{c}Abdullāh.
767	Death of jurisconsult Abū Ḥanīfa.
775-785	Reign of Caliph al-Mahdī.
785-786	Reign of Caliph al-Hādī.
786-809	Reign of Caliph Hārūn al-Rashīd.
792	al-Amīn designated successor to Hārūn al-Rashīd.
793	Death of jurisconsult Mālik b. Anas.
799	al-Ma'mūn designated second successor to Hārūn al-Rashīd.
800-909	Aghlabid Dynasty of North Africa.
803	Fall of Barmakid family.
806	Major Muslim attack against Byzantium.
809-813	Reign of Caliph al-Amīn. Fourth Civil War.
812	Siege of Baghdad by Ṭāhir.
813-833	Reign of Caliph al-Ma'mūn.
816-838	Revolt of Babak, primarily in Azerbaijan.
817	al-Ma'mūn designates ^{c}Alī al-Riḍā (d. 818) successor.
819	al-Ma'mūn enters Baghdad.
820	Death of jurisconsult al-Shāfi^{c}ī.
821-873	Ṭāhirid Dynasty of Khurāsān.
827	al-Ma'mūn establishes Mu^{c}tazilite doctrines as "orthodoxy."
829-831	Revolt of Copts in Egypt.
833-842	Reign of Caliph al-Mu^{c}taṣim.
836-889	Samarra ^{c}Abbāsid capital.
842-847	Reign of Caliph al-Wāthiq.
847-861	Reign of Caliph al-Mutawakkil.
855	Death of jurisconsult Aḥmad b. Ḥanbal.
861-908	Most active period of Ṣaffārid Dynasty led by Ya^{c}qub al-Saffār (d. 879).
864	Zaydī Shī^{c}ite Dynasty established in Daylam.
868	Death of writer al-Jāḥiẓ.
868-905	Ṭūlūnid Dynasty of Egypt founded by Aḥmad b. Ṭūlūn (808-884).
869-892	Reign of Caliph al-Mu^{c}tamid, Regent. al-Muwaffaq takes charge of ^{c}Abbāsid army.
869-883	Zanj revolt.
870	Conquest of Malta.
870	Death of collector of ḥadīth al-Bukhārī.

871	Zanj sack Basra.
873	Death of philosopher al-Kindī.
873	Death of translator Ḥunayn b. Isḥāq.
ca. 873	Disappearance of Twelfth Shīᶜite Imām.
874-999	Sāmānid Dynasty of Transoxiana.
877	Aḥmad b. Ṭūlūn begins building mosque in al-Qaṭāᶜi.
ca. 880's	Rise of Qarmatians.
886	Peace agreement between Ṭūlūnid Khumārawayh and Caliph al-Muᶜtamid.
890-1008	Major line of Ḥamdānid Dynasty of Iraq and Syria.
901	Establishment of Shīᶜite Zaydī State in Yemen.
902-908	Reign of Caliph al-Muktafī.
908	Dec. 17: Caliphate of Ibn al-Muᶜtazz for one day.
908	Revolt in name of Fāṭimid Dynasty in North Africa.
909-1171	Fāṭimid Dynasty.
922	Execution of mystic al-Ḥallāj.
923	Death of historian al-Ṭabarī.
925	Death of physician al-Rāzī.
928	Qarmatians steal Black Stone from Kaᶜba, holding it until 951.
929	ᶜAbd al-Raḥmān III (912-961) of Umayyads of Spain takes title of Caliph.
932-1062	Būyids of Iraq and Iran.
935-969	Ikhshīdid Dynasty of Egypt founded by Muḥammad b. Ṭughj.
935	Death of theologian al-Ashᶜarī.
936	Ibn Rā'iq becomes amīr al-umarā'.
944	Peace agreement between Muḥammad b. Ṭughj al-Ikhshīd and Caliph al-Muttaqī.
945-1055	Būyids occupy Baghdad.
950	Death of philosopher al-Fārābī.
953-975	Reign of al-Muᶜizz, Fāṭimid Caliph.
956	Death of historian al-Masᶜūdī.
962-1186	Ghaznavid Dynasty.
962	Alptegīn in Ghazna.
965	Death of poet al-Mutanabbī.
966-968	Kāfūr rules Egypt.
969	Jawhar conquers Egypt for Fāṭimids and founds Cairo.
973	al-Azhar founded.
975-996	Reign of al-ᶜAzīz, Fāṭimid Caliph.
996-1021	Reign of al-Ḥākim, Fāṭimid Caliph.
998-1030	Maḥmūd of Ghazna.
1020	Death of poet Firdawsi, author of Shāhnāma.
1030	Death of historian Miskawayh.
1036-1094	Reign of al-Mustanṣir, Fāṭimid Caliph.
1037	Death of philosopher Ibn Sīnā (Avicenna).
1048	Death of savant al-Bīrūnī.
1055-1063	Ṭughril Beǧ enters Baghdad as head of Seljuks.
1058	Death of political theorist al-Māwardī.
1059	Shīᶜite revolt in Iraq led by al-Basāsīrī.
1063-1072	Reign of Alp Arslān, Seljuk Sultan.

1064	Death of philosopher Ibn Ḥazm.
1071	Aug. 26: Battle of Manziḳert (Malazgirt) and Byzantine defeat.
1072-1092	Reign of Malik Shāh, Seljuk Sultan.
1075	Seljuks of Rūm make Iznik (Nicaea) their capital.
1092	Niẓām al-Mulk murdered by Assassins.
1095	Nov.: Pope Urban at Clermont calls for First Crusade.
1097	First Crusade at Constantinople; then take Iznik. Konya becomes capital of Seljuks of Rūm.
1098	Crusaders capture Antioch.
1099	July 15: Jerusalem conquered by Crusaders.
1100	Baldwin becomes King of Jerusalem.
1111	Death of philosopher and mystic al-Ghazzālī.
1118-1157	Reign of Seljuk Sanjar.
1123	Death of poet and astronomer ʿUmar Khayyām.
1124	Death of al-Ḥasan b. al-Ṣabbāḥ, leader of Assassins.
1144	Zangī (1127-1146) captures Edessa (Urfa) from Crusaders.
1147	Second Crusade led by Conrad II and Louis VII.
1148-1215	Ghūrid Dynasty of Afghanistan.
1154	Nūr al-Dīn (1146-1174) captures Damascus.
1169-1193	Ṣalāḥ al-Din (Saladin) controls Egypt.
1171-1250	Ayyūbid Dynasty in Egypt.
1171	Ṣalāḥ al-Dīn ends Fāṭimid Dynasty and establishes Ayyūbid Dynasty.
1176	Sept.: Kilij Arslān defeats Byzantine forces at Myriokephalon.
1180-1225	Reign of al-Nāṣir, ʿAbbāsid Caliph.
1187	July 4: Ṣalāḥ al-Dīn victorious over Crusaders at Battle of Ḥaṭṭīn.
1189-1192	Third Crusade led by Frederick Barbarossa, Philip Augustus and Richard I.
1200-1218	Reign of al-Malik al-ʿĀdil, Ayyūbid Sultan.
1198	Death of philosopher Ibn Rushd (Averroes).
1204-1261	Fourth Crusade and Latin occupation of Constantinople.
1206	Temuchin takes title of Chingiz Khān.
1218	Fifth Crusade lands at Damietta.
1218-1238	Reign of al-Malik al-Kāmil, Ayyūbid Sultan of Egypt.
1220	Khwarazm Shāhs defeated by Chingiz Khān.
1220-1231	Reign of Khwarazm Shāh Jalāl al-Dīn.
1229	Death of geographer Yāqūt.
1229	Peace treaty between Sixth Crusade led by Frederick II and al-Malik al-Kāmil.
1234	Death of historian Ibn al-Athīr.
1238-1492	Naṣrid Dynasty of Granada.
1240	Death of philosopher Ibn ʿArabī.
1242-1258	Reign of al-Mustaʿṣim, last ʿAbbāsid Caliph of Baghdad.
1243	Mongols defeat Seljuks of Rūm at Kösedagh near Sivas.
1244	Jerusalem taken by Khwarazmian troops.
1249	Seventh Crusade led by St. Louis (Louis IX) lands at Damietta.
1250-1517	Mamlūk Dynasty in Egypt.
1250	Shajar al-Durr, female ruler of Egypt.

1256	Hūlāgū takes Assassin stronghold of Alamūt.
1256-1349	Īl-Khānid Dynasty of Persia.
1258	Feb.: Hūlāgū sacks Baghdad and ends ᶜAbbāsid caliphate.
1260	Sept. 3: Mamlūk victory at ᶜAyn Jālūt over Mongols.
1260-1277	Reign of Baybars, Mamlūk Sultan.
1265	Death of Hūlāgū.
1271	Journey of Marco Polo through Persia to China.
1273	Death of mystic Jalāl al-Dīn al-Rūmī.
1274	Death of astronomer Nāṣir al-Dīn al-Tūṣī.
1279-1290	Reign of Qalā'ūn, Mamlūk Sultan.
1282	Death of biographer Ibn Khallikān.
1291	Fall of last Crusader stronghold in Levant, during Mamlūk sultanate of al-Ashraf Khalīl (1290-1293).
1291	Death of poet Saᶜdī.
1294	Marco Polo in Persia on return to Europe.
1295-1304	Reign of Ghāzān Khān, Īl-Khānid ruler.
1317-1335	Reign of Abu Saᶜīd, Īl-Khānid ruler.
1318	Death of historian Rashīd al-Dīn.
1324-1360	Reign of Orhān, Ottoman sultan.
1326	Ottoman capture of Bursa.
1331	Ottoman conquest of Nicaea (Iznik).
1337	Ottoman conquest of Nicomedia (Izmit).
1345	First Ottoman campaign in Europe.
1354	Ottoman conquest of Ankara.
1354	Ottoman occupation of Gallipoli.
c.1360-1389	Reign of Murād I, Ottoman Sultan.
1361	Murād captures Adrianople (Edirne).
1369	Tīmūr conquers Khurāsān and Transoxiana.
1371	Battle of Chermanon and Ottoman victory over Serbs.
1378-1469	Qara Qoyunlu (Black Sheep) Dynasty in Armenia and Azerbayjan.
1378-1502	Aq Qoyunlu (White Sheep) Dynasty in Iraq and Armenia.
1382-1517	Circassian or Burji Mamlūk rule of Egypt and Syria.
1382-1398	Reign of Barqūq, Mamlūk Sultan.
1385	Ottoman conquest of Sofia.
1386	Ottoman conquest of Nish.
1387	Ottoman conquest of Salonika.
1389	June 15: Battle of Kosovo and Ottoman victory over Serbs.
1389-1402	Reign of Bāyezīd I, Ottoman Sultan.
1389	Death of poet Ḥāfiẓ.
1391-1398	First Ottoman siege of Constantinople.
1395	June: Wallachia becomes an Ottoman vassal state.
1396	Sept. 25: Battle of Nicopolis. Ottoman victory over Venice, Hungary, Byzantium and Crusaders.
1397	Ottomans annex Karamān lands, including Konya.
1398	Ottoman conquest of Vidin in Europe and Sivas in Anatolia.
1398-1399	Tīmūr attacks India and sacks Delhi.
1400-1401	Tīmūr attacks Syria and Asia Minor. Captures Sivas.
1402	July 28: Battle of Ankara. Tīmūr captures Bāyezīd.
1403	Ottomans lose Salonika.
1405	Death of Tīmūr.

1405-1447	Reign of Shāh Rukh of the Tīmūrids.
1413	Meḥmet I unifies Ottoman territories.
1415	Meḥmet reconquers Smyrna (Izmir).
1421-1451	Reign of Murād II, Ottoman Sultan.
1422	Second Ottoman siege of Constantinople.
1422-1437	Reign of Barsbāy, Mamlūk Sultan.
1425-1430	Ottoman - Venetian War.
1430	Ottomans reconquer Salonika.
1440	Ottomans fail to take Belgrade.
1442	Death of historian al-Maqrīzī.
1443	Iskender Beğ [Scanderbeğ/Georges Kastriote] rebels in northern Albania.
1444	Murād II abdicates in favor of Meḥmet II.
1444	Nov. 10: Battle of Varna and defeat of Hungarian King Ladislas and John Hunyadi by Ottomans.
1446	Murād II's second accession to Ottoman sultanate.
1448	Oct. 17-19: Second battle of Kosovo. Ottomans defeat Hungarians.
1451	Feb. 3: Death of Murād II.
1451-1481	Reign of Meḥmet II, Ottoman Sultan.
1452	Erection of Ottoman fortress of Rumeli Hisari.
1453	April 6-May 29: Ottoman siege and capture of Constantinople.
1455	Ottomans make Moldavia a tribute state.
1456	Ottomans fail again to take Belgrade.
1459	Ottoman final defeat of Serbs after death of George Brancovich.
1460	Meḥmet II conquers Morea.
1461	Ottoman conquest of Trebizond.
1463-1479	Ottoman - Venetian War.
1464	Completion of Topkapi Sarayi in Istanbul.
1466-1470	Inconclusive war between Mamlūks and Ottomans.
1468	Meḥmet II re-annexes Karamān lands in Anatolia.
1468-1495	Reign of Qāyitbāy, Mamlūk Sultan.
1468	Jan. 17: Death of Iskender Beğ.
1469	Death of historian Ibn Taghrī Birdī.
1471-1478	Uzun Ḥasan, Aq Qoyunlu ruler, active with European support against Ottomans.
1472	Venetian, Cypriot and Uzun Ḥasan alliance against Ottomans.
1475	Ottoman conquest of Genoese colonies in Crimea. Ottoman suzerainty over khānate of Crimea.
1479	Ottoman - Venetian peace.
1480-1481	Ottomans occupy Otranto, Italy.
1481	May 3: Death of Meḥmet II.
	May 20: Accession of Bāyezīd II.
	June 20: Battle of Yenişehir. Bāyezīd II defeats Cem, his brother and rival.
1481-1512	Reign of Bāyezīd II, Ottoman Sultan.
1483	Ottomans annex Herzegovina.
1484	Ottomans annex Kilia and Akkerman.
1487	Bartholomew Diaz rounds Cape of Good Hope by vessel.
1492	Fall of Naṣrid Dynasty in Granada to Christians.
1495	Death of Ottoman Prince Cem in Naples.
1497	Bābur, eventual founder of Mughal Dynasty, captures Samarqand.

1499 Ismāᶜīl establishes Ṣafavid Dynasty in Iran. Ottoman conquest of Lepanto.
1499-1502 Ottoman war with Venice.

1500-1516 Reign of Qānṣūh al-Ghawrī, Mamlūk Sultan.
1502 Ṣafavid capital established at Tabriz.
1504 Ṣafavid Shāh Ismāᶜīl takes Baghdad.
1505 Bābur active in India establishing Mughol Dynasty.
1507 Portuguese attack Hormuz.
1512-1520 Reign of Selīm I, Ottoman Sultan after deposing his father, Bāyezīd II.
1512 Withdrawal of Bābur from Central Asia.
1514 Aug. 23: Selīm I defeats Shāh Ismāᶜīl and his Qizilbash troops at Chāldirān.
1516 Portuguese under d'Albuquerque take Hormuz.
1516 Aug. 24: Ottoman victory over Mamlūks at Marj Dābiq.
1517 Jan.: Ottoman conquest of Egypt.
1520-1566 Reign of Süleymān I, Ottoman Sultan.
1521 Ottoman conquest of Belgrade.
1522 Ottoman conquest of Rhodes.
1524-1576 Reign of Ṭahmāsp, Ṣafavid Shāh.
1524-1525 Revolt of Aḥmad Pāṣhā in Egypt. Suppressed by Ottoman Grand Wazīr Ibrāhīm.
1526 Aug. 29: Ottoman victory over Hungarians at Battle of Mohács.
1528 Ottoman capture of Buda.
1529 Sept.-Oct.: Ottoman siege of Vienna.
1530 Death of Bābur.
1533 Armistice of Istanbul between Süleymān and Hapsburg Archduke Ferdinand. War between Ṣafavids and Ottomans. Barbarossa made Ottoman Grand Admiral.
1534 Ottomans capture Tabriz and Baghdad.
1535 Ottoman - French alliance.
1537-1540 Ottoman - Venetian War.
1538 Ottoman annexation of Hungary and third capture of Buda.
1547 Ottoman - Hapsburg peace.
1548 Ottoman - Ṣafavid War.

1550 Süleymāniye mosque built by Sinan in Istanbul.
1551-1562 Ottoman - Austrian War.
1552 Ottoman failure to dislodge Portuguese from Hormuz.
1553-1555 Ottoman war with Ṣafavids.
1555 May 29: Ottoman - Ṣafavid Peace Treaty at Amasya.
1561 Ṭahmāsp makes Qazvīn Ṣafavid capital.
1566 Sept. 6: Süleymān's death before fortress of Szigetvár.
1566-1574 Reign of Selīm II, Ottoman Sultan.
1569 Ottoman campaign against Russians. Ottoman campaign in Yemen.
1571 Ottoman conquest of Famagusta, Cyprus.
Oct. 7: Ottoman naval loss to Holy League at Lepanto.
1578-1639 Ottoman - Ṣafavid wars.
1578 Ottoman annexation of Georgia and Derbent.
1588-1629 Reign of ᶜAbbās I, Ṣafavid Shāh.
1590 Ottoman - Ṣafavid peace.
1593-1606 Ottoman - Austrian War.

1600 Shāh ᶜAbbās makes Iṣfahān Ṣafavid capital.
1602 Shāh ᶜAbbās captures Baḥrain from Portuguese.
1603 Shāh ᶜAbbās captures Tabriz.
1606 Ottoman - Austrian Peace Treaty at Zsitva-Török.
1622 English capture Hormuz.
1623 Shāh ᶜAbbās I captures Baghdad.
1638 Ottomans recapture Baghdad.
1639 Ottoman - Ṣafavid peace with Treaty of Zuhāb (Qaṣr-i Shīrīn).
1645-1670 Ottoman - Venetian War.
1645 Ottomans attack Crete.

1656 Venice conquers Lemnos.
1656-1661 Meḥmet Köprülü, Ottoman Grand Wazīr.
1661-1676 Aḥmed Köprülü, Ottoman Grand Wazīr.
1663 Austria joins Venice against Ottomans.
1664 Ottomans defeated at St. Gotthard. Twenty-year truce concluded at Vasvár with Austria.
1670 Ottoman - Venetian peace with almost all of Crete in Ottoman hands.
1672-1676 Ottoman - Polish War.
1676 Peace of Zurawno. Ottomans gain Podolia and Eastern Ukraine from Poland.
1676-1683 Kara Muṣṭafā, Ottoman Grand Wazīr.
1677-1681 First Ottoman - Russian War.
1679 Death of Ottoman traveler Evliya Chelebi.
1681 Peace of Radzyn. Ottomans lose Eastern Ukraine.
1682-1699 Ottoman - Austrian War.
1683 July-Sept.: Second siege of Vienna. Ottoman defeat.
1684 Holy League of Papacy, Austria, Poland and Venice against Ottomans.
1686 Ottomans lose Battle of Zenta to Austria.
1686 Venice captures most of Morea. Russia joins Holy League.
1687 Ottomans lose Battle of Mohács to Austrians.
First Russian siege of Azov.
1689-1691 Muṣṭafā Köprülü, Ottoman Grand Wazīr.
1688 Ottomans lose Belgrade.
1689 Ottomans lose Szigetvár and Vidin.
1690 Ottomans gain land against Austria, including Belgrade.
1691 Battle of Szalánkamén. Ottomans lose to Austria. Death of Muṣṭafā Köprülü.
1696 Russians under Peter the Great take Azov.
1697 Ottoman defeat at Zenta by Prince Eugene of Savoy.
1699 Jan. 26: Peace of Carlowitz. First permanent loss of territory by Ottomans.

1710-1711 Ottoman - Russian War.
1711 Ottomans win Battle of Pruth against Russians and regain Azov.
Peace of Pruth.
1716-1718 War with Venice and Ottomans retake Morea.
1716 Ottoman - Austrian War.
1717 Austrian conquest of Belgrade.
1718 Peace of Passarowitz. Ottomans lose lands to Austria.
1722 March 8: Battle of Gulnābād. Rout of Ṣafavid forces by Afghan Maḥmūd. Peter the Great takes Derbent.

1722	Afghan Maḥmūd takes Isfahan. Effective end of Ṣafavid Dynasty.
1725-1730	Ismāʿil Pāshā al-ʿAẓm, Governor of Damascus.
1726-1729	Ottomans attack Persia, but peace arranged by Afghan Shāh of Persia, Ashrāf.
1729-1730	Nādir Khān Afshār drives Afghans from Persia.
1729	First Turkish printing press.
1736-1747	Nādir Khān becomes Nādir Shāh.
1736-1739	Ottoman war with Austria and Russia.
1736	Russia retakes Azov.
1739	Treaty of Belgrade with Austria. Ottomans acquire Belgrade. Nādir Shāh attacks Delhi.
1740	Nādir Shāh attacks Bukhara.
1745	Establishment of Wahhābīs, Darʿīya, Arabia.
1747	Assassination of Nādir Shāh.
1750	Karīm Khān Zand, sole ruler in southern Iran.
1757-1773	Reign of Muṣṭafā III, Ottoman Sultan.
1758-1779	Karim Khān Żand, undisputed ruler of Persia.
1768-1774	Ottoman - Russian War.
1769	Russians capture Jassy and Bucharest.
1770	Russian naval victory over Ottomans at Chesme.
1770-1773	ʿAlī Bey active in Egypt.
1770-1789	Yūsuf Shihāb, Amīr of Lebanon.
1773-1789	Reign of ʿAbdülhamīd I, Ottoman Sultan.
1774	Treaty of Küçük Kaynarci between Russia and Ottomans.
1775	Aḥmad Pāshā al-Jazzār (d.1804), Governor of Sidon; later of Acre.
1783	Russia annexes Crimea.
1787-1792	Ottoman - Russian War.
1788	Austria joins war.
1789-1807	Reign of Selīm III, Ottoman Sultan.
1789	Austria invades Bosnia and Serbia. Russians invade Moldavia and Wallachia.
1789-1840	Bashīr II Shihāb, Amīr of Lebanon.
1791	Peace of Sistova between Austria and Ottomans re-establishing 1788 borders.
1792	Peace of Jassy between Russians and Ottomans with Dniester as new Russian - Ottoman border.
1796	Āghā Muḥammad Qājār becomes Shāh of Persia.
1797-1834	Reign of Fatḥ ʿAlī, Qājār ruler.
1798	July: Bonaparte's victory at Battle of Pyramids outside Cairo.
	July: Admiral Nelson destroys French fleet at Abū Qir.
1799	Napoleon invades Palestine, but fails to capture Acre.
1800	Russia annexes Georgia.
1801	French evacuation of Egypt.
1802	Wahhābī raid on Karbala.
1803-1804	Wahhābī capture of Mecca and Medina.
1804	Serbian revolt.
1805-1848	Muḥammad ʿAlī, Viceroy of Egypt.
1806-1812	Ottoman - Russian War.
1807	Treaty of Finkenstein between Persia and Russia.
	Treaty of Tilsit between Napoleon and Russia.
	British occupy Alexandria.

1808-1839	Reign of Maḥmūd II, Ottoman Sultan.
1811	March 1: Massacre of Egyptian Mamlūks by Muḥammad ᶜAlī.
1811-1818	Muḥammad ᶜAlī's campaigns against Wahhābīs.
1813	Treaty of Gulistan between Persia and Russia.
1815-1817	Second Serbian uprising.
1816-1831	Dā'ūd Pāshā, Governor of Baghdad.
1818	Persian attack on Afghanistan.
1820's	British pacts with Persian Gulf shaykhs.
1820-1821	Sudanese campaigns of Muḥammad ᶜAlī.
1821-1830	Greek War of Independence.
1821	Insurrections in Wallachia.
ca. 1822	Establishment of Būlāq press in Egypt.
1821-1823	Ottoman - Persian War.
1823	Khartoum founded.
1824-1827	Muḥammad ᶜAlī's campaigns in Greece led by Ibrāhīm.
1825-1828	Persian - Russian War.
1826	June 15: Massacre of Janissaries in Istanbul.
1827	Establishment of medical schools in Istanbul and Cairo.
	July 6: Treaty of London (Britain, France, Russia) concerning their support of Greece against Ottomans.
	Oct. 20: Battle of Navarino. Ottoman - Egyptian navy defeated by Admiral Codrington and Western forces.
1828	Egyptians evacuate Greece.
	Treaty of Turkmanchai between Persia and Russia.
1828-1829	Ottoman - Russian War.
1829	Sept.: Treaty of Adrianople between Ottomans and Russians.
1830	French invade Algeria.
1832-1841	Egyptian involvement in Syria under Ibrāhīm.
1832	Battle of Konya. Ottomans defeated by Egyptians.
1833	April 8: Convention of Kütahya between Ottomans and Egyptians.
	July 8: Treaty of Unkiar Skelessi between Ottomans and Russia.
1834	Arabic press in Beirut established.
1837-1838	Persian siege of Herat.
1839	June 24: Battle of Nezib. Ibrāhīm's victory over Ottoman forces trained by von Moltke.
1839-1861	Reign of ᶜAbdülmecīd, Ottoman Sultan.
1839	Nov. 3: Promulgation of Hatt-i Sherif Gülhane in Istanbul.
1840	July: Treaty of London (Britain, Austria, Prussia, Russia) on Eastern question.
1841	Feb.: Hereditary viceroyalty of Egypt for Muḥammad ᶜAlī.
	July: Straits Convention (Britain, France, Prussia, Russia, Austria).
1842	Shihābī amirate of Lebanon ended.
1842-1858	Stratford de Redcliffe, British ambassador in Istanbul.
1843	Dual Qaimaqamate in Lebanon established.
1844	Sayyid Muḥammad ᶜAlī of Persia proclaims himself the Bāb. This is considered the beginning of the Bahā'i Movement.
1848-1854	ᶜAbbās Ḥilmī I, Viceroy of Egypt.
1848-1896	Nāṣir al-Dīn, Qājār Shāh.
1850	Execution of the Bāb. Bābī uprisings.
1852	Persecution in Iran of Bābīs, who flee West.
1853	Oct.: Ottomans declare war on Russia.

1854-1856 Crimean War (Ottoman - Russian War) with participation of a number of European states on the Ottoman side.

1854-1863 Saᶜīd, Viceroy of Egypt.

1854 Oct. 25: Battle of Balaklava and "charge of the Light Brigade."

Nov. Ferdinand de Lesseps receives concessions to build the Suez Canal.

1855 Sept.: Sebastopol taken from Russians.

1856 Feb. 18: Hatt-i Hümayun promulgated in Istanbul.

Feb.-March: Treaty of Paris ending Crimean War.

Persian occupation of Herat.

1857 Alexandria - Cairo railroad completed.

Afghanistan's independence recognized by Britain and Persia.

1860-1861 Civil War in Lebanon.

1860 Founding of Robert College in Istanbul.

1860-1861 French expeditionary force in Lebanon.

1861 Organic Regulation of Lebanon establishing semi-autonomous self-government in Mt. Lebanon area.

1861-1876 Reign of ᶜAbdülezīz, Ottoman Sultan.

1863-1879 Ismāᶜīl, Viceroy and then Khedive of Egypt.

1864 Ottoman Law of Vilayets.

1865 Establishment of Ottoman National Debt Administration.

1866 Ismāᶜīl of Egypt acquires title of Khedive from Ottoman Sultan.

American University of Beirut, originally called Syrian Protestant College, founded.

1866-1868 Uprising on Crete against Ottomans.

1869 University of Istanbul founded.

Nov. 17: Suez Canal officially opened.

1869-1872 Midhat Pāshā, Governor of Baghdad.

1872 Sweeping Persian concessions to Baron Julius de Reuter revoked by Qājār government.

1873 Nāṣir al-Dīn, Qājār ruler, visits Europe.

1874-1879 General Charles Gordon, Governor of the Sudan.

1875 Establishment of Mixed Courts in Egypt.

Britain acquires Khedive's shares in Suez Canal Company.

Uprisings in Herzegovina and Bosnia.

1876 May: Establishment of *Caisse de la Dette* and Dual Control in Egypt. ᶜAbdülezīz, Ottoman Sultan, deposed.

Aug.: Murād V, Ottoman Sultan, deposed.

1876-1909 Reign of ᶜAbdülḥamīd II, Ottoman Sultan.

1876 Dec. 23: Ottoman Sultan ᶜAbdülḥamīd promulgates a Constitution.

1877 Feb.: Midhat Pāshā dismissed from Ottoman government.

March: Opening of Ottoman Parliament.

1877-1878 Ottoman - Russian War.

1878 Feb. 13: Ottoman Parliament dismissed; Constitution suspended.

March: Treaty of San Stefano between Ottomans and Russians.

June-July: Congress of Berlin modifies Treaty of San Stefano.

Uprising in Crete. Russians organize Cossack Brigade in Persia.

1879-1892 Muḥammad Tawfīq, Khedive of Egypt.

1881 French occupy Tunisia. Outbreak of Sudanese Mahdia.

First Zionist *Aliya* to Palestine.

1881-1882 ᶜUrābī revolt in Egypt.

1882 Jan. 8: British-French Gambetta Note on developments in Egypt.

July: British bombard and occupy Alexandria.

1882	Sept.: British defeat Egyptians at Battle of Tal al-Kābir.
1883-1907	Lord Cromer, British Consul General in Egypt.
1883	Nov.: General Hicks and Egyptian forces defeated by Mahdī.
1885	Fall of Khartoum and death of General Gordon.
1888	Convention of Constantinople concerning Suez Canal.
1889	Uprising in Crete. Imperial Bank of Persia founded.
1890-1897	Armenian revolts against Ottomans.
1891	Muscat and Oman under British protection.
1890	Persian tobacco concession.
1890-1898	Reconquest of the Sudan by Kitchener.
1892-1914	Reign of ᶜAbbās Ḥilmī II, Khedive of Egypt.
1896-1897	Uprising in Crete.
1896-1907	Muẓaffar al-Dīn, Qājār ruler.
1897	Ottoman - Greek War.
1898	Fashoda Incident.
1899	Anglo-Egyptian Condominium established in the Sudan.
	Concessions by Ottomans to Germans to build railroads.
	British agreement with Shaykh of Kuwait.
1900-1908	Hejaz railroad built.
1900	First Persian oil concession to d'Arcy.
1901	Ibn Saᶜūd and Wahhābīs take Riyadh.
1902	Congress of Ottoman Liberals meet in Paris.
1902-1903	Uprising in Macedonia.
1904	April: Entente Cordiale between Britain and France.
1905	Persian Revolution. Death of Muḥammad ᶜAbduh.
1906	May: Sinai officially part of Egypt after Taba-Aqaba frontier dispute between Ottomans and Britain.
	June 13: Dinshawāy Incident in Egypt.
	August: Qājār ruler, Muẓaffar al-Dīn, promulgates a Constitution.
	Dec.: Persian Constitution ratified.
1907	Anglo-Russian Convention dividing Persia.
	Young Turk movements unite under name of Committee of Union and Progress.
1907-1909	Muḥammad ᶜAlī, Qājār ruler.
1907-1911	Gorst, British Consul General in Egypt.
1908	Ottoman Third Army Corps in Salonika revolts; ᶜAbdülḥamīd reactivates 1876 Constitution. Crete annexed by Greece.
	Death of Egyptian political leader Muṣṭafā Kāmil.
1909	April: Ottoman Third Army deposes ᶜAbdülḥamīd II.
	Formation of Anglo-Persian Oil Company to exploit d'Arcy concession. Russian intervention in Persia.
1909-1924	Aḥmad, Qājār ruler.
1910	Assassination of Buṭrus Ghālī in Egypt.
	Uprising in Albania against Ottomans.
1911-1914	Kitchener, British Consul General in Egypt.
1911-1912	Ottoman - Italian War over Libya and Ottoman loss.
1911	American financial expert Shuster appointed as Persian Treasurer General; then dismissed after Russian intervention.
	Abadan refinery completed.
1912	Proclamation of Albanian independence.
1912-1913	First Balkan War.

1913		C.U.P. takes over direct control of Ottoman government.
		Arab Congress in Paris. Second Balkan War.
	Sept.:	Treaty of Constantinople between Ottomans and Bulgaria.
1914		Formation of Arab *al-^{c}Ahd*, Nationalist secret society.
	Aug.:	Secret treaty between C.U.P. and Germany.
		Outbreak of World War I.
	Nov. 1:	Ottomans declare war on Britain, France and Russia.
	Nov. 5:	Britain declares war on Ottomans and annexes Cyprus.
	Nov. 22:	British forces land at Fao, Iraq.
	Dec. 18:	British declaration of a protectorate over Egypt.
1914-1917		Ḥusayn Kāmil, Sultan of Egypt.
1915	Feb.:	Ottomans attack Suez Canal.
	Mar. 18:	"Constantinople Agreement" among Britain, France and Russia on division of Ottoman lands.
	Apr. 25:	Allied landing on Gallipoli Peninsula.
	Apr. 26:	Treaty of London among Britain, France, Russia, Italy.
	July:	Ḥusayn-MacMahon correspondence begins.
	Sept. 28:	Turks defeat British at Kūt al-Amāra, Iraq.
	Oct. 24:	Major British reply to Ḥusayn's proposals.
	Dec.:	Agreement between Britain and Ibn Sa^{c}ūd.
1916	Jan. 9:	Allied withdrawal from Gallipoli Peninsula.
	Apr. 29:	British surrender to Turks at Kūt al-Amāra, Iraq.
	May:	Sykes - Picot Agreement.
	June 5:	Arab revolt, popularly associated in the West with T.E. Lawrence (Lawrence of Arabia).
	July 19:	Second Ottoman campaign against Suez Canal.
	Dec. 15:	British recognize Ḥusayn as King of the Hejaz only.
1917	Mar. 11:	British occupy Baghdad.
	Mar-Apr:	British battle Ottomans in Gaza.
	April:	Agreement of St. Jean de Maurene among Britain, Italy and France.
	Nov. 2:	Balfour Declaration.
	Nov. 7:	Bolshevik Revolution in Russia.
	Dec. 5:	Soviets renounce all claims to Ottoman lands.
	Dec. 9:	Allenby takes Jerusalem.
1917-1936		Aḥmad Fu^{c}ād, King of Egypt.
1918	Mar. 3:	Treaty of Brest Litovsk between Soviets - Central Powers.
	Oct. 1:	British and Arabs capture Damascus.
	Oct. 7:	French troops land at Beirut.
	Oct. 26:	Aleppo captured by British and Arabs.
	Oct. 30:	Mudros Armistice concluded between Ottomans and Allies.
	Nov. 11:	Armistice in Europe.
	Nov.:	Egyptian leader Zaghlūl leads *wafd* to British High Commissioner.
	Nov. 13:	Allied fleet arrives in Istanbul.
1919	January:	Peace Conference opened in Paris.
	February:	Greek Premier Venizelos issues claims to Izmir and part of Anatolia.
	March 8:	Zaghlūl deported from Egypt. Popular uprising.
	March:	Italians land in Anatolia.
	May:	Ibn Sa^{c}ūd defeats troops of Ḥusayn of Mecca.
	May 15:	Greeks land at Izmir (Smyrna).
	May 19:	Mustafa Kemal (b. 1880) arrives at Samsun.

1919 July 23: Turkish Nationalist Congress at Erzurum.

Aug. 9: Anglo-Persian Agreement; never ratified by Persian Majlis.

Sept. 13: Turkish National Pact at Sivas; declaration of National Pact.

October: General Gouraud, French High Commissioner for Lebanon and Syria.

December: Lord Milner mission to Egypt.

1920 Mar. 20: Syrian "National Congress" proclaims Fayṣal King of Syria and Palestine.

April: Provisional Turkish government established in Ankara.

April: San Remo Conference establishing mandate system.

May: Soviets in Gilan.

July: Sir Herbert Samuel, High Commissioner for Palestine.

July: French occupation of Damascus.

Jul-Aug: Major Arab insurrection in Iraq.

August: Ibn Sa^{c}ūd annexes ^{c}Asīr.

Aug. 20: Ottoman government in Istanbul signs Treaty of Sevrés.

Aug. 31: French High Commissioner creates Greater (Modern) Lebanon.

1921 Jan. 20: Turkish Fundamental Law adopted by Grand National Assembly in Ankara.

Feb. 21: Persian *coup d'ētāt* led by Reza Khān.

Feb. 26: Russo-Persian Treaty signed.

March: Cairo Conference run by Winston Churchill.

Mar. 13: Italians agree to withdraw from Turkey.

Mar. 16: Treaty of Moscow between Soviets and Mustafa Kemal.

April 1: ^{c}Abdullāh made ruler of the newly created State of Transjordan by Britain.

May: Major anti-Zionist riots in Palestine.

Aug. 23: Fayṣal proclaimed King of Iraq.

Aug. 24- Sept. 16: Battle of Sakarya between Turks and Greeks.

Oct. 20: French agree to withdraw from Turkey.

1922 Feb. 28: Britain declares Egyptian independence.

Mar. 15: Fu^{c}ād takes title of King of Egypt.

July: Churchill White Paper for Palestine.

July 24: League of Nations approves British and French mandates for Palestine, Transjordan, Iraq, Lebanon and Syria.

Sept. 11: Turks retake Izmir.

Nov. 1: Mustafa Kemal abolishes the sultanate.

Nov. 20: Lausanne Conference begins with Turkish delegation headed by İsmet.

1922-1927 First Millspaugh mission to Iran.

1923 April: Egyptian Constitution promulgated.

May 26: Transjordan officially organized as autonomous state under ^{c}Abdullāh by the League of Nations.

July 24: Treaty of Lausanne signed with Turkey.

Sept. 29: Mandate system comes into official effect.

Oct. 13: Ankara made capital of Turkey.

Oct. 29: Turkish Republic formally proclaimed.

1924-1925 Druze Rebellion in Syria.

1924 March 3: Caliphate abolished.

Oct. 3: Ḥusayn of Mecca forced to abdicate to his son ^{c}Alī.

1924 Nov. 22: Murder in Egypt of Sir Lee Stack and Allenby's ultimatum.
1925 April: Hebrew University in Jerusalem opened.
August: Polygamy abolished in Turkey.
October: Persian Majlis deposes last Qājār Shāh.
Nov.: Wearing of "fez" in Turkey is forbidden.
Dec. 12: Reza Khān becomes Reza Shāh, founder of Pahlavi Dynasty of Iran.
Dec. 19: ^{c}Alī, King of the Hejaz, abdicates.
1925-1927 Major insurrection of Druze in Syria.
1926 January: Ibn Sa^{c}ūd proclaimed King of the Hejaz.
April: Reza Shāh crowns himself.
1927 Death of Zaghlūl. Egyptian *wafd* headed by al-Naḥḥās.
European dress required for men in Iran.
May: British recognition of Ibn Sa^{c}ūd's kingdom.
1928 April: Turkey declared a secular state.
Nov.: Turkey adopts the Latin alphabet.
Abolition of capitulations in Iran.
1929 August: Wailing Wall Incident and riots in Palestine.
1930 March: Official "Turkification" of names of all Turkish cities.
May: Shaw Report for Palestine.
October: Passfield White Paper for Palestine.
1931 Feb.: British Prime Minister MacDonald's letter on Palestine.
1932 August: Turkey joins League of Nations.
Sept.: Saudi Arabia's new official name of Kingdom of the Hejaz and Nejd.
October: Iraq joins League of Nations.
1933 Sept.: Death of Fayṣal of Iraq; Ghazi succeeds (1933-1939).
1934 Jan. 1: Family names required of all Turkish citizens. Mustafa Kemal becomes Atatürk.
1935 Mar. 21: Iran official name for Persia.
Oct. 3: Italian invasion of Ethiopia.
1936 Apr-Oct: Arab general strike in Palestine.
July: Montreaux Convention gives Turkey complete control of the Straits of Dardanelles.
Aug. 26: Anglo-Egyptian Treaty.
Sept. 9: Franco-Syrian Treaty; never ratified.
Oct. 29: First military *coup d'état* in Iraq led by Bakr Ṣidqī.
1936-1952 Fārūq, King of Egypt, including period of his minority.
1937 July 8: Peel Commission Report on Palestine.
July 9: Saadabad Pact among Iran, Iraq, Afghanistan, Turkey.
Sept. 8: Pan-Arab Congress at Bludan.
1938 Nov. 9: Woodhead Commission Report on Palestine.
Nov. 10: Atatürk dies; succeeded as President of Turkey by İsmet Inönü.
1939 Feb.: Anglo-Arab Conference on Palestine held in London.
May 17: British White Paper on Palestine.
June 23: Alexandretta (Hatay) Province incorporated into Turkey.
Sept.: Outbreak of World War II with German attack on Poland.
1940 June 22: Franco-German Armistice.
1941 Apr-Jun: Rashīd ^{c}Alī in power in Iraq ending with British occupation.
June: Allies occupy Syria and Lebanon; governed by Vichy administrators.

1941	Aug. 25:	Anglo - Soviet troops move into Iran.
	Sept. 16:	Reza Shāh of Iran forced to abdicate; succeeded by his son, Muḥammad Reza Shāh.
1942	Feb. 4:	Britain forces Egyptian government to accept al-Naḥḥās as Prime Minister.
	May 11:	Zionist Biltmore program.
	July 1:	Rommel's German army reaches al-Alamayn, Egypt.
	October:	German defeat at al-Alamayn, Egypt.
1943	January:	German defeat at Stalingrad.
	National	Pact between Sunnī and Maronite leaders of Lebanon.
	Dec. 1:	Tehran Declaration by Churchill, Roosevelt and Stalin.
1943-1945	Mission of American financial expert Millspaugh to Iran.	
	Oct. 5:	"Protocol of Alexandria" issued by Arab leaders, laying basis for Arab League.
	Nov. 4:	Lord Moyne assassinated in Cairo by "Stern Gang."
	Dec.:	Jebel Druze absorbed into Syrian state.
1945	Mar. 22:	Arab League created.
	Nov.:	Anglo - American Committee of Inquiry formed to investigate future of Palestine.
	Dec. 12:	Proclamation of Autonomous Republic of Azerbayjan.
1946	January:	Democratic Party of Turkey founded.
	Jan. 19:	Iran presents appeal to UN Security Council for withdrawal of Soviet troops from Azerbayjan.
	Mar. 19:	Second Iranian appeal to Security Council.
	May 1:	Report issued by Anglo - American Committee of Inquiry on Palestine.
	May 9:	Evacuation of Soviet troops from Iran.
	Dec. 11:	Collapse of Autonomous Republic of Azerbayjan.
1947	Mar. 12:	Truman Doctrine for maintaining governments in Greece and Turkey.
	May:	UN Security Council on Palestine created.
	Oct. 22:	Iranian Majlis rejects Soviet - Iranian oil concession.
	Nov. 27:	UN Partition Plan for Palestine passed by UN General Assembly.
1948	Apr. 10:	Massacre of Arabs at Deir Yassin by Irgunists.
	May 14:	Establishment of State of Israel.
	May 14-15:	End of British Mandate for Palestine.
	May 15 -	June 11: Open warfare between Arabs and Israelis.
	Jul. 8-18:	Second phase of open warfare between Arabs and Israelis.
	Sept. 17:	Count Bernadotte assassinated by "Stern Gang."
	Nov. 19:	Establishment of U.N.R.P.R.
	Dec. 1:	^{c}Abdullāh renames state Arab Ḥāshimite Kingdom of Jordan.
1949	Jan. 31:	Jordan joined the United Nations.
	Feb. 24:	Israel - Egyptian armistice.
	Mar. 7:	Israel - Lebanese armistice.
	Mar. 11:	Israel joins the United Nations.
	Mar. 30:	Syrian *coup d'ētāt*; civilian government of Shukri al-Quwatli replaced by Colonel Ḥusnī Za^{c}īm.
	April 3:	Israel - Jordan armistice.
	July 20:	Israel - Syrian armistice.
	Aug. 14:	Syrian *coup d'ētāt* led by Colonel Sāmī al-Ḥinnawī.
	Dec. 20:	Syrian *coup d'ētāt* led by Colonel Adīb Shīshaklī.

1950	March:	National Front led by Dr. Mosaddeq makes significant gains in election for Iranian Majlis.
	May 1:	Democratic Party replaces People's Republic Party in Turkish election; Menderes Prime Minister and Bayar President.
	May 25:	Britain, France and United States issue Tripartite Declaration.
	Sept. 19:	Turkey joins North Atlantic Organization.
1951	March 7:	Iranian Prime Minister. Razmara shot to death.
	Apr. 29:	Dr. Muḥammad Mosaddeq, Iranian Prime Minister.
	May 2:	Shāh signs oil nationalization bill.
	July 20:	King ^{c}Abdullāh of Jordan assassinated.
	Dec. 24:	Libya becomes independent.
1952	Jan. 25:	British involved in "Battle of Ismā^{c}īlīya" against Egyptian police.
	Jan. 26:	"Black Saturday" in Cairo.
	July 23:	Egyptian Revolution led by RCC led by Gamāl ^{c}Abd al-Nāṣir (Nasser).
	July 26:	Fārūq compelled to abdicate.
	Aug. 3:	Iranian Majlis gives Prime Minister Mosaddeq full dictatorial powers for 6 months.
	Aug. 11:	al-Ḥusayn (Hussein) becomes King of Jordan, replacing his father Talāl.
	Sept.:	Major Land Reform Act promulgated in Egypt.
1953	Jan. 19:	Iranian Majlis votes to extend Mosaddeq's power for a year.
	Feb.:	Anglo - Egyptian Agreement on British evacuation of Sudan.
	June 18:	RCC abolishes Egyptian monarchy.
	Aug. 13:	Iranian Shāh dismisses Mosaddeq.
	Aug. 16:	Iranian Shāh flees Iran to Iraq.
	Aug. 22:	Iranian Shāh returns to power in Iran. Mosaddeq placed under arrest.
	October:	Major Israeli raid against Jordan.
	Nov. 3:	Moshe Sharett becomes Prime Minister of Israel, replacing Ben-Gurion.
	Nov. 9:	^{c}Abd al-^{c}Azīz b. Sa^{c}ūd dies; Sa^{c}ūd becomes King of Saudi Arabia.
1954	Feb. 24:	Shīshaklī removed from power in Syria by military.
	Aug. 5:	Compensation Agreement between Iran and AIOC.
	Oct. 19:	Egyptian - British Agreement on evacuation of British Suez bases.
	Oct. 26:	Muslim Brotherhood attempts to assassinate Nasser.
	Nov. 1:	Algerian rebellion begins.
1955	Feb. 17:	Ben-Gurion becomes Israel's Defense Minister.
	Feb. 24:	Iraq - Turkish Agreement. Start of Baghdad Pact.
	Feb. 28:	Israeli raid on Gaza.
	April:	Britain joins Baghdad Pact.
	Apr. 18-24:	Afro - Asian Conference at Bandung.
	Sept.:	Pakistan joins Baghdad Pact.
	Sept. 27:	Nasser announces Russian arms deal.
	Oct. 11:	Iran officially joins Baghdad Pact.

1955	Nov. 3:	Ben-Gurion becomes Israeli Prime Minister.
	Dec.:	Major Israeli raid against Syria.
1956	Jan. 1:	Proclamation of Sudanese independence.
	March 1:	Ḥussein of Jordan removes General John Glubb from command of Arab Legion.
	May 16:	Egypt recognizes government of Mainland China.
	July 19:	Secretary of State Dulles announces no United States aid for building Egyptian High Dam.
	July 26:	Nasser nationalizes Suez Canal.
	Oct. 11:	Major Israeli raid against Jordan.
	Oct. 24:	Jordan joins Egypt and Syria in a defense pact.
	Oct. 29:	Israel invades Sinai.
	Oct. 30:	Anglo-French ultimatum issued to Egypt and Israel.
	Oct. 31:	Britain bombs Egyptian military bases.
	Nov. 5:	Israeli military operations in Sinai effectively ended. Anglo-French force invades Canal Zone.
	Nov. 6:	Eden and Mollet accept cease-fire effective next day.
	Dec. 22:	Withdrawal of Anglo-French contingents from Suez completed; replaced by U.N.E.F. troops.
1957	Jan. 5:	Eisenhower Doctrine announced.
	March 7:	Last Israeli troops withdraw from Sinai and Gaza Strip.
	March 13:	Jordan terminates 1948 Anglo-Jordanian Treaty.
1958	Feb. 1:	United Arab Republic of Egypt and Syria created.
	April:	Amīr Fayṣal comes to power in Saudi Arabia.
	May:	Increasing internal turmoil in Lebanon.
	July 14:	Iraqi Revolution led by al-Qāsim (Kaseem).
	July 15:	U.S. Marines land in Lebanon.
	Oct. 25:	U.S. troops withdrawn from Lebanon.
	Nov. 17:	Ibrāhīm ᶜAbbūd leads *coup* in the Sudan.
1960	May:	First serious violence in Turkey, inspired by Democratic Party against former President Ismet Inönü.
	May 27:	Turkish military led by General Gürsel overthrows government of Celal Bayar and Adnan Menderes; establishes N.U.C.
1961	June 19:	Kuwait declared free and independent of British control.
	June 25:	Iraqi threat against Kuwait.
	July:	Major socialization and nationalization laws promulgated in Egypt.
	Sept. 28:	Syria withdraws from United Arab Republic.
	Oct. 25:	Second Turkish Republic established under Pres. Gürsel.
1962	July:	Algeria becomes independent.
	July:	Shāh of Iran announces White Revolution for internal reform.
	Sept. 19:	Muḥammad al-Badr becomes Imām of Yemen.
	Sept. 26:	Beginning of Yemeni Civil War with Republican forces led by ᶜAbdullāh Sallāl.
1963	January:	Aden joins Federation of South Arabia.
	Feb. 8:	*Coup d'état* in Iraq led by ᶜAbd al-Salām ᶜArīf.
	March 8:	*Coup d'état* in Syria led by Baᶜthists.
	June 16:	Levi Eshkol becomes Israeli Prime Minister.
1964	May 28:	Establishment of PLO with Aḥmad Shuqary as head.
	Nov. 2:	Fayṣal officially replaces Saᶜūd as Saudi Arabian king.

1965	October:	Süleymān Demirel, head of Justice Party, becomes Turkish Prime Minister.
1966	Feb. 23:	Military *coup* in Syria led by General Ṣalāḥ Jadīd.
	Mar. 28:	General Cevdet Sunay becomes President of Turkey.
	Apr. 13:	ᶜAbd al-Salām ᶜArīf of Iraq dies in helicopter crash; succeeded by brother, Maj. Gen. ᶜAbd al-Raḥmān ᶜArīf.
	October:	Failure of Intra Bank of Beirut.
	Nov. 13:	Palestinian fidā'īyīn mine kills Jews near Hebron.
	Nov. 13:	Israel reprisal attack on Jordanian border village of al-Samu.
1967	April 7:	Israeli - Syrian air clash.
	May 14:	Nasser reinforces Sinai forces.
	May 16:	Egyptian troops replace U.N.E.F. in Sinai.
	May 21:	Partial mobilization of Israeli and Egyptian troops.
	May 22:	Nasser announces blockade of Straits of Tiran.
	May 30:	Jordan joins Arab Defense Pact of Egypt and Syria.
	June 1:	Moshe Dayan is made Israeli Defense Minister.
	June 5:	Arab - Israeli War begins with Israeli air strikes.
	June 10:	End of Third Arab - Israeli War (Six-Day War).
	July 28:	Israel "annexes" Old Jerusalem.
	Aug. 29 - Sept. 1:	Arab summit meeting at Khartoum.
	Oct. 21:	Egypt sinks Israeli naval destroyer "Elath."
	Oct. 22:	Israel attacks Egyptian Suez oil refineries.
	Nov. 4:	ᶜAbd al-Raḥmān al-Iryānī leads *coup* in Yemen against ᶜAbdullāh Sallāl.
	Nov. 22:	U.N. Resolution 242 on Arab - Israeli problem.
	Nov. 30:	Last British troops leave Aden.
	Dec. 24:	Resignation of Aḥmad Shuqary as head of P.L.O.
1968	Jan. 23:	Last Egyptian - Israeli prisoner exchange after June War.
	Mar. 21:	Israel attacks Karameh, Jordan and fight against Palestinian fidā'īyīn and Jordanian troops.
	July 17:	*Coup d'état* in Iraq; Gen. Aḥmad Ḥasan al-Bakr becomes President.
	July 23:	El-Al Israel airliner hijacked to Algeria.
	Aug. 4:	Israel raid near Salt, Jordan.
	Oct. 26:	Gen. Ḥāfiẓ al-Asad, Syrian leader, in bloodless *coup*.
	Oct. 27:	Israeli raid deep into Egyptian territory.
	Dec. 26:	Attack on El-Al Israel airliner in Athens.
	Dec. 28:	Israeli raid on Beirut airport; destroy 13 planes.
1969	Feb. 3:	Yāsir ᶜArafāt becomes head of P.L.O.
	Feb. 18:	Attack on Israeli airliner in Zürich.
	Feb. 28:	Gen. Ḥāfiẓ al-Asad takes over direct control of Syrian government.
	Mar. 8:	Intensive fighting along Suez Canal; "War of Attrition" begins, lasting until August 1970.
	Mar. 17:	Golda Meir becomes Israeli Prime Minister.
	May:	Gen. Jaᶜfar al-Numayrī seizes power in the Sudan.
	June:	PFLP blows up Tapline in Golan Heights.
	July 1:	Israel moves major government offices to Old Jerusalem.
	Aug. 11:	Israel attacks Lebanese villages which Israel claims were fidā'īyīn bases.
	Aug. 21:	Fire at al-Aqsa Mosque in Jerusalem.
	Aug. 29:	TWA airliner hijacked by fidā'īyīn.

1969	Sept. 1:	Revolution in Libya led by Colonel Mu^{c}ammar al-Qadhāfī (Qaddafi).
	October:	Palestinian - Lebanese clashes.
	November:	Cairo Agreement between Lebanese and Palestinians.
	Dec. 9:	U.S. Secretary of State Rodgers proposes Middle East peace plan.
1970	Feb. 12:	Israeli jets raid Cairo suburbs.
	March 11:	Major agreement between Iraqi government and Kurds.
	June:	Widespread fighting in Jordan between fidā'īyīn and Hussein's troops.
	July 21:	Completion of Aswan High Dam.
	July 26:	Qabus b. Sa^{c}īd overthrows his father in palace *coup* in Oman.
	August 7:	Cease-fire along Suez Canal between Egypt and Israel ending "War of Attrition."
	Sep. 6-12:	PFLP hijack and blow up U.S. and Swiss airliners in Jordan and Egypt, releasing last hostages September 29.
	Sept.:	Civil War in Jordan between Hussein and fidā'īyīn.
	Sept. 23:	Süleymān Faranjiya becomes President of Lebanon.
	Sept. 27:	Truce in Jordan signed between al-Ḥusayn and Palestinian leader ^{c}Arafāt; second truce signed October 13.
	Sept. 28:	Gamāl ^{c}Abd al-Nāṣir dies; Anwar al-Sādāt becomes President of Egypt.
	Nov. 16:	General Ḥāfiẓ al-Asad consolidates his power in Syria.
1971	March 7:	Sādāt ceases renewing Egyptian - Israeli Cease-Fire Agreement.
	May 27:	Soviet - Egyptian Treaty of Friendship signed.
	July 18:	Elimination of last fidā'īyīn positions in Jordan.
	Jul.19-22:	*Coup d'état* in Sudan led by Hāshim al-^{c}Atā falls to counter-*coup* led by Numayrī.
1972	Feb. 25-28:	Major Israeli raid into southern Lebanon.
	April 9:	Soviet - Iraq Treaty of Friendship signed.
	May:	Marxist-oriented, urban guerillas active in Turkey.
	May 30:	Three Japanese men open fire on civilians at Lod Airport, Tel Aviv, killing 26 persons.
	July 18:	President Sādāt of Egypt orders Soviet advisers and experts to leave Egypt.
	Sept. 5:	Eleven members of Israeli Olympic team in Munich killed while hostages of eight fidā'īyīn, five of whom killed.
	Oct. 5:	OPEC sets goal of 51% ownership in oil companies.
1973	Feb. 21:	Israel shoots down Libyan civilian airliner over Sinai.
	March 1:	"Black Septemberists" seize Saudi Embassy in Khartoum; ultimately three American diplomats killed.
	March 26:	Sādāt announces Soviet - Egyptian relations again solid.
	April 6:	Fahri Korutürk elected President of Turkey.
	April 10:	Israeli commandos raid Sidon and Beirut.
	July 1:	Attempt to overthrow al-Bakr's Iraqi government fails.
	July 5:	President Ḥāfiẓ al-Asad of Syria inaugurates Euphrates Dam at al-Ṭabqa, which is renamed Madīnat al-Thawra.
	Sept. 13:	Air clashes between Israel and Syria.
	Oct. 6:	Egyptian and Syrian troops attack Israeli forces; detachments from other Arab states eventually join in.
	Oct. 14:	U.S. begins resupplying Israel to balance continuing

1973 Soviet aid to Arab forces.

Oct. 16: Israelis cross Suez Canal.

Oct. 18: OAPEC announces decision to cut back oil production; oil price is raised during this period.

Oct. 22: UN Security Council passes Resolution 338 calling for a cease-fire "in place."

Oct. 23: UN Security Council passes Resolution 339 reconfirming call for cease-fire; Israel and Egypt accept it, while Syria accepts it "with conditions."

Oct.25-31: United States troops on alert.

Oct. 27: United Nations observers on Suez front.

Oct. 28: Israel-Egyptian negotiations begin at Kilometer 101 on Suez - Cairo Road.

Nov. 5: OAPEC announces embargo of all oil to United States and Netherlands.

Nov. 6-9: U.S. Secretary of State Henry Kissinger travels back and forth between Cairo and Jerusalem.

Nov. 11: Israel and Egypt sign a Cease-Fire Accord and continue negotiations.

1974 January: Turkish Prime Minister Bulent Ecevit of the RPP seeks support of new important Turkish political party, the National Salvation Party (NSP).

Jan. 18: Israel and Egypt sign a Disengagement Agreement.

March 5: Israel completes withdrawal from area West of Suez Canal.

March 11: "War of Attrition" between Israel and Syria begins.

March 14: Fighting in Iraq between Iraq government and Kurds reported.

March 18: Arab oil embargo of United States lifted.

April 11: PFLP General Command fidā'īyīn attack Qiryat Shmona, Israel, followed by Israeli raids into Lebanon.

April 28: Kissinger begins "peace mission" traveling between Damascus, Jerusalem and other Near East capitals.

May 29: Israel and Syria agree to a Disengagement Agreement.

May 31: Kissinger returns to the United States.

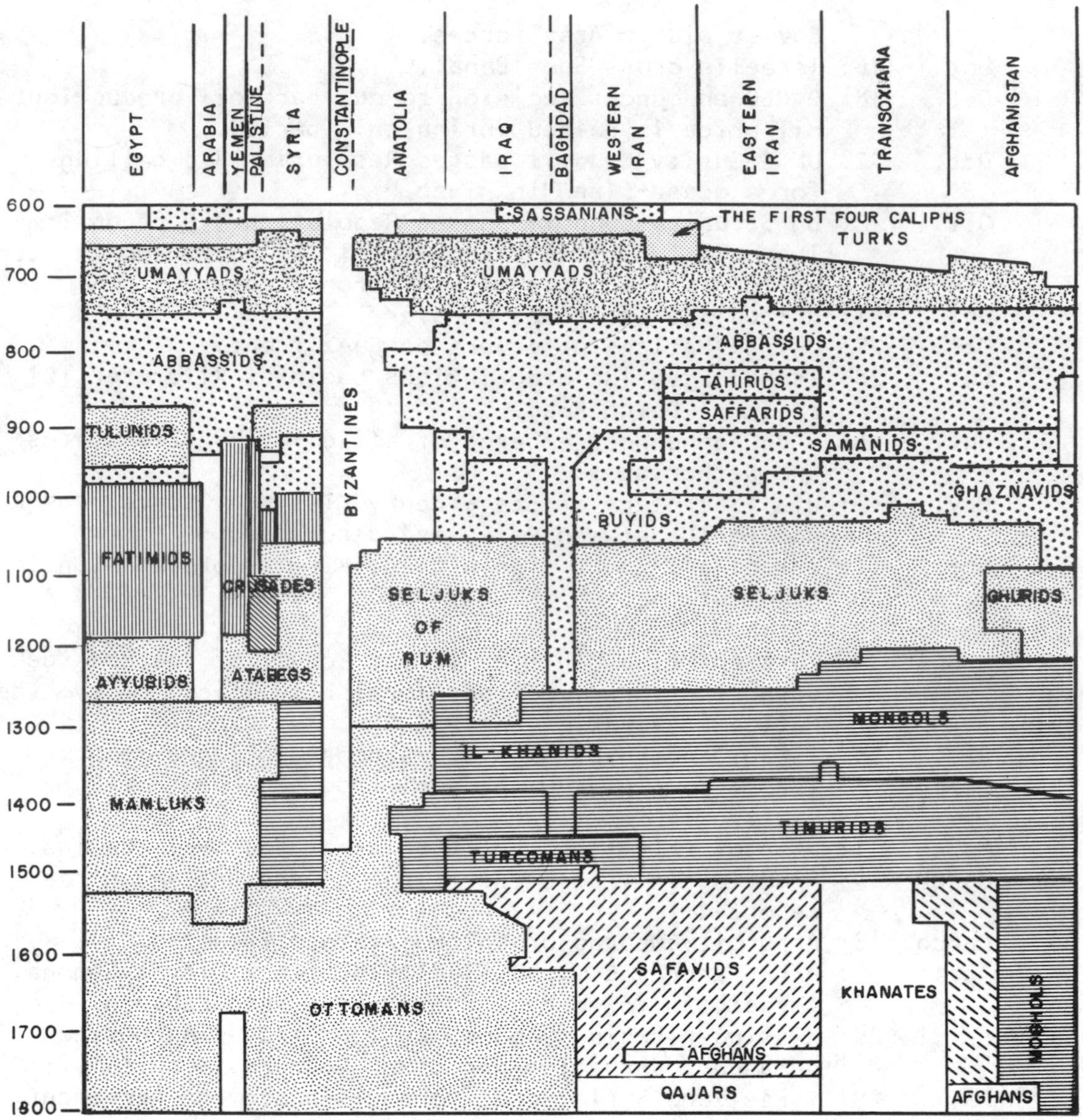

TIME CHART, 600-1800.

INDEX TO MAPS